RETIREMENT
RESOURCE GUIDE

ESSENTIAL ERISA EDUCATION & BEST PRACTICES
FOR CPAs, ADVISORS & OTHER FINANCIAL PROFESSIONALS

Disclaimer

The material presented in this text has been drawn from sources believed to be reliable. Every effort has been made to ensure the accuracy of the material. However, the accuracy of this information is not guaranteed. The laws and regulations governing IRAs and retirement plans change frequently, and sometimes with limited or no advance notice. The Retirement Resource Guide is sold with the understanding that the publisher and editor are not engaging in the practice of law or accounting. The information provided here is for general informational purposes only, and should not be considered as personalized investment advice.

The text is designed to answer most questions related to IRAs as employer-sponsored retirement plans. However, it may be necessary to refer to a more comprehensive text or other source to answer some questions. If the reader is unsure of an answer, it is best to consult a competent professional.

Copyright 2014 Retirement Learning Center, LLC

Published by the Retirement Learning Center, LLC

206 North 7th Street

Brainerd, MN 56401

www.RetirementLC.com

Printed in the United States of America

ISBN: 978-0-9831785-9-0

RETIREMENT
RESOURCE GUIDE

INTRODUCTION

The Importance of Understanding Your Clients' Retirement DNA

We all have distinct physical DNA, and while we can't change what we are made of— we can make the most of it through our actions and behaviors. For example, we can make conscious decisions to eat more wholesome foods, consume vitamins and antioxidants, and exercise with some consistency in order to maximize our physical DNA.

Like our physical DNA, each of us has distinct retirement DNA that develops with us throughout our adult lives as we move from employer to employer during our working careers. A person's physical DNA may dictate blue eyes and blond hair while his/her retirement DNA may reveal a 401(k) plan, simplified employee pension (SEP) or savings incentive match plan for employees (SIMPLE) plan. And just as there are ways to maximize one's physical DNA, there are ways to maximize one's retirement DNA through our actions and behaviors.

The fact of the matter is—most people spend little to no time understanding their retirement DNA, let alone how to maximize it. We at the Retirement Learning Center are dedicated to providing financial professionals with the knowledge and tools that will help them map and maximize their clients' retirement DNA. This knowledge can serve as the basis for making thoughtful, well-informed and prudent retirement planning decisions.

This text is designed to be a practical, business-building guide for financial professionals, like yourself, who seek to differentiate themselves and excel in the retirement plans marketplace. Each chapter begins by covering the essential rules and regulations that affect retirement plans, and concludes with practice management applications that you can implement in your day-to-day operations.

We at the Retirement Learning Center understand the highly competitive nature of the market, and have focused our efforts on helping financial professionals effectively differentiate and position themselves to their clients. The Retirement Learning Center is the independent thought leader in the retirement and rollover space. We offer multi-dimensional, business-building solutions to the financial services industry, designed to help asset managers, broker dealers, financial advisors, CPAs and independent financial planners better serve their clients in the great quest to retire with confidence.

Specifically, the Retirement Learning Center delivers

- Educational solutions,

- Content development services, and

- ERISA consulting expertise.

With over 150 years of combined retirement industry experience among our consultants, our depth and breadth of knowledge and experience is superior. To learn more about the Retirement Learning Center, please visit our web site at www.retirementlc.com.

–John Carl, President and Founder
The Retirement Learning Center

Instructions

The Retirement Resource Guide self-study course is available exclusively through Columbia Management. The following represents the instructions for taking the course.

1 The Columbia Management wholesaler e-mails an invitation to potential students, which contains a registration web link.

2 Students use the web link to register for the self-study course with Broker Education Sales and Training (BEST, Columbia Management's continuing education (CE) administrator). You must complete the self-study course and take the final exam within one year of enrolling.

3 Once BEST receives the student's registration, BEST sends the self-study book (the Retirement Resource Guide) to the student's business address via two-day UPS, with instructions to read the material.

4 The student reads the book and completes the chapter review questions, which include evaluative feedback. The student then communicates his or her readiness to take the final exam.

5 The Columbia Management wholesaler, who is an approved exam monitor for BEST, will provide a date and location for an appropriate testing site. All required documentation and sealed tests will be distributed on site to those students who have registered to take the exam.

6 Best will collect the exam materials and process the students' scores.

7 Students that post a score of 70% or higher on the exam receive a CE certificate from BEST. BEST and the Columbia Management wholesaler will notify any who did not post a passing score, and instruct the individual on how to retake the exam.

CHAPTER 1

Redefining Retirement

Each day, millions of US workers begin transitioning out of their wealth accumulation years, and into an extended (and often anxious) period in their lives marked by the onset of wealth harvesting in varying degrees, depending on their life plan. They are not "retiring" in the conventional sense of the word—they are re-inventing themselves; perhaps working fewer hours, starting a new career or perhaps launching a new business. These individuals are often unprepared—financially and emotionally—for the transition from the asset accumulating to asset harvesting phase of their lives. This dramatic shift affects how financial professionals work with these clients. The change can be viewed as a generational shift in managing client assets.

Chapter Goal

Upon completion of this chapter the reader will understand the changing retirement landscape, and the key differences in investment focus between wealth accumulators and wealth harvesters. With this knowledge, financial professionals will be better equipped to address the unique financial needs and emotional concerns of wealth harvesters.

Learning Objectives

✓ Identify from a list of options key reasons why the burden for saving for retirement is shifting from employers to employees.

✓ Recognize from a list of options unique financial pressures applicable to the Baby Boomer generation.

✓ Differentiate between the investment focus of wealth accumulators vs. wealth harvesters.

Retirement Market at a Glance

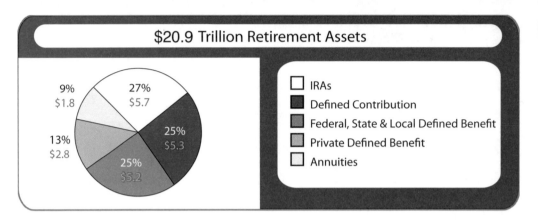

$20.9 Trillion Retirement Assets

9% $1.8
27% $5.7
25% $5.3
13% $2.8
25% $5.2

☐ IRAs
■ Defined Contribution
☐ Federal, State & Local Defined Benefit
☐ Private Defined Benefit
☐ Annuities

Sources: Investment Company Institute, June 30, 2013

The value of total assets held in retirement plans as of June 30, 2013 was $20.9 trillion. This represents a 10 percent increase in the amount of assets over June 30, 2012 ($18.9 trillion).

As the pie chart illustrates, defined benefit (DB) plans (federal, state, local and private plans combined) claim the largest percentage of the total, 38 percent, which represents $8 trillion. In second place is the IRA segment, with 27 percent of the total assets, or $5.7 trillion. In a close third is the defined contribution (DC) plan segment with 25 percent of the total, or $5.3 trillion. Retirement savings accounted for 36 percent of all household financial assets in the United States as of December 31, 2012.

Sixty percent of households headed by persons age 55 to 64 (soon-to-be wealth harvesters) owned at least one retirement account.[1]

What is "Retirement?"

Until recently, many have viewed retirement as an event that goes something like this. A worker reaches age 65 and announces his or her retirement. The employing firm throws a retirement party and bestows a gold watch upon the retiree, and the individual marches off to play endless rounds of golf, stopping only to cash his or her monthly pension checks. As the saying goes, that was then, this is now. Retirement today is a multi-year, transitional process, sometimes called "phased retirement," for a growing number of workers.

As better health and medical advancements have extended the length of time retirees spend in retirement, the concept of retirement itself has changed. Today, most people

[1] Federal Reserve Bulletin, Vol. 98, No. 2, June 2012

view retirement as an opportunity to have greater control over their lives. When the American Association of Retired Persons (AARP) polled pre-retirees, most said that they planned to stay active and work in retirement, but on their terms. For some, this meant changing occupations, achieving a better balance between work and their personal lives, or learning something new. The good news is that the desire and ability to work in retirement can greatly ease the financial burden for those making the transition.

Who are the Baby Boomers?

In 2008, Kathleen Casey Kirschling officially retired at age 62. She was born January 1, 1946 at 12:01 AM, giving her the title of first Baby Boomer. In 2011, the first of the Baby Boomers reached the full Social Security retirement age of 65.

The Baby Boomers are the generation born between 1946 and 1964, and constitute 78.2 million individuals.[2] Department of Labor (DOL) research has characterized the typical Baby Boomer as someone who is an independent, well-educated risk taker, who distrusts authority and seeks out alternative solutions to problems. Unfortunately, the DOL also found that the average Baby Boomer is financially challenged when it comes to retirement income planning.

Historically, the financial services industry has focused on helping Baby Boomers accumulate wealth for retirement. Investment strategies have focused almost exclusively on asset accumulation. As a result, Baby Boomers own 80 percent of U.S. household assets totaling $38 trillion.[3] But the tide is changing from accumulation to distribution as Baby Boomers begin crossing the retirement threshold.

Starting in 2011, the first of the Boomers turned age 65, and could begin receiving full Social Security benefits. As Boomers contemplate retirement, their attention will turn away from wealth accumulation as their primary goal, to wealth harvesting. The change in the client psyche from wealth accumulator to wealth harvester affects the client/financial professional relationship. During the wealth accumulation years, the average investor will use the services of several financial professionals. In preparation for the shift to wealth harvesting, investors reduce the number of financial professionals utilized.[4]

Baby Boomers' Unique Financial Pressures

Arguably, the leading concern held by a wealth harvester is the fear of outliving one's assets in retirement. This fear is a legitimate one, because Baby Boomers face financial pressures that previous generations have not had to deal with to the same degree. They face unique financial pressures as a result of

- an increased responsibility to fund their own retirement;

[2] U.S. Census Bureau [3] 2012 Statistical Abstract, Household Financial Assets and Liabilities
[4] McKinsey & Company, The Retirement Journey: *Pathways to Success in the New Retirement Market*

- the uncertainty of Social Security;

- a low savings rate;

- unrealistic expectations for retirement;

- rising health care costs;

- longer life expectancies;

- a growing elderly population; and

- an increased responsibility to care for elderly family members and returning adult children.

Responsible for Funding Their Own Retirement

In the past several decades, employers have increasingly adopted defined contribution plans in which the risk of having enough for retirement is transferred to employees. At the same time, many defined benefit plans have been phased out or cut back in an effort to reduce employer expenses. Consequently, employees today are more responsible than ever for financing their own retirements.

Defined benefit plan access has dropped from 32 percent in 1993 to 19 percent in 2012. The industry has seen defined contribution plan access rise from a 35 percent in 1993 to a 59 percent in 2012.

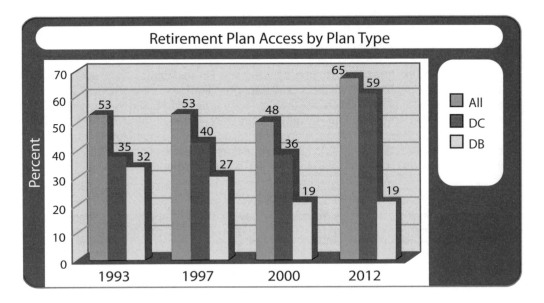

Sources: National Compensation Survey, March 2013, U.S. Bureau of Labor Statistics

Uncertainty of Social Security Benefits

Another leading Baby Boomer financial concern is the uncertainty of Social Security. On average, according to the Employee Benefits Research Institute, Social Security accounts for the largest share (37%) of a retiree's income.

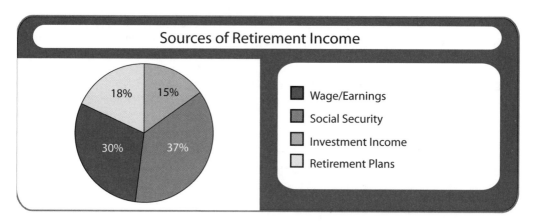

Sources: Social Security Administration, Fast Facts & Figures About Social Security, 2013

Social Security is a "pay as you go" benefits system, which means that Social Security taxes paid by or on behalf of today's workers are used to pay benefits to today's retirees and beneficiaries. Some interesting statistics: in 1945 there were roughly 42 workers supporting each retiree, in 1950 there were 16, today there are three, and the Social Security Administration predicts there will be slightly over two workers supporting each retiree by 2030.

According to the Social Security Administration's 2013 Trustees Report, the Social Security system faces an uncertain financial future unless Congress acts to ensure its financial solvency. If no legislative changes are made, under the long-range intermediate assumptions, the Trustees project the combined OASI and DI Trust Fund assets will increase through 2020, begin to decline in 2021, and become exhausted and unable to pay scheduled benefits in full on a timely bass in 2033. After the depletion of reserves, continuing tax income would be sufficient to pay 77 percent of scheduled benefits in 2033 and 72 percent in 2087.

The uncertainty of the Social Security system's ability to pay promised benefits for the next generation undermines the public's confidence in this vital and respected program. Seventy percent of workers are not too or not at all confident that Social Security will continue to provide benefits of at least equal value to the benefits retirees receive today.[5]

[5] *2013 Retirement Confidence Survey*, Employee Benefits Research Institute

Low Savings Rate

Baby Boomers are—or at least should be—concerned about a low savings rate.

Personal saving is the amount left over from disposable personal income after expenditures on personal consumption, interest, and net current transfer payments. The U.S. savings rate was negative in 1932 and 1933 — two years when the country was struggling to cope with the Great Depression, a time of massive business failures and job layoffs.[6] A negative savings rate means that Americans spent all their disposable income, and dipped into their savings—including their retirement savings—to finance their purchases. From an all-time high of 14.6 percent on May 1, 1975, the personal savings rate has declined steadily to reach a low of 0.8 percent on April 1, 2008. As of June 2013, the savings rate was 4.4%, after rising to 6.5% in December 2012.

Unrealistic Expectations for Retirement

Many individuals have unrealistic expectations with respect to their anticipated retirement income. The Employee Benefits Research Institute's (EBRI's) 2013 annual *Retirement Confidence Survey*, revealed several intriguing statistics that support this supposition.

- Fifty-one percent are confident to some degree that they will have enough income in retirement, yet only 44 percent have actually done a retirement-needs calculation.

- Fifty-seven percent of workers believe they will be receiving pension plan payments in retirement, when in reality, only 32 percent participate in a pension plan that could provide such payments.

- Fifty-seven percent of workers have accumulated less than $25,000 for retirement.

As a rule of thumb, the financial services industry has perpetuated the idea that one should plan on needing roughly 70 percent of one's pre-retirement income in retirement. This is a retiree's "income replacement ratio." An EBRI survey revealed that 86 percent of workers expect they will need an income replacement ratio of less than 70 percent.

The Department of Labor recommends that Baby Boomers will need at least a 75-percent income replacement ratio, primarily because of rising health care costs, longer life spans, and elder and child care expenses.

What is the right income replacement ratio? Many factors affect the number, including current level of income. A person earning $60,000 annually, will need roughly 78 percent of his/her preretirement income, while a person earning $250,000 annually will need 88 percent.[7]

Clearly, many workers have an unrealistic picture of what their income and expenses will be during their retirement years. Investors who consult advisors or use on-line calculators set more realistic retirement savings targets. As reported in its March 2013 issue of Notes, the Employee Benefits Research Institute (EBRI) found that both the use

[6] U.S. Department of Commerce, February 2013
[7] Aon Consulting, 2008 Replacement Ratio Study

of on-line calculators and the advice of financial advisors resulted in employees being able to set more realistic estimated retirement savings targets. This, in turn, increased the estimated probability of the group saving sufficient amounts to meet their retirement income needs. That's the good news.

The bad news: Only about a quarter of the sample studied by EBRI (i.e., 25.6%) used either of these two advice methods. The majority simply guessed at what they would need, and those who did guess were less likely to choose an adequate retirement savings target. The findings were based on data generated by EBRI's Retirement Confidence Survey and a modified version of the EBRI Retirement Security Projection Model. The results of the survey are available free of charge on EBRI's web site (ebri.org).

Another survey found that Working with a financial advisor makes a significant difference in Baby Boomer confidence regarding financial preparation for retirement. According to the Insured Retirement Institutes' (IRI's) third annual survey, "Boomer Expectations for Retirement, 2013,

- 48% of Baby Boomers who work with a financial professional are very or extremely confident with their financial preparations for retirement, compared to only 28% working on their own.
- 71% of Baby Boomers working with an advisor have determined a retirement savings goal and 94% have retirement savings. This compares to only 34% and 64%, respectively, of Boomers who have not consulted an advisor.
- Baby Boomers working with an advisor are more engaged with their retirement plans, as measured by rebalancing of retirement savings accounts. Nearly two-thirds rebalance their portfolios yearly or every few years, while conversely, 61% of Boomers who have not consulted an advisor rarely or never rebalance their portfolios.

Rising Health Care Costs

Rising health care costs are of great concern to Baby Boomers. Health care cost risk is the risk that rises in health care expenses will lead to earlier than expected portfolio depletion. In other words, it is the risk that increases in the cost of paying for health care could cause a retiree to run out of money. Based on data from the U.S. Department of Health and Human Services, we can expect health care costs to rise an average of 6.1 percent annually until 2019.

Rising health care costs become a great threat when one considers that Medicare, although improved as a result of the Affordable Care Act, is still financially strained, and that it does not cover the cost of long-term care, in most cases. According to the 2013 Trustee's Report on Medicare, The hospital portion of the trust fund is expected to be depleted by 2026.

And Medicaid is not the answer. Medicaid is reserved for low-income individuals only. In order to receive Medicaid benefits, retirees are often required to spend-down their assets to reach poverty level.

Adding insult to injury, as a result of rising health care costs, fewer employers are providing health care benefits to their retirees. Private-sector employers are less likely to offer retiree health benefits than in the past. The percentage of employers that currently expect to continue offering health benefits to future early retirees declined from 46 percent in 1993 to 17.7 percent in 2011, while the portion expecting to offer such benefits to Medicare-eligible retirees declined from 40 percent in 1993 to 15.9 percent in 2011.[8]

Without employment-based health insurance, a 65-year-old couple can expect to spend $260,000 on remaining lifetime health care costs with a five-percent probability of costs exceeding $570,000. Less than 15 percent of households approaching retirement have accumulated that much in total financial assets.[9]

Living Longer

Because of better nutrition and medical services early in life and throughout, U.S. citizens are living longer, healthier lives. Life expectancy at birth in the U.S. in 1900 was 47.3 years. Today, life expectancy at birth in the U.S. is 78.49 years.[10] In many respects, a longer life expectancy is a good thing, but a longer life expectancy means the risk of outliving ones assets in retirement is very real without proper planning.

Longevity risk is the risk of outliving one's savings. As a rule of thumb, financial planners have, in the past, indicated that a person should plan for 20 years of income in retirement. However, according to life expectancy figures from the National Center for Health Statistics, and based on U.S. Life Tables, a 65-year-old has a 50 percent chance of living another 20 years to age 85; and a 25 percent chance of living another 27 years to age 92. For a married couple, at least one spouse has a 50 percent chance of reaching age 92; and a 25 percent chance of reaching age 97. For someone to plan on spending just 20 years in retirement would be not only unrealistic, but a real gamble.

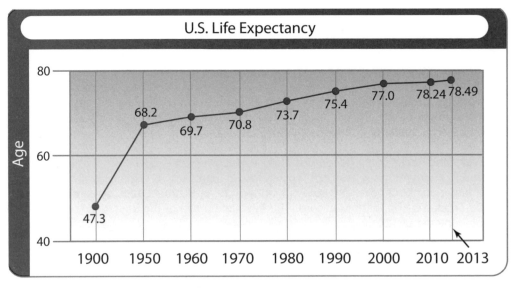

Source: Central Intelligence Agency (CIA) Factbook, 2013

[8] Employee Benefit Research Institute, Issue Brief, October 2012, No. 377 [9] Webb and Zhivan, What is the Distribution of Lifetime Health Care Costs From Age 65½, Center for Retirement Research at Boston College, March, 2010 [10] Central Intelligence Agency (CIA) Factbook, 2013

A Growing Elderly Population

Longer life expectancies mean our elderly population is growing—and growing dramatically. As a percent of total population, the elderly segment, especially women, continues to increase, which expands the eldercare needs and burdens on social programs. According to the 2013 CIA Factbook, the number of Americans age 65 and older was 43.9 million, or 13.9 percent of the population. By 2030, this population is expected to grow to 71.5 million, representing 20 percent of the population.[11]

With an aging population many Baby Boomers are already providing eldercare for an aged family member, and this will continue to increase. An estimated 29 percent of the current adult population has some responsibility for care giving—a number expected to increase.[12] Consider that

- there are 65.7 million unpaid caregivers in the U.S.;
- the value of family care giving is estimated at $450 billion annually; and
- the typical caregiver is a 48-year-old female who is providing 22 hours of care for a 61-year-old female relative.[13]

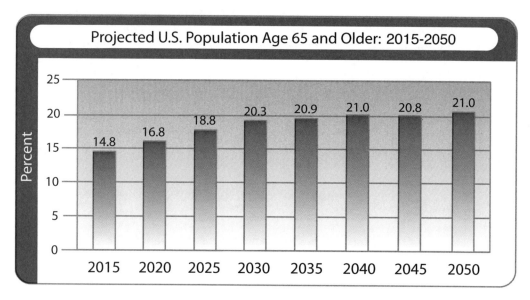

Projected U.S. Population Age 65 and Older: 2015-2050

Source: Population Division, U.S. Census Bureau, 2012

Dependent Adult Children

In addition to the eldercare issue, many Baby Boomers are supporting or partially supporting adult children who are saddled with student loan debt or are under-employed or unemployed, and cannot make it on their own. U.S. Census Bureau figures show that 56 percent of men and 43 percent of women ages 18 to 24 today live with one or both parents.

[11] U.S. Census Bureau, 2010   [12] Family Caregiver Alliance, November 2012
[13] Family Caregiver Alliance, November 2012

Client Fears

In light of these financial concerns, the fear of running out of money is very real to clients nearing and in their wealth harvesting years. Financial professionals must address this fear in order to preserve the client/financial professional relationship. Retirees are often unprepared financially and emotionally for the transition from the asset accumulation phase to the asset harvesting phase of their lives. Financial professionals have a clear opportunity to educate clients, and realistically manage their fears and expectations related to retirement income. In order to be effective, financial professionals must be able to

- properly position themselves to wealth harvesters; and
- help clients execute retirement income strategies that address wealth harvesters' unique needs and concerns.

Wealth Accumulators Vs. Wealth Harvesters

A wealth accumulator's goal is to save enough between now and his or her anticipated retirement date to cover his or her anticipated expenses during retirement. The amount that must be saved depends on the anticipated average return the wealth accumulator hopes to earn on the savings, the level of retirement income desired, the wealth accumulator's risk tolerance, and how long he or she has to save before his or her planned retirement.

A wealth harvester has reached the point in life where he or she will begin drawing down the assets built up during the wealth accumulating years. Typically, wealth harvesting begins at retirement, but some job changers may need to begin harvesting on an interim basis when caught between employers. Although wealth harvesting involves many of the same investment concepts used for wealth accumulation, there is a distinct change in investment focus and risk management strategies, which we will explore in the following sections.

There are several differences in the investment focus between wealth accumulators and wealth harvesters. Some of these differences include a focus on

- fixed vs. variable investment timeframes,
- average vs. probable rates of returns on investments, and
- accumulation vs. harvesting asset allocation strategies.

Fixed Vs. Variable Investment Timeframes

Saving projections for the wealth accumulation stage are typically calculated on the basis of how old the worker is currently, and at what age he or she would like to retire; therefore, the number of saving years are known, or "fixed." A typical investment strategy for a wealth accumulator would initially be more aggressive and equity-based in the early accumulation years, gradually shifting toward less volatile investments as the worker approaches his or her targeted retirement date. The shift toward investments with more stable returns near the end of the accumulation period is a defense mechanism intended to avoid delaying retirement as a result of drastic market downturns.

The timeframe for wealth harvesting, on the other hand, is not known, because no one knows for sure how long he or she will live, and the risk that an investor will live longer than planned for is known as "longevity risk." Longevity risk and management strategies will be covered in greater detail later in this text.

Average vs. Probable Rates of Return

During the wealth accumulation stage, investment returns are generally estimated based on historical averages over a similar period of time. Since investment returns have historically been more stable over longer time periods, as long as a reasonable rate of return is selected, having many years before one needs to start harvesting one's savings usually provides an ample opportunity to weather and rebound from bear markets. As an accumulator nears retirement, however, avoiding drastic losses becomes a significant concern, because losses at the end of the accumulation period can significantly delay the ability of a wealth accumulator to comfortably retire at the desired time. Projection errors occur when the rate of return used to calculate a savings return does not match up with actual returns and can make the difference between retiring on schedule, and having to work several additional years.

During the wealth harvesting stage, the investment model shifts drastically with regard to how rates of return are estimated. Making projections based on average rates of return during the wealth harvesting stage can quickly result in premature depletion of savings—particularly if losses occur early in retirement. This is why most financial advisers have switched from using projectors that base returns on average returns to "Monte Carlo" simulations to simulate investment outcomes for hundreds of possible historical returns. Monte Carlo simulations allow a wealth harvester to pick a rate of return that has a higher probability for providing income throughout the entire anticipated retirement period.

Accumulation vs. Harvesting Asset Allocation Strategies

As alluded to earlier, wealth accumulators are often initially encouraged to take advantage of longer investment time horizons by investing more aggressively in higher potential return, equity-based products. However, the concern for asset preservation grows as a person reaches the wealth harvesting stage.

Because a retiree will be dependent on his or her retirement savings to pay for current expenses, taking distributions when retirement assets are depressed in value to pay for necessary living expenses can significantly shorten how long retirement assets will last. It would be a mistake; however, to think that investing in an overly conservative manner is more likely to result in the best outcome for the harvesting investor.

Consider, for example, that it is entirely probable that many who retire at age 65 will spend 30 plus years in retirement. This investment time horizon is nearly as long as the wealth accumulation stage for many individuals! Why, then, should wealth harvesters behave as if they will need all of their retirement assets in the first years of retirement by investing in stable, but low-return investments? The key to responsible asset allocation during the wealth harvesting stage is to create an asset allocation mixture that allows for more aggressive long-term investing, while diverting a portion toward investments that offer a more stable return to pay for fixed living expenses.

After the Baby Boomers come the "X" and "Y" generations, which include 116 million Americans aged 20-47. Retirement may seem a long way off for them, but given the fact the majority will need to rely on their own personal savings to finance their retirements—even more so than Baby Boomers have had to—knowing a few "tips" may help improve their chances of building a secure retirement.

Research conducted by the Life Insurance and Market Research Association (LIMRA), released April 18, 2013, reveals five steps Gen Xers and Yers can take now to improve their chances of building a sufficient retirement nest egg.

Tip	Why Important?
1. Improve financial knowledge	60% of Gen X and 54% of Gen Y consumers admit to having little to no knowledge about financial products and services.
2. Get help	Investors who worked with an advisor were more likely to contribute to a retirement plan (78% vs. 43%), more likely to save at a higher rate (61% vs. 38%), and feel more confident about their retirement prospects (71% vs. 43%).
3. Participate in employer-sponsored retirement savings plans or start an IRA	56% of younger Americans, (ages 18-34) are not currently contributing to a retirement plan. 75% of Gen X and Gen Y workers have access to 401(k) plans, which often include employer-matching contributions.
4. Steadily increase retirement plan contributions annually	Automatic contribution escalation helps improve a worker's savings rate.
5. Don't withdraw retirement savings early	One of the biggest factors that undermine investors' ability to reach their retirement savings goals are early cash-outs, loans and withdrawals.

Practice Management: Becoming the "Go-To" Financial Professional

Baby Boomers are nearing retirement, and are often unprepared financially and emotionally for the shift from wealth accumulator to wealth harvester. Because many will spend more than 20 years in retirement, and face unique financial pressures (e.g., skyrocketing medical costs), many Baby Boomers fear they will outlive their retirement assets. If financial professionals can effectively position themselves to their wealth accumulator clients, and allay client fears with respect to retirement income, they will experience a greater possibility of successfully preserving the client/financial professional relationship throughout the wealth harvesting years.

A financial professional can help ensure he or she will be the "go-to" person during the wealth harvesting years through proper positioning to the client—during the wealth accumulating years. This is done through two processes: differentiation and association.

Differentiation

The first step in winning the financial professional survivor game is differentiation. A financial professional must differentiate himself or herself from the competition. This can be accomplished in several ways, including the following.

1 Begin retirement income-related discussions with clients during their wealth accumulation years, well before their target retirement date.

2 Address clients' fears about running out of money in retirement by discussing possible risk management strategies (e.g. purchasing long-term care insurance to help reduce the risk of portfolio depletion as a result of rising health care costs or considering a phased-approach to retirement to allow for another source of retirement income to stave off the risk of over spending).

3 Treat the wealth harvesting years as a new financial planning phase, and use it as an opportunity for one-on-one consulting sessions.

4 Discuss financial topics with clients that other financial professionals may ignore or about which they may be uninformed (e.g., the tax benefits of net unrealized appreciation in company stock, IRA consolidation strategies, 403(b) changes, in-service retirement plan distributions, beneficial changes as a result of the Pension Protection Act of 2006, etc.).

5 Offer to "quarterback" a client's team of financial planning professionals. Be willing to coordinate a client's team of tax, legal, and legacy planning professionals.

6 Stay current with technical rules that affect clients' retirement income plans. The IRS' web site www.irs.gov and the Department of Labor's web site www.dol.gov are excellent sources of free information.

Association

Once a financial professional has differentiated himself or herself from the competition by applying the suggested tactics listed above, clients generally begin to associate the financial professional with wealth harvesting planning. Association is complete when clients identify the professional as the financial planning partner who will help them prepare for and successfully navigate their wealth harvesting years. This can allow the financial professional to begin helping clients develop customized retirement income strategies.

Feedback for the review questions can be found at the end of the chapter.

1 Which type of employer-sponsored retirement plan puts the burden of saving for retirement on the *EMPLOYEE*?

    A Defined contribution
    B Defined benefit plan
    C Individual Retirement Account
    D All of the above

2 With respect to wealth harvesters, which of the following statements is *TRUE*?

    A Risk management strategies are more important to wealth harvesters than wealth accumulators.
    B Wealth harvesters have a fixed investment time frame.
    C Wealth harvesters should apply an average rate of return.
    D The asset allocation strategy for a wealth harvester should be the same as that of a wealth accumulator.

3 The Department of Labor (DOL) recommends Baby Boomers have what percent of their current income as a minimum retirement income replacement ratio?

    A 55%
    B 60%
    C 75%
    D 85%

4 Who is responsible for the investment risk in a private defined benefit plan?

    A Employer
    B Employee
    C IRS
    D Department of Labor

5 For the average American, what is the leading source of income an individual will reply upon in retirement?

    A Income from wages and earnings
    B Income from retirement plans
    C Income from investments
    D Income from Social Security benefits

Chapter Review Questions Feedback

1 Which type of employer-sponsored retirement plan puts the burden of saving for retirement on the *EMPLOYEE*?

    A Defined contribution
    B Defined benefit plan
    C Individual Retirement Account
    D All of the above

    A *Correct, because a defined contribution plan does not guarantee a specific retirement benefit to the employee.* Chapter 1, Page 4

    B *Incorrect, because a defined benefit plan guarantees a specific retirement benefit to the employee, which is financed by the employer.*

    C *Incorrect, because this is not a type of employer-sponsored retirement plan.*

    D *Incorrect, because options B and C are incorrect.*

2 With respect to wealth harvesters, which of the following statements is *TRUE*?

    A Risk management strategies are more important to wealth harvesters than wealth accumulators.
    B Wealth harvesters have a fixed investment time frame.
    C Wealth harvesters should apply an average rate of return.
    D The asset allocation strategy for a wealth harvester should be the same as that of a wealth accumulator.

    A *Correct, wealth harvesters are more concerned with preserving their assets and, therefore, reducing their risk.* Chapter 1, Page 10-11

    B *Incorrect, wealth harvesters have a variable investment time frame because they do not know how long their retirement will last.*

    C *Incorrect, wealth harvesters should apply probable rates of return to simulate a variety of investment outcomes.*

    D *Incorrect, the concern for asset preservation grows as a person becomes a wealth harvester, necessitating a different asset allocation strategy than a wealth accumulator.*

3 The Department of Labor (DOL) recommends Baby Boomers have what percent of their current income as a minimum retirement income replacement ratio?

    A 55%
    B 60%

C 75%

D 85%

A *Incorrect, because the DOL has estimated that 55% would be insufficient to cover retiree expenses.*

B *Incorrect, because the DOL has estimated that 60% would be insufficient to cover retiree expenses.*

C **Correct, because the DOL has estimated that in order to cover rising health care costs, longer life spans and elder care costs, 75% would be the minimum income replacement ratio.** Chapter 1, Page 6

D *Incorrect, because the DOL recommends a MINIMUM income replacement ratio of 75%.*

4 Who is responsible for the investment risk in a private defined benefit plan?

A Employer
B Employee
C IRS
D Department of Labor

A **Correct, because the employer makes all investment decisions for a defined benefit plan.** Chapter 1, Page 4

B *Incorrect, because the employer makes all investment decisions for a defined benefit plan; the employee has no responsibility for investment selection or performance in a defined benefit plan.*

C *Incorrect, because the employer makes all investment decisions for a defined benefit plan; the IRS has no responsibility for investment selection or performance in a private defined benefit plan.*

D *Incorrect, because the employer makes all investment decisions for a defined benefit plan; the Department of Labor has no responsibility for investment selection or performance in a defined benefit plan.*

5 For the average American, what is the leading source of income an individual will reply upon in retirement?

A Income from wages and earnings
B Income from retirement plans
C Income from investments
D Income from Social Security benefits

A *Incorrect, income from wages and earnings account for 30%.*

B *Incorrect, income retirement plans account for 18%.*

C *Incorrect, income from investments accounts for 15%.*

D **Correct, income from Social Security benefits accounts for 37%.** Chapter 1, Page 5

CHAPTER 2

Understanding Retirement Plans

Chapter Goal

Upon completion of this chapter the reader will understand the various types of retirement plans, and will be better able to suggest the appropriate plan type and provisions that will meet each employer's unique retirement plan goals.

Learning Objective

✓ Differentiate between the following 14 types of retirement plans: defined benefit, profit sharing, 401(k), money purchase pension, target benefit, employee stock ownership plan (ESOP), stock bonus, Taft-Hartley, 412(i), 403(b), 457(b), 457(f), and Thrift Savings Plans.

✓ Determine the appropriate usage of the following seven contribution allocation methodologies: flat dollar, pro rata, integrated, age weighted, new comparability, 401(k) safe harbor, and Roth 401(k).

✓ Identify optional plan features based on employer needs, considering the following 10 options: automatic enrollment, automatic deferral increases, vesting, elapsed time vs. hours of service, statutory and/or class exclusions, a last day requirement, loans, in-service and/or hardship distributions, default investments, and Fiduciary Advisers.

✓ Determine maximum contribution limits for various plans.

Defined Benefit Plans

A defined benefit plan defines how much a participant will receive at retirement based on the plan's specific provisions, as well as statutory limitations. A participant's age, years of service, and compensation, can all come into play, depending upon the terms of the plan, when determining what the "defined benefit" will be. These plans tend to be funded with employer contributions, but may include employee contributions in some cases. Because defined benefit plans "promise" a specific benefit, the investment risk is borne by the employer, who either manages the investments personally, or hires an investment manager for the job. Also, because plan assumptions regarding mortality, turnover, etc., can have a significant impact a plan's ability to pay benefits, these plans generally require the services of an enrolled actuary, who makes sure that reasonable assumptions are made with respect to funding requirements. In some cases, a defined benefit plan can be invested in insurance contracts (e.g., a 412(e) plan), which can remove a great deal of administrative burden from the employer who is funding the plan.

Defined benefit plans can offer employers an opportunity to maximize their retirement savings in a relatively short period of time, but they can also be tremendously expensive if the demographic profile of the employer's workforce reveals that workers are older, long-tenured, and/or highly compensated.

As a result of the Pension Protection Act of 2006 (PPA), plan funding requirements for defined benefit plans have been accelerated. Highlights of the changes appear next.

For purposes of determining current liability for the 2006 and 2007 plan years, the inter- est rate used were required to be 90 to 100 percent of the weighted average of the rates of interest on amounts invested conservatively in long-term investment-grade corporate bonds during the four-year period ending on the last day before the plan year begins.

Effective for 2008 and later years, defined benefit plan funding rules changed completely. The funding target for single-employer plans is 100 percent of current liability.

A three-segment yield-curve replaced the corporate bond interest rate used to determine a plan's current liability. The yield-curve is based on a 24-month average of the rates of investment grade corporate bonds with varying maturities that are in the top three quality levels available.

Plans that are severely underfunded, and considered "at risk," must accelerate their funding as compared to other plans, resulting in higher required contributions.

On July 6, 2012, President Obama signed into law H.R. 4348, Moving Ahead for Progress in the 21st Century Act (MAP–21). Included were funding stabilization meas- ures for defined benefit plans, effective for plan years beginning after December 31, 2011. Presently, the minimum funding rules for single-employer defined benefit plans specify the interest rates and other actuarial assumptions that must be used in determining the present value of benefits. Present value may be determined using three interest rates (referred to as segment rates), each of which applies to benefit payments expected to be made from the plan during a certain period. Each segment rate is a single interest rate determined monthly on the basis of a corporate bond yield curve, which reflects the average for the 24-month period ending with the preceding month. The IRS publishes the segment rates each month.

MAP–21 modifies the method for determining the interest rate used to calculate the actuarial value of benefits earned under the defined benefit plan. This interest rate is critical in determining the plan's funding requirements. The rate has an inverse relationship to the required funding: The higher the interest rate, the lower the funding requirement. When MAP-21 is fully phased in over the next few years (by 2016), plan sponsors and actuaries will use a 25-year average corporate interest rate to determine the applicable interest rate range available to the plan for funding purposes. The plan's 24-month average interest rate must fall within this range or be adjusted upward or downward so that it does. Under this determination method, interest rates for plan funding purposes will generally be higher than current rates, resulting in lower funding requirements and, therefore, lower tax deductions for plan sponsors. Consequently, plan sponsors will contribute less money to their plans when actual interest rates are at historical lows, as is the present situation.

Funding Formulas

Defined benefit plan funding formulas take into consideration plan assets, rate of return, mortality, estimated benefit, and valuation date. Although there may be variations, the following is a list of the most common defined benefit funding methods.

- Unit Credit (or Accrued Benefit) Funding Method,

- Aggregate Funding Method,

- Individual Aggregate (or Individual Spread Gain) Funding Method,

- Entry Age Normal Funding Method,

- Frozen Initial Liability Funding Method,

- Attained Age Normal Funding Method, and

- Individual Level Premium Funding Method.

Contribution Limits

The maximum contribution to a defined benefit plan is dependant upon several variables, including the funding formula, annual compensation cap, participant annual additions limit, and employer deductibility limit.

Compensation Cap

The amount of compensation that can be considered when calculating a participant's accrued benefit according to the plan's formula is limited under Internal Revenue Code (IRC) Section (Sec.) 401(a)(17). The limit is $255,000 for 2013 and $260,000 for 2014 This amount may be indexed periodically for cost-of-living increases.

IRC Sec. 415 Limit (Annual Benefit Limit)

The maximum annual benefit for a defined benefit plan participant for 2013 is $205,000 and for 2014 is $210,000.

For 2006 and later years, for purposes of determining average compensation for a participant's high three years, the high three years are the period of consecutive calendar years (not more than three) during which the participant had the greatest aggregate compensation from the employer. The limit is reduced if the normal retirement age is younger than 62. It is also reduced if participation in the plan is less than ten years.

The dollar limit generally applies to a benefit payable in the form of a straight life annuity. If the benefit is in the form of a lump sum payment, then the benefit must be adjusted to an equivalent straight life annuity. Effective for years beginning after 2005, for purposes of adjusting a benefit in a form that is subject to the minimum value rules, such as a lump-sum benefit, the interest rate used generally must be not less than the greater of

1 5.5 percent;

2 the rate that provides a benefit of not more than 105 percent of the benefit that would be provided if the rate (or rates) applicable in determining minimum lump sums were used; or

3 the interest rate specified in the plan.

IRC Sec. 404 Deductibility Limit

Employers with defined benefit plans may receive tax deductions for contributions up to the prescribed limits under IRC Sec. 404(a)(1)(A)(i)-(iii). Typically, an employer will be allowed to deduct contributions needed to meet the minimum funding requirement for the plan as determined by the funding formula.

The Pension Protection Act of 2006 (PPA) provides increases in deduction limits for contributions to defined benefit plans. For taxable years beginning in 2006 and 2007, in the case of contributions to a single-employer defined benefit plan, the maximum deductible amount was determined as follows.

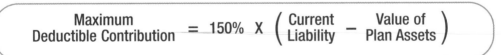

$$\text{Maximum Deductible Contribution} = 150\% \times \left(\text{Current Liability} - \text{Value of Plan Assets} \right)$$

For taxable years beginning after 2007, in the case of contributions to a single-employer defined benefit pension plan, the maximum deductible amount is the greater of

1 (Funding Target + Target Normal Cost + Cushion) − Plan Assets; or

2 the minimum required contribution for the plan year.

However, in the case of a plan that is not in at-risk status, the first amount above is:

(Funding Target + Target Normal Cost determined as if the plan was in at-risk status) − Value of Plan Assets

The cushion amount for a plan year is:

(50% of the plan's Funding Target for the plan year) + (the amount by which the plan's Funding Target would increase if determined by taking into account increases in participants' compensation for future years)

Participant Eligibility

An employer can limit participation in a defined benefit plan as long as the plan satisfies the minimum coverage and participation requirements set forth in the IRC.

Age Requirement

Under minimum participation rules, the age requirement that an employer may impose through the terms of the defined benefit plan for participation eligibility is no greater than age 21 (IRC Sec. 410(a)(1)(A)(i)).

Service Requirement

An employer may require employees to complete a specified amount of service (up to two years) before becoming eligible to participate in a defined benefit plan. If the plan imposes a year of service requirement, each participant's accrued benefit may be subject to a risk of forfeiture according to the plan's vesting schedule. If the plan imposes two years of service, a participant's benefit may not be subject to a vesting schedule, meaning each participant must have an immediate nonforfeitable right to 100 percent of his/her accrued benefit under the plan.

Sponsoring Employer Characteristics

Employers that sponsor defined benefit plans are typically large, well-established corporations that are able to guarantee retirement benefits to their employees. However, defined benefit plans are also popular with small, professional firms (e.g., attorneys, dentists, architects, etc.).

PPA Changes To Defined Benefit Lump Sum Distributions

The defined benefit plan changes under PPA essentially require faster funding of plan benefits and alter how liabilities and benefits are calculated. One of the key changes is how the value of a lump sum distribution is determined. Plans must use statutory interest rate and mortality assumptions in determining the value of a lump sum distribution. Historically, the applicable interest rate was based on 30-year Treasury securities, and the applicable mortality table was the 1994 Group Annuity Reserving Table ("94 GAR"), projected through 2002. Provisions of PPA-06 change the interest rate and mortality table used in calculating lump sums. Going forward, the interest rate used is derived from a corporate bond yield curve, and the mortality table will be the same as that used to determine minimum funding for the plan, as prescribed by the Secretary of the Treasury. As a result of using an interest rate based on a corporate bond yield curve, typically, a higher interest rate will apply for payments made further out in the future. Long term, the result will probably yield somewhat smaller lump sum benefits. Transition rules applied for the calculation of lump sum distributions in 2008 through 2011. During this period, lump sum distributions were calculated using a weighted average of the old calculation method and the new calculation method.

412(e) Plans

Important Note: 412(e) plans were formerly known as 412(i) plans.

IRC Sec. 412(e)(3) plans are a unique type of defined benefit plan, that do not require the services of an enrolled actuary because they are funded exclusively by the purchase of life insurance contracts or fixed annuity contracts or a combination of the two. Plans funded only with life insurance rather than a combination of life insurance and annuities will invite greater scrutiny by the IRS. The life insurance and annuity contracts must be part of the same series and use the same mortality tables and rate assumptions for all participants. IRC Sec. 412(e) plans are subject to the same qualification requirements that apply to traditional defined benefit plans, with two exceptions. First, if the insurance contracts meet the requirements of Treasury Regulation 1.412(i)-1(b)(2), the plan is exempt from the normal minimum funding requirements. Those contract requirements are as follow.

1 The plan must be funded exclusively by the purchase from an insurance company or companies (licensed under the law of a State or the District of Columbia to do business with the plan) of individual annuity or individual insurance contracts, or a combination thereof. The purchase may be made either directly by the employer or through the use of a custodial account or trust. A plan shall not be considered to be funded otherwise than exclusively by the purchase of individual annuity or individual insurance contracts merely because the employer makes a payment necessary to comply with the provisions of section 411(c)(2) (relating to accrued benefit from employee contributions).

2 The individual annuity or individual insurance contracts issued under the plan must provide for level annual, or more frequent, premium payments to be paid under the plan for the period commencing with the date each individual participating in the plan became a participant, and ending not later than the normal retirement age for that individual or, if earlier, the date the individual ceases his participation in the plan. Premium payments may be considered to be level even though items such as experience gains and dividends are applied against premiums. In the case of an increase in benefits, the contracts must provide for level annual payments with respect to such increase to be paid for the period commencing at the time the increase becomes effective. If payment commences on the first payment date under the contract occurring after the date an individual becomes a participant or after the effective date of an increase in benefits, the requirements of this sub division will be satisfied even though payment does not commence on the date on which the individual's participation commenced or on the effective date of the benefit increase, whichever is applicable. If an individual accrues benefits after his normal retirement age, the requirements of this subdivision are satisfied if payment is made at the time such benefits accrue. If the provisions required by this subdivision are set forth in a separate agreement with the issuer of the individual contracts, they need not be included in the individual contracts.

3 The benefits provided by the plan for each individual participant must be equal to the benefits provided under his individual contracts at his normal retirement age under the plan provisions.

4 The benefits provided by the plan for each individual participant must be guaranteed by the life insurance company, described in paragraph (b)(2)(i) of this section, issuing the individual contracts to the extent premiums have been paid.

5 Except as provided in the following sentence, all premiums payable for the plan year, and for all prior plan years, under the insurance or annuity contracts must have been paid before lapse. If the lapse has occurred during the plan year, the requirements of this subdivision will be considered to have been met if reinstatement of the insurance policy, under which the individual insurance contracts are issued, occurs during the year of the lapse and before distribution is made or benefits commence to any participant whose benefits are reduced because of the lapse.

6 No rights under the individual contracts may have been subject to a security interest at any time during the plan year. This subdivision shall not apply to contracts which have been distributed to participants if the security interest is created after the date of distribution.

7 No policy loans, including loans to individual participants, on any of the individual contracts may be outstanding at any time during the plan year.

This subdivision shall not apply to contracts which have been distributed to participants if the loan is made after the date of distribution. An application of funds by the issuer to pay premiums due under the contracts shall be deemed not to be a policy loan if the amount of the funds so applied, and interest thereon, is repaid during the plan year in which the funds are applied and before distribution is made or benefits commence to any participant whose benefits are reduced because of such application.

Second, a 412(i) plan will automatically satisfy the accrued benefit test if the plan satisfies items 1 through 4 above, plus provides that an employee's accrued benefit at any time is not less than what the cash surrender value of his/her insurance contracts would be if all premiums due are paid, no rights under the contracts have been subject to a security interest at any time, and no policy loans are outstanding at any time during the year.

Abusive Sales Practices

The Treasury Department and the IRS have issued guidance to shut down abusive transactions involving specially designed life insurance policies in 412(i) plans. The guidance designates certain arrangements as "listed transactions" for tax-shelter reporting purposes.

The guidance covers three specific issues. First, proposed regulations (REG-126967-03) state that any life insurance contract transferred from an employer or a tax-qualified plan to an employee must be taxed at its full fair market value (not necessarily its cash surrender value). Some firms have promoted an arrangement where an employer establishes a 412(i) plan under which the contributions made to the plan, which are deducted by the employer, are used to purchase a specially designed life insurance contract. Generally, these special policies are made available only to highly compensated employees. The insurance contract is designed so that the cash surrender value is temporarily depressed, so that it is significantly below the premiums paid. The contract is distributed or sold to the employee for the amount of the current cash surrender value during the period the cash surrender value is depressed; however, the contract is structured so that the cash surrender value increases significantly after it is transferred to the employee. Use of this "springing" cash value life insurance gives employers tax deductions for amounts far in excess of what the employee recognizes in income. These regulations prevent taxpayers from using artificial devices to understate the value of the contract. Revenue Procedure 2004-16 provided a temporary safe harbor for determining fair market value. The IRS replaced this valuation guidance with Revenue Procedure 2005-25.

Second, Revenue Ruling 2004-20 states that an employer cannot buy excessive life insurance (i.e., insurance contracts where the death benefits exceed the death benefits provided to the employee's beneficiaries under the terms of the plan, with the balance of the proceeds reverting to the plan as a return on investment) in order to claim large tax deductions. These arrangements generally will be listed transactions for tax-shelter reporting purposes.

Third, Revenue Ruling 2004-21 states that a 412(i) plan cannot use differences in life insurance contracts to discriminate in favor of highly paid employees.

On August 1, 2012, U.S. Telemangement Inc., filed a putative class action lawsuit in the District of Connecticut challenging the propriety of certain insurance contracts used to fund IRC Sec. 412(e) defined benefit plans [see U.S. *Telemanagement, Inc. v. Fidelity Security Life Insurance Co. et al.,* No. 3:12-cv-1110 JBA (D. Conn.)]. The complaint challenges the appropriateness of the contracts for the retirement plan, and also alleges that the insurance company that sold the annuities acted as an ERISA fiduciary of the plans. The case could have industry-wide impact, perhaps resulting in other non-412(e)(3) lawsuits claiming that other life insurance or annuity-based retirement products and services are "too expensive" or "unsuitable" for retirement plans.

Sponsoring Employer Characteristics

The most likely candidates for a 412(i) plan are small, professional businesses that want to maximize contributions for their owners. They work best for business that are well established and highly-profitable.

Cash Balance Plans

A cash balance plan is a type of hybrid defined benefit plan that looks somewhat like a defined contribution plan. Under a cash balance plan, benefits are determined by reference to a hypothetical account balance. An employee's hypothetical account balance is determined by reference to hypothetical annual allocations to the account based on a certain percentage of the employee's compensation for the year and hypothetical earnings on the account. In a typical cash balance plan, a participant's account is credited each year with a pay credit (such as 5 percent of compensation from his or her employer) and an interest credit (either a fixed rate or a variable rate that is linked to an index such as the one-year Treasury bill rate). Increases and decreases in the value of the plan's investments do not directly affect the benefit amounts promised to participants. Thus, the investment risks and rewards on plan assets are borne solely by the employer. Participant eligibility is similar to traditional defined benefit plans. Many employers have converted their traditional pensions to cash-balance plans. Consequently, two issues of particular concern have come to light:

1 employer practices in disclosing the impact of the pension conversions, and

2 the effect of conversions on older and long-service employees.

PPA affirms that cash balance plans are not, by nature, age discriminatory.

In October 2010, the Treasury Department issued final regulations (Treasury Decision 9505) for cash balance and other hybrid plans, applicable for plan years beginning on or after January 1, 2011. Among other things, the final regulations interpret rules for an age-discrimination safe harbor, conversion protection for employees, and a three-year minimum vesting requirement. The Treasury Department also issued proposed regulations (REG–132554–08), applicable for plan years beginning on or after January 1, 2012, that are intended to enhance the availability of cash balance defined benefit retirement plans by minimizing funding issues.

On October 11, 2011, the IRS published Notice 2011-85, which extends the effective date for the regulations relating to interest crediting rates under cash balance plans. These rules require that the rate of any interest credit for any plan year cannot exceed a market rate of return. The regulations, when finalized, will apply for plan years that begin on or after a date to be specified in the regulations that is not earlier than January 1, 2013. In addition, related provisions of the final hybrid plan regulations that are effective January 1, 2012, are also postponed.

The notice also extends the deadline for sponsors of cash balance and other hybrid plans to adopt certain amendments, such as those covering vesting and age non-discrimination provisions. The deadline for adopting these amendments is now the last day of the plan year before the plan year for which these rules, once finalized, will apply to their plan. However, the amendment deadline extension does not apply to the elimination of a "whipsaw" provision under this type of plan.

Even though these amendment deadlines are delayed, plans must continue to operationally comply with the requirements.

Profit-Sharing Plans

A profit-sharing plan allows employers to share profits with their employees for the purpose of helping them save for retirement. Contributions to a profit sharing plan are tax deductible to the employer, and an employer need not have profits in order to actually make a contribution to a profit sharing plan. However, because contributions to a profit sharing plan generally are not mandatory for any given year, employers often will choose to reduce contributions, or forego making contributions in years when profits are down or nonexistent.

Contribution Formulas

Profit-sharing plan contributions are discretionary in most cases, and they must be made according to a nondiscriminatory allocation formula. The most common formula used is a formula which allocates contributions based on a percentage of each participant's compensation, but there are several others, as described in the following paragraphs. The actual formula that must be used will be selected in the plan document that governs the profit sharing plan.

Flat Dollar

A plan sponsor who uses a flat dollar contribution formula in its profit sharing plan must contribute the same dollar amount to each eligible employee.

Pro Rata

An allocation formula that provides eligible participants with a contribution based on the same percentage of compensation is known as a pro rata formula.

Integrated

An integrated allocation formula—allows a plan sponsor to provide higher contributions for eligible participants who earn amounts over a set threshold, as long as the "permitted disparity rules" of IRC Sec. 401(1) are satisfied. Integrated plans are also known as "Social Security-based" or "permitted disparity" plans. The permitted disparity rules allow plan sponsors to give eligible participants who earn compensation above the "integration level," which is typically the Social Security Taxable Wage Base, an additional contribution. This additional contribution is equal to the lesser of

- two times the base contribution percentage, or
- the base contribution percentage plus the "permitted disparity factor."

If the plan sponsor sets the integration level at the Social Security Taxable Wage Base, then the permitted disparity factor equals 5.7 percent. Note that the plan sponsor may set the integration level at an amount lower than the Social Security Taxable Wage Base. If this is done, however, the plan sponsor must then reduce the permitted disparity factor according to the following table.

Integration Level	Applicable Permitted Disparity Factor
The Taxable Wage Base (TWB)	5.7%
81-99% of the TWB	5.4%
21-80% of the TWB	4.3%
0-20% of the TWB	5.7%

EXAMPLE

Integrated Systems, Inc. maintains an integrated profit sharing plan for its employees. The integration level is the taxable wage base (i.e., $117,000 for 2014). For 2014, Integrated Systems will make a 6% contribution (i.e., the base contribution) up to the taxable wage base for all eligible participants. For those participants with compensation above the taxable wage base, Integrated Systems will make an 11.7% contribution (which is the lesser of twice the base contribution [12%] or the base contribution plus 5.7% [11.7%]).

Profit sharing plans typically satisfy general nondiscrimination rules by comparing the amount of contributions given to participants. The IRS allows plan sponsors to prove their plans are nondiscriminatory under a testing alternative known as the "cross-testing method." Under the cross-testing method, contributions are converted to equivalent benefits payable at normal retirement age, and then compared to determine whether or not the benefits unduly favor highly compensated employees over nonhighly compensated employees. This is similar to defined benefit plan testing. A complete discussion of the cross-testing method is beyond the scope of this manual.

Common businesses that use cross-tested plans are those that want to provide more favorable benefits for certain segments of employees. Typically, these are professional businesses such as chiropractors, doctors, and lawyers. The most common types of cross-tested plans are age-weighted and new comparability plans.

An age-weighted or age-based plan takes into consideration both the age of the plan participant and his/her compensation in determining the contribution amount. Consequently, age-weighted formulas favor older participants. Age-weighted allocation formulas are particularly well suited for small businesses and professional practices where the owners are markedly older than the rank-and-file employees.

New comparability plans permit plan sponsors to favor select groups of participants. Under the new comparability rules, plan sponsors are allowed to define and assign employees to different contribution "rate groups" within the plan. The contribution level for each rate group may vary, as long as the plan proves nondiscriminatory under the cross-testing method.

As the following comparison chart for 2014 illustrates, cross-tested allocation formulas can allow substantially higher contribution amounts for owners and key employees.

Employee	Age	Compensation	Discretionary Profit Sharing (*pro rate*)	Discretionary Profit Sharing (*integrated @ 81%*)	Discretionary Profit Sharing (*age weighted*)	Discretionary Profit Sharing (*cross tested*)
Owner A	48	$260,000.00	$52,000.00	$52,000.00	$52,000.00	$52,000.00
Owner B	60	$260,000.00	$52,000.00	$52,000.00	$52,000.00	$52,000.00
Participant C	43	$60,000.00	$12,000.00	$10,119.00	$9,238.33	$3,540.00
Participant D	50	$60,000.00	$12,000.00	$10,119.00	$15,326.84	$3,540.00
Participant E	32	$30,000.00	$6,000.00	$5,060.00	$2,084.83	$1,770.00
Total		$670,000.00	$134,000.00	$129,298.00	$130,650.00	$112,850.00

Contribution Limits

In addition to contributions being limited by the terms of the plan document, there are also statutory limits that apply to profit sharing plan contributions. These limits include the compensation cap, the IRC Sec. 415 limit, and the employer's IRC Sec. 404 limit for deductibility of plan contributions. A brief discussion of each of these limits follows.

Compensation Cap

The maximum amount of compensation that can be considered when calculating a plan participant's contribution is determined under IRC Sec. 401(a)(17) and IRC Sec. 404(l). The limit under these sections for 2013 is $255,000 and for 2014 is $260,000. This amount may be indexed periodically based on cost-of-living adjustments.

EXAMPLE

Janet Green, a participant in the ACE profit sharing plan, has annual compensation of $270,000. For 2014, Janet's employer decides to make a 10% pro rata profit sharing contribution to the plan. How large will Janet's contribution be?

ANSWER

Even though 10% of $270,000 would be $27,000, Janet's contribution will be $26,000 because only the maximum compensation amount of $260,000 for 2014 can be considered when making plan contributions.

IRC Sec. 415 Limit (Annual Additions Limit)

The maximum dollar amount that can be contributed to a profit sharing plan on behalf of an individual participant is the lesser of

- 100 percent of compensation, or
- the applicable dollar limit ($51,000 for 2013 and $52,000 for 2014)

This limit is known as the annual additions limit. Although it is possible that the 100 percent of compensation limit will be the limiting factor for making a contribution in some cases, it is far more likely that a participant's contribution will be limited by the annual dollar limit or the employer's deductibility limit before the 100 percent of compensation limit is reached.

EXAMPLE

Joe Brown, a participant in the Spade Company profit sharing plan, has annual compensation of $210,000. For the 2014 tax year, the Spade Company makes a 25%, pro rata profit sharing contribution to the plan. How large will Joe's contribution be?

ANSWER

Even though 25% of $210,000 is $52,500, Joe may receive a maximum contribution of only $52,000 in order to stay within the annual additions limit for 2014.

IRC Sec. 404 Deductibility Limit

Although the annual additions limit specifies that the maximum contribution that may be made on behalf of any one plan participant cannot exceed 100 percent of compensation, it is rare that this 100 percent of compensation limit will be applied, because a plan sponsor may only receive a tax deduction for contributions up to 25 percent of eligible payroll (i.e., the total compensation of all eligible participants in the plan). As long as a plan is using a pro rata formula, this limit is easily maintained by simply choosing an allocation percentage that does not exceed 25 percent of compensation. However, if, for example, an age-weighted formula is used, and the older participants in the plan happen to also be the most highly compensated participants, there is a greater likelihood that the contributions will exceed the deductibility limit.

EXAMPLE

Under an age-weighted profit sharing plan allocation formula, Stephen Fox, one of the older, and more highly compensated employees in his firm, is to receive a contribution equal to 30% of his compensation. Will his employer be able to deduct such a large contribution?

ANSWER

If, when Stephen's contribution is added to the contributions made to all the other eligible participants in the plan, the total of all contributions do not exceed 25% of total eligible compensation, then the employer will be able to deduct a contribution of 30% of compensation made on Stephen's behalf.

Participant Eligibility

An employer can limit participation in a profit sharing plan as long as the plan satisfies the minimum coverage and participation requirements set forth in the IRC.

Age Requirement

The maximum age requirement that a plan sponsor may impose through the terms of the profit sharing plan for participation eligibility is age 21 (IRC Sec. 410(a)(1)(A)(i)).

Service Requirement

A plan sponsor may require employees to complete a specified amount of service (up to two years) before becoming eligible to participate in a profit sharing plan. If the plan imposes a year of service requirement, each participant's accrued benefit may be subject to a risk of forfeiture according to the plan's vesting schedule, if one applies. However, if the plan imposes two years of service, a participant's benefit may not be subject to a vesting schedule, meaning each participant must have an immediate non-forfeitable right to 100 percent of his/her accrued benefit under the plan.

Sponsoring Employer Characteristics

The employer most likely to sponsor a profit sharing plan is one that is employee-oriented, and wants to help participants save for retirement, but desires the flexibility of discretionary contributions from year to year.

Money Purchase Pension Plans

Money purchase pension plans are quite similar to profit sharing plans, in terms of contribution limits, with one main difference—contributions to money purchase pension plans are mandatory, and are determined by the terms of the plan document. In this respect, although the ultimate benefit in a money purchase pension plan is not "defined," the plans are subject to minimum funding requirements based on the contribution that is promised in the plan document.

Prior to 2002, employers commonly paired money purchase pension plans with profit sharing plans (referred to as "paired plans"), because the level of deductible contributions that could be made to a profit sharing plan (15 percent of compensation) was lower than that allowed under a money purchase pension plan (25 percent of compensation). By combining a profit sharing plan with a money purchase pension plan, an employer could give itself the ability to maximize contributions by making, for example, a nondiscretionary 10 percent contribution in the money purchase pension plan, and a discretionary contribution up to 15 percent in the profit sharing plan.

However, with pension law changes that occurred in 2001, effective in 2002, the profit sharing plan deductible contribution limit was brought into parity with the money purchase pension plan limit, making paired plans essentially obsolete. Since most employers prefer contribution flexibility, when all other features are equal, many employers have discontinued their money purchase pension plans in recent years.

However, there are still some reasons why an employer might prefer a money purchase pension plan over a profit sharing plan, or other plan type. For example, the mandatory employer contribution in a money purchase pension plan sends a strong message to employees that their employer is dedicated to helping them save for retirement. From an employee's perspective, a money purchase pension plan is definitely preferable to a profit sharing plan because the participant will know in advance how much will be contributed on a year-to-year basis. This message may help bolster employee loyalty. Another reason an employer may desire a money purchase pension plan might be in the case of a leasing company that wants to allow its clients the ability to exclude their leased employees from participation under the clients' own retirement plans.

Contribution Formula

The contribution formulas used in money purchase pension plans are pro rata or integrated.

Pro Rata

An allocation formula that provides eligible participants with a contribution based on the same percentage of compensation is known as a pro rata formula.

An integrated allocation formula allows a plan sponsor to provide higher contributions for eligible participants who earn amounts over a set threshold, as long as the "permitted disparity rules" of IRC Sec. 401(1) are satisfied. Integrated plans are also known as "Social Security-based" or "permitted disparity" plans. The permitted disparity rules allow plan sponsors to give eligible participants who earn compensation above the "integration level," which is typically the Social Security Taxable Wage Base, an additional contribution. This additional contribution is equal to the lesser of

- two times the base contribution percentage, or
- the base contribution percentage plus the "permitted disparity factor."

Integration Level	Applicable Permitted Disparity Factor
The Taxable Wage Base (TWB)	5.7%
81-99% of the TWB	5.4%
21-80% of the TWB	4.3%
0-20% of the TWB	5.7%

If the plan sponsor sets the integration level at the Social Security Taxable Wage Base, then the permitted disparity factor equals 5.7 percent. Note that the plan sponsor may set the integration level at an amount lower, than the Social Security Taxable Wage Base. If this is done, however, the plan sponsor must then reduce the permitted disparity factor according to the table on the following page.

Contribution Limits

In addition to contributions being limited by the terms of the plan document, there are also statutory limits that apply to money purchase pension plan contributions. These limits include the compensation cap, the IRC Sec. 415 limit, and the employer's IRC Sec. 404 limit for deductibility of plan contributions. A brief discussion of each of these limits follows.

Compensation Cap

The maximum amount of compensation that can be considered when calculating a plan participant's contribution is determined under IRC Sec. 401(a)(17) and IRC Sec. 404(l). The limit under these sections for 2013 is $255,000 and for 2014 is $260,000. This amount may be indexed periodically based on cost-of-living adjustments.

Joel Ward, a participant in the Delightful Deli Money Purchase Pension Plan, which has a pro rata contribution rate of 10%, has annual compensation of $270,000. How large will Joel's contribution be?

Even though 10% of $270,000 would be $27,000, Joel's contribution will be $26,000, because the plan may only consider the maximum compensation amount of $260,000 when determining contributions for 2014.

IRC Sec. 415 Limit (Annual Additions Limit)

The maximum dollar amount that can be contributed to a money purchase pension plan on behalf of an individual participant is the lesser of

- 100 percent of compensation, or
- the applicable dollar amount ($51,000 for 2013 and $52,000 for 2014).

This limit is known as the annual additions limit. Although it is possible that the 100 percent of compensation limit will be the limiting factor for making a contribution in some cases, it is far more likely that a participant's contribution will be limited by the annual dollar limit or the employer's deductibility limit before the 100 percent of compensation limit is reached.

Ashley Rose, a participant in the Sprout Money Purchase Pension Plan, has annual compensation of $210,000. For the 2014 tax year, the Sprout Company makes a 25%, pro rata contribution to the money purchase pension plan. How large will Ashley's contribution be?

Even though 25% of $210,000 is $52,500, Ashley may receive a maximum contribution of only $52,000 in order to stay within the annual additions limit for 2014.

IRC Sec. 404 Deductibility Limit

Although the annual additions limit specifies that the maximum contribution that may be made on behalf of any one plan participant cannot exceed 100 percent of compensation up to a set dollar limit, it is rare that this 100 percent of compensation limit will be applied, because a plan sponsor may only receive a tax deduction for contributions up to 25 percent of eligible payroll (i.e., the total compensation of all eligible participants in the plan). As long as a plan is using a pro rata formula, this limit is easily maintained by simply choosing an allocation percentage that does not exceed 25 percent of compensation.

Participant Eligibility

An employer can limit participation in a money purchase pension plan as long as the plan satisfies the minimum coverage and participation requirements set forth in the IRC.

Age Requirement

The maximum age requirement that a plan sponsor may impose through the terms of the money purchase pension plan for participation eligibility is age 21 (IRC Sec. 410(a)(1)(A)(i)).

Service Requirement

A plan sponsor may require employees to complete a specified amount of service (up to two years) before becoming eligible to participate in a money purchase pension plan. If the plan imposes a year of service requirement, each participant's accrued benefit may be subject to a risk of forfeiture according to the plan's vesting schedule, if one applies. However, if the plan imposes two years of service, a participant's benefit may not be subject to a vesting schedule, meaning each participant must have an immediate nonforfeitable right to 100 percent of his/her accrued benefit under the plan.

Sponsoring Employer Characteristics

Employers that sponsor money purchase pension plans are typically well-established business that are able to guarantee an annual contribution to their employees.

Target Benefit Plan

A target benefit plan is a special type of money purchase pension plan under which contributions to a participant's account are determined by reference to the amounts needed to fund the stated "target" benefit under the plan. The plan bears some resemblance to a defined benefit plan, because contributions are based on projected retirement benefits, but actual benefits received at retirement are based on the investment performance of the contributions, and are not guaranteed, as they are in the case of a defined benefit plan.

Contribution Formula

In a target benefit plan, allocations are generally weighted for age and compensation. Consequently, contributions on behalf of older, more highly-paid employees tend to be greater than those provided to younger, lower-paid employees, when expressed as a percentage of compensation.

Contribution Limits

Contributions to a target benefit plan are limited by the formula specified in the plan document, the applicable compensation cap (IRC Sec. 401(a)(17)), the annual additions limit (IRC Sec. 415), and the employer's contribution deductibility limit (IRC Sec. 404).

Compensation Cap

The maximum amount of compensation that can be considered when calculating a plan participant's contribution is determined under IRC Sec. 401(a)(17) and IRC Sec. 404(l). The limit under these sections for 2013 is $255,000 and for 2014 is $260,000. This amount may be indexed periodically based on cost-of-living adjustments.

IRC Sec. 415 Limit (Annual Additions Limit)

The maximum dollar amount that can be contributed to a target benefit plan on behalf of an individual participant is the lesser of

- 100 percent of compensation, or
- the applicable dollar amount ($51,000 for 2013 and $52,000 for 2014).

This limit is known as the annual additions limit. Although it is possible that the 100 percent of compensation limit will be the limiting factor for making a contribution in some cases, it is far more likely that a participant's contribution will be limited by the annual dollar limit or the employer's deductibility limit before the 100 percent of compensation limit is reached.

IRC Sec. 404 Deductibility Limit

A plan sponsor may only receive a tax deduction for contributions to a target benefit plan of up to 25 percent of eligible payroll (i.e., the total compensation paid to all eligible participants in the plan).

Participant Eligibility

An employer can limit participation in a target benefit plan as long as the plan satisfies the minimum coverage and participation requirements set forth in the IRC.

Age Requirement

The maximum age requirement that a plan sponsor may impose through the terms of the target benefit plan for participation eligibility is age 21 (IRC Sec. 410(a)(1)(A)(i)).

Service Requirement

A plan sponsor may require employees to complete a specified amount of service (up to two years) before becoming eligible to participate in a target benefit plan. If the plan imposes a year of service requirement, each participant's accrued benefit may be subject to a risk of forfeiture according to the plan's vesting schedule, if one applies. However, if the plan imposes two years of service, a participant's benefit may not be subject to a vesting schedule, meaning each participant must have an immediate non-forfeitable right to 100 percent of his/her accrued benefit under the plan.

Sponsoring Employer Characteristics

Target benefit plans appeal to employers that want to benefit older employees.

Taft-Hartley Plans

Taft-Hartley plans are established by unions under Sec. 302(c)(5) of the Taft-Hartley Act. Taft-Hartley plans

- are funded by one or more participating employers;
- are collectively bargained with each participating employer;
- are managed by a joint board of trustees equally representing both labor and management;
- hold plan assets in a trust fund; and
- provide pension portability and consistent coverage to employees who change employers as long as the new employer participates in the same Taft-Hartley fund.

Taft-Hartley plans generally allow individual employees to gain credits toward pension benefits from work with multiple employers, as long as each employer has a collective bargaining agreement requiring plan contributions.

Most Taft Hartley plans are defined benefit plans, although they could also be defined contribution plans such as money purchase pension or profit sharing plans.

Contributions

Unlike most employer-sponsored retirement plans, where the employer decides what level of contribution will be made to the plan, or which benefit funding formula will be used, contributions to a Taft-Hartley plan are negotiated through collective bargaining.

Also, contributions are often based on a flat-rate per hour of covered service. For example, one employer under the plan might pay $1.50 per hour of covered service, while another employer might pay $1.00 per hour of covered service, depending on the collective bargaining agreement.

Contribution Limits

Contribution limits to a Taft-Hartley plan will depend upon the type of plan established (e.g., defined benefit or money purchase pension), and the terms negotiated as part of the collective bargaining agreement.

Eligibility Requirements

The age and service requirements applicable to plans sponsored by single employers, also apply to Taft-Hartley plans, but most plans tend not to impose initial eligibility requirements for plan participation. If eligibility requirements do apply, the number of hours of service required for eligibility to participate in a Taft-Hartley plan is determined by the collective bargaining agreement. It is not uncommon for a collective bargaining agreement to require nonunion participants to satisfy a higher number of hours per week than it requires of union participants in order to receive a contribution.

Sponsoring Employer Characteristics

Often, many employers in the same industry in a geographic area contribute to the same Taft-Hartley plan. Taft-Hartley plans are very common in the construction trades, where workers rotate from employer to employer and experience periodic unemployment between jobs. Without Taft-Hartley plans, these mobile workers would not only have great difficulty becoming eligible for participation in an individual employer's pension plan, they would often not be eligible for annual contributions because they would not accrue enough hours of service at any one employer to be eligible for a contribution.

Stock Bonus Plan

A stock bonus plan is defined in Treasury regulations under IRC Sec. 401(a) as a plan established and maintained to provide benefits similar to those of a profit sharing plan, except that benefits must be distributable in stock of the sponsoring employer. A stock bonus plan is subject to the same general qualification requirements, contribution limits, and eligibility requirements as a profit sharing plan.

There are some distinctions between a profit sharing plan and a stock bonus plan, however. For example, contributions to a stock bonus plan generally will be made in stock of the sponsoring employer, and if cash contributions are made, they are typically used to buy more employer stock.

Benefits from a stock bonus plan must be distributable in whole shares of employer stock, although the value of any fractional shares may be paid in cash. If the employer stock is not readily tradable on an established market, participants must have the right to require the employer to repurchase the stock.

Participants in a stock bonus plan have voting rights with respect to the employer stock, if the stock is not publicly traded. Profit sharing plans are not subject to this requirement.

Employee Stock Ownership Plan

An employee stock ownership plan (ESOP) is a stock bonus plan that is designed to invest primarily in stock of the sponsoring employer. The basic purpose of an ESOP is to transfer ownership of employer stock to the employees without having to resort to the sale of the business to outside persons. According to the National Center for Employee Ownership, there are about 11,300 ESOPs covering approximately 14 million employees.

An ESOP operates through a trust and allows a company to make tax deductible contributions to the trust for the purpose of purchasing company stock, which will subsequently be allocated to participants' accounts. Contributions may either be made in cash, which will be used to buy shares of the company, or existing company stock may be contributed directly to the trust.

ESOPs have many tax advantages for sponsoring companies, and a "leveraged ESOP" is often used as a corporate financing method. In a leveraged ESOP, the plan's trust borrows money from an outside lender (e.g., bank), and purchases employer stock, which is held in a suspense account within the plan. The company repays the loan by making tax-deductible contributions to the ESOP. As contributions are made by the employer to repay the loan, a portion of the stock in the suspense account is released and allocated to the participants' accounts in accordance with the allocation formula in the plan.

The loan proceeds can then be used for various corporate purposes, including financing new equipment, acquiring a new company, buying out an owner, or virtually any other legitimate business purpose.

Eligibility for an ESOP is generally quite liberal, since one of the main purposes of an ESOP is to encourage employees to take ownership in the company, as research has shown that companies that "share the wealth" and encourage open communication tend to grow faster than companies that do not take such an approach.

Generally, an ESOP is subject to the same overall qualification requirements, contribution limits, and eligibility requirements as a profit sharing plan, except ESOPs may not be tested for nondiscrimination using a safe harbor age and service allocation formula, nor can they use the cross-testing method.

401(k) Plans

An IRC Sec. 401(k) plan is a profit sharing or stock bonus plan with an employee funding feature known as a "cash or deferred arrangement" or CODA.

Contributions

The CODA allows participants to make pre-tax contributions to the 401(k) plan from their salary (i.e., salary deferrals). Effective January 1, 2006, 401(k) plans may contain a designated Roth contribution program (or Roth 401(k)).

In a Roth 401(k), participants may elect to treat their salary deferrals as designated Roth (after-tax) contributions. Roth 401(k) contributions must be

1. specifically designated as Roth contributions,

2. made to separate accounts and separately tracked within the plan,

3. made on an after-tax basis, and

4. limited, to where the combined total of pre-tax salary deferrals and Roth after-tax contributions does not exceed the annual limit.

For 2013 and 2014, the limit is $17,500 for participants under age 50, and $23,000 for those age 50 or greater. Employers may make profit sharing contributions to a 401(k) plan, as well as matching contributions based on participants' salary deferrals and/or designated Roth contributions.

Contribution Limits

As with all qualified retirement plans, 401(k) plans must satisfy certain tests to assure that contributions to the plan are nondiscriminatory. Because of the various types of contributions allowed under a 401(k) plan, and their interactions, these nondiscrimination tests are generally significantly more complicated than those that apply to other types of plans. The specific details of nondiscrimination testing for 401(k) plans is beyond the scope of this text. However, in order to be able to consider certain plan design strategies, it is necessary to be aware of the two nondiscrimination tests that are unique to 401(k) plans: the actual deferral percentage (ADP) test, which tests whether employee salary deferrals and designated Roth contributions discriminate in favor of highly compensated employees, and the actual contribution percentage (ACP) test, which tests whether employer matching and employee after-tax contributions discriminate in favor of highly compensated employees.

The basic contribution limits applicable to 401(k) plans follow.

Annual Deferral Limit

For participants under age 50, the annual deferral limit under IRC Sec. 402(g)(1) for IRC Sec. 401(k) plans is the lesser of 100 percent of compensation or $17,500 for 2013 and 2014. Unlike profit sharing contributions made by the employer, deferrals are not considered when determining whether an employer has exceeded his or her deductibility limit. Also, this limit is an individual limit, not a plan limit. Therefore, if an individual participates in two or more plans that are subject to the annual deferral limit, all annual deferrals must be added together for the purpose of determining whether the limit has been exceeded (except those deferrals made to 457 plans.)

EXAMPLE

Doug White, age 36, works part time for a company that offers a 401(k) plan, in which he is eligible to participate. His annual salary is $14,500. How much of his salary may he defer to his employer's 401(k) plan for 2014?

ANSWER

If Doug only participates in this employer's plan, he could defer up to $14,500, as long as the plan itself does not cap the maximum deferral at a lesser amount. However, if Doug participates in another employer's 401(k) plan for the year, he must aggregate the salary deferrals, and contribute no more than the maximum amount of $17,500 between the two plans for 2014.

Catch-Up Contribution for Participants Age 50 or Older

In the year a 401(k) participant turns age 50, and thereafter, catch-up contributions may be allowed under a 401(k) plan. A catch-up contribution allows participants who have already reached their annual deferral limit, a plan-imposed limit or a statutory limit to contribute an additional amount as a salary deferral contribution. For 2013 and 2014 the maximum additional amount is $5,500. As with conventional salary deferral amounts, catch-up contributions are not considered when determining deductibility limits for employers. Catch up contributions also do not count toward a participant's annual additions limit (explained later).

EXAMPLE

If Mary Marble turns 50 years old on December 20, 2014, and her plan allows participants to make catch-up contributions, how much may she contribute to her 401(k) plan as a salary deferral if she earns $50,000 in eligible compensation?

ANSWER

Mary may elect to defer up to $23,000 of her compensation to her 401(k) plan for 2014 (i.e., $17,500 as a standard salary deferral, and $5,500 as a catch-up contribution).

IRC Sec. 415 Limit (Annual Additions Limit)

The maximum dollar amount that can be deposited to a defined contribution plan on behalf of an individual participant is the lesser of 100 percent of compensation, or

$51,000 for 2013 and $52,000 for 2014. In the case of a 401(k) plan, salary deferrals, designated Roth and employer contributions are taken into account when determining this limit. If catch-up contributions are allowed under the plan, catch-up contributions essentially increase the IRC Sec. 415 limit to equal the annual additions limit plus the annual catch-up limit ($52,000 + $5,500 = $57,500 for 2014).

EXAMPLE

If Sam Black is age 53 in 2014, and has compensation of $200,000, how much may Sam defer to his 401(k) plan?

ANSWER

Sam may defer up to $23,000 to the plan. If Sam defers the entire $23,000, then Sam's employer may not contribute more than $34,500 to Sam, to assure that Sam does not exceed his annual additions limit of $57,500.

IRC Sec. 404 Deductibility Limit

Under IRC Sec. 404, a plan sponsor may only receive a tax deduction for contributions to a 401(k) plan of up to 25 percent of eligible payroll for the taxable year (i.e., the total compensation paid to all eligible participants in the plan). Employee salary deferrals are not treated as employer contributions for purposes of determining the maximum deductible contribution limit. Therefore, elective contributions are always fully deductible by the employer.

Participant Eligibility Requirements

An employer can limit initial participation in a 401(k) plan as long as the plan satisfies the minimum coverage and participation requirements set forth in the IRC.

Age Requirement

The maximum age requirement that a plan sponsor may impose through the terms of the 401(k) plan for participation eligibility is age 21 (IRC Sec. 410(a)(1)(A)(i)).

Service Requirement

A plan sponsor may require employees to complete a specified amount of service (up to one year) before becoming eligible to make employee salary deferrals to the 401(k) plan. Employee salary deferrals are always immediately vested.

If a 401(k) plan also provides for employer contributions, the plan may require employees to complete up to two years of service before becoming entitled to receive those contributions. If the plan imposes two years of service for employer contribution eligibility, a participant's benefit may not be subject to a vesting schedule, meaning each participant must have an immediate nonforfeitable right to 100 percent of his/her accrued benefit attributable to employer contributions under the plan.

If the plan imposes a year of service requirement to be eligible to receive employer contributions, each participant's accrued benefit with respect to employer contributions may be subject to a risk of forfeiture according to the plan's vesting schedule, if one applies.

Sponsoring Employer Characteristics

Employers that sponsor traditional 401(k) plans are typically businesses with more than 25 employees, that want to encourage their workers to take on some personal responsibility for preparing for retirement through making employee salary deferrals.

Tax-exempt organizations may offer 401(k) plans; however, governmental entities are not allowed to have 401(k) plans. (IRC Sec. 401(k)(4)(B)).

Solo or individual 401(k) plans appeal to owner-only businesses because they allow owners to maximize retirement plan contributions.

Combining insight it has gained from thousands of 401(k) plan audits and the recently completed 401(k) Compliance Check Questionnaire project, the IRS has identified the following 11 compliance problems as "most common" among 401(k) plans. They are the failure to

- Amend the plan document on a timely basis for federal law changes;
- Follow the terms of the plan document;
- Use the plan's definition of compensation, especially if the definition is different for some employees;
- Include all eligible employees, for example, if there is confusion about the definitions of eligibility and entry dates or who is an employee;
- Follow the plan's loan provisions and the requirements of Internal Revenue Code (IRC) Section (§) 72(p) regarding the maximum loan amount or the maximum loan repayment term;
- Satisfy the per-participant maximum annual plan contribution limit under IRC § 415, especially for 403(b) plans;
- Timely deposit elective deferrals;
- Follow the plan's terms on hardship distributions,
- Follow the plan's matching contribution provisions,
- Satisfy nondiscrimination testing for deferrals or matching contributions, and
- Cap elective deferrals to comply with IRC § 402(g) limits (i.e., $17,500 for those under age 50 and $23,000 for those age 50 and above).

The good news regarding these common compliance problems is the IRS has provided guidance on how plan sponsors may correct these errors (as well as others) through its Employee Plans Compliance Resolution System (EPCRS, contained in Revenue Procedure 2013-12) and the 401(k) Plan Fix-It Guide (both available on line at the IRS's web site www.irs.gov). The bad news—the IRS learned through the 401(k) Compliance Check Questionnaire project, that only 65 percent of plan sponsors were aware of EPCRS and only 41 percent were aware of the 401(k) Plan Fix-It Guide.

Safe Harbor 401(k) Plans

As noted earlier, nondiscrimination testing for 401(k) plans (i.e., the ADP and ACP tests) can be quite complicated, and if an employer's plan fails one or both of these tests, the employer must take corrective measures or face potential plan disqualification. Also, if a 401(k) plan is top heavy (where more than 60 percent of the plan's assets are held by key employees), it must satisfy minimum contribution and vesting requirements. One way for employers to avoid ADP and ACP testing, and satisfy top-heavy requirements, is by adopting what are known as safe harbor provisions in their 401(k) plans. A safe harbor 401(k) plan has certain implementation and operational requirements that an employer must follow. Safe harbor 401(k) plans must satisfy an employee notice requirement, a mandatory contribution requirement and a 100 percent vesting requirement.

Notice Requirement

The employer satisfies the notice requirement if at least 30 days (and no more than 90 days) before the beginning of each plan year, the notice is given to each eligible employee for the plan year. The notices must provide information on contributions that will be made; the type and amount of compensation that may be deferred under the plan; how to make cash or deferred elections; the periods available under the plan for making cash or deferred elections; withdrawal and vesting provisions; and how to obtain more information on the plan.

Mandatory ADP Safe Harbor Contribution

The employer must contribute either a basic matching contribution, an enhanced matching contribution, or a nonelective contribution each year.

100 Percent Vesting

Regardless of which type of safe harbor contribution is made (i.e., basic match, enhanced match, or nonelective contribution), it must be 100 percent vested (i.e., non-forfeitable). If the employer makes other, non-safe harbor contributions to the plan, they may be subject to a vesting schedule.

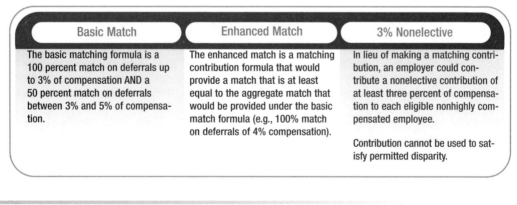

Basic Match	Enhanced Match	3% Nonelective
The basic matching formula is a 100 percent match on deferrals up to 3% of compensation AND a 50 percent match on deferrals between 3% and 5% of compensation.	The enhanced match is a matching contribution formula that would provide a match that is at least equal to the aggregate match that would be provided under the basic match formula (e.g., 100% match on deferrals of 4% compensation).	In lieu of making a matching contribution, an employer could contribute a nonelective contribution of at least three percent of compensation to each eligible nonhighly compensated employee. Contribution cannot be used to satisfy permitted disparity.

Distributions

Safe harbor contributions must not be distributed earlier than separation from service, death, disability, plan termination, or the attainment of age 59½. Safe harbor 401(k) contributions may not be made available for in-service withdrawal before age 59½ for any reason (including hardship).

ACP Safe Harbor Requirements

A plan satisfies the ACP safe harbor if the plan limits matching contributions to one of the following formulas.

- The basic match, with no additional matching contributions
- The enhanced match, where matching contributions do not exceed six percent of the employee's compensation, and no other matching contributions are made
- A matching formula where matching contributions are based on elective deferrals and/or employee after-tax contributions which, in aggregate, do not exceed six percent of the employee's compensation, the rate of matching does not increase as the rate of deferrals/after-tax contributions increases, and the rate for a highly compensated employee is not greater than the rate that applies to a nonhighly compensated employee with the same rate of deferrals/after-tax contributions.

Furthermore, regardless of which matching formula is used, additional limits must apply to other contributions in order to avoid the ACP test, such as the following.

- Discretionary matching contributions of any kind cannot exceed four percent of compensation.
- Deferrals representing more than six percent of compensation may not be matched.
- The rate of match may not increase as the deferral percentage increases.
- The rate of matching contributions for highly compensated employees may not be greater than for nonhighly compensated employees.

Note that, unlike the safe-harbor matching contributions, any additional contributions may be subject to a vesting schedule, and may be eligible for in-service withdrawals. If made, after-tax contributions would be subject to the ACP test, despite safe harbor provisions.

Eligibility Requirements

The safe harbor matching contribution requirement is satisfied if, under the terms of the plan, safe harbor matching contributions under either the basic matching formula or an enhanced matching formula are made on behalf of each nonhighly compensated employee who is eligible to make and has made employee salary deferrals.

The nonelective contribution requirement is satisfied if, under the terms of the plan, the employer makes a safe harbor nonelective contribution on behalf of each nonhighly compensated employee who is eligible to make employee salary deferrals, regardless of whether amounts are actually deferred.

The plan may not require a minimum number of hours be worked during the plan year, or employment on the last day of the plan year, to accrue the safe harbor contribution once the initial eligibility requirements to participate have been satisfied.

Sponsoring Employer Characteristics

Employers with existing 401(k) plans who consistently fail the ADP and/or ACP tests are prime candidates for adopting safe harbor provisions.

If an employer is considering establishing a 401(k) plan, and wants to avoid ADP and/or ACP testing from the get go, it should consider a safe harbor 401(k) plan.

DB(k)

A new hybrid defined benefit/401(k) plan, referred to as the "DB(k)" is available for plan years beginning on or after January 1, 2010. The DB(k) plan

- will automatically satisfy the defined benefit nondiscrimination requirements;
- is available to employers with 500 or fewer employees;
- is subject to IRS Form 5500 filing;
- would be required to include an automatic enrollment feature with a safe harbor match or nonelective contribution; and
- would automatically satisfy the 401(k) nondiscrimination testing.

DB(k) Requirements

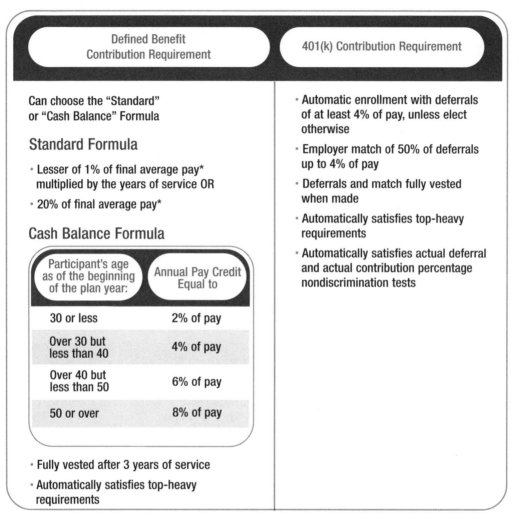

Defined Benefit Contribution Requirement	401(k) Contribution Requirement
Can choose the "Standard" or "Cash Balance" Formula	• Automatic enrollment with deferrals of at least 4% of pay, unless elect otherwise
Standard Formula	• Employer match of 50% of deferrals up to 4% of pay
• Lesser of 1% of final average pay* multiplied by the years of service OR	• Deferrals and match fully vested when made
• 20% of final average pay*	• Automatically satisfies top-heavy requirements
Cash Balance Formula	• Automatically satisfies actual deferral and actual contribution percentage nondiscrimination tests

Cash Balance Formula

Participant's age as of the beginning of the plan year:	Annual Pay Credit Equal to
30 or less	2% of pay
Over 30 but less than 40	4% of pay
Over 40 but less than 50	6% of pay
50 or over	8% of pay

• Fully vested after 3 years of service
• Automatically satisfies top-heavy requirements

*Final average pay is determined using the consecutive-year period (up to 5) during which the participant received the greatest aggregate compensation

Other DB(k) Details

- A sponsor of a DB/k need only file one Form 5500 annually for the plan.
- DB/k plans may use the safe harbors offered by qualified default investment alternatives.
- The Pension Benefit Guaranty Corporation only insures the defined benefit portion.

403(b) Plan

An IRC Sec. 403(b) plan is similar to an IRC Sec. 401(k) plan; however, employer eligibility for an IRC Sec. 403(b) plan is more limited. An employer is allowed to have an IRC Sec. 403(b) plan if it is a

- public school, college or university,
- church,
- public hospital, or
- tax-exempt entity under IRC Sec. 501(c)(3).

When 403(b) arrangements were first introduced, salary deferrals had to be invested in an annuity contract, which is why some people refer to 403(b) arrangements as tax-sheltered annuities (TSAs). However, 403(b) arrangements are no longer limited to annuity contracts. In addition to allowing assets to be invested in annuity contracts, IRC Sec. 403(b)(7) also allows assets to be invested in custodial accounts investing in mutual funds. For the purpose of this chapter, when we use the term 403(b) plan, it should be taken to apply to both annuity contracts and custodial accounts, unless otherwise specified.

403(b) plans are very similar to 401(k) plans with a few minor variations in operating rules, and some unique terminology, such as the "maximum amount contributable."

Plan Document Requirement

The 403(b) final regulations require that an eligible employer maintain its 403(b) plan pursuant to a written plan document. It is intended that the formal plan document include all of the material provisions regarding eligibility, benefits, applicable limitations, the contracts available under the plan, and the time and form under which benefit distributions would be made. The Department of Labor (DOL) has advised that the extent to which the plan document requirement subjects the employer to Title I of ERISA will be determined on a case-by-case basis. The regulations took effect January 1, 2009. All employers offering 403(b) arrangements must adopt a written plan no later than December 31, 2009. However, employers must operationally comply with the final rules as of January 1, 2009.

The IRS has compiled and posted on its web site (irs.gov) a Voluntary Correction Program Submission Kit for 403(b) plan sponsors who missed the December 31, 2009, deadline to adopt a written plan document.

The IRS also created a program to pre-approve 403(b) plan documents. From June 28, 2013, to April 30, 2014, the IRS will accept applications from plan document vendors seeking opinion and advisory letters (i.e., approval letters) for prototype and volume submitter 403(b) plans respectively, pursuant to the guidelines detailed in Revenue Procedure (Rev. Proc.) 2013-22. The IRS will not issue determination letters for individually designed 403(b) plans at this time. Entities sponsoring 403(b) plans that want reliance that the terms of their plans are in compliance with the Internal Revenue Code and Treasury regulations will need to restate them using pre-approved plan documents obtained from a document vendor (i.e., either a prototype plan sponsor or a volume submitter plan practitioner). Rev. Proc. 2013-22 states organizations with 403(b) plans will not be required to adopt pre-approved plans until sometime after April 30, 2015.

In conjunction with the release of Rev. Proc. 2013-22, the IRS made available sample 403(b) plan provisions [known as a listing of required modifications (LRMs)]. The sample provisions address requirements the IRS will consider in reviewing 403(b) plan documents submitted through the pre-approval program. Both Rev. Proc. 2013-22 and the 403(b) plan LRMs are available on the IRS's web site (irs.gov).

Contribution Formula

Depending upon how the plan is structured, 403(b) plans may allow participants to make employee salary deferrals, provide employer matching contributions, and/or provide profit sharing-like contributions.

Contribution Limits

Because only tax-exempt and not-for-profit organizations may offer 403(b) plans, they are not subject to the deductibility limits associated with 401(k) plans, which are generally offered by for-profit employers. However, similar rules apply regarding annual salary deferral and annual addition limits, with the addition of a concept that is unique to 403(b) plans, which is known as the maximum amount contributable (MAC). The basic rule for determining the MAC, is quite simple. Generally, if both elective deferrals and nonelective (employer) contributions are allowed to a 403(b) plan, contributions are limited to the lesser of the limit on

- annual additions, or
- annual salary deferrals.

Keep in mind, however, that if a 403(b) plan only allows for elective deferrals, the MAC is based on the limit on salary deferrals only, not the lesser of the limit on annual additions or the limit on salary deferrals. Similarly, if a 403(b) plan does not allow for elective deferrals (which would be unusual, but possible), the MAC will be based only on the limit on annual additions.

IRC Sec. 415 Limit (Annual Additions Limit)

The maximum dollar amount that can be contributed to a 403(b) plan on behalf of an individual participant is the lesser of 100 percent of includible compensation for the most recent year of service, or $51,000 for 2013 and $52,000 for 2014. (Note: The dollar limit may increase for later years as a result of cost-of-living increases.) In the case of a 403(b) plan, both salary deferrals and employer contributions are taken into account when determining this limit. If catch-up contributions are allowed under the plan, catch-up contributions essentially increase the IRC Sec. 415 limit to equal the annual additions limit plus the annual catch-up limit ($52,000 + $5,500 = $57,500 for 2014).

Under IRC §415, a participant generally is considered to exclusively control and maintain his or her own 403(b) plan. Consequently, in the situation where a 403(b) plan participant also participates in another employer's qualified retirement plan, contributions to a 403(b) plan the are not combined or aggregated with contributions to the qualified plan *except when the 403(b) participant controls the other employer* [Treas. Reg. 1.415-8(d)(1)]. It is important to note that an individual has only one salary deferral limit pursuant to IRC §402(g), regardless of the number of qualified plans in which he or she participates. Where a participant controls any business (defined as owning more than 50 percent of the business), the contributions to the 403(b) plan are combined with contributions to the qualified plan of the controlled employer or any affiliated employer [See Treasury Regulation 1.415-8(d)(2)].

Annual Deferral Limit (General Limit)

The annual deferral limit under IRC Sec. 402(g)(1) for IRC Sec. 403(b) plans is the lesser of 100 percent of compensation or $17,500 for 2013 and 2014. This limit is an individual limit, not a plan limit. Therefore, if an individual participates in two or more plans that are subject to the annual deferral limit, all salary deferrals must be added together for the purpose of determining whether the limit has been exceeded (except those deferrals made to 457 plans.)

Catch-Up Contribution for Participants Age 50 or Older

In the year a 403(b) participant turns age 50, and thereafter, catch-up contributions may be allowed under the 403(b) plan, just as they are with a 401(k) plan. A catch-up contribution allows participants who have already reached their annual deferral limit to contribute an additional amount as a salary deferral. For 2013 and 2014 this additional amount is $5,500. These contributions are added to what is otherwise allowable under the MAC.

15-Year Rule

Another unique feature available to 403(b) plan participants is the option to increase the limit on salary deferrals if the participant has at least 15 years of service with a public school system, hospital, home health service agency, health and welfare service agency, church, or convention or association of churches (or associated organization).

For participants in these professions with at least 15 years of service, the limit on salary deferrals to a 403(b) plan may be increased by the lesser of

- $3,000,
- $15,000, reduced by the sum of

- the increases to the general limit allowed in earlier years due to the application of this rule, plus

- the aggregate amount of designated Roth contributions for prior tax years, or

- $5,000 times the number of years of service for the sponsoring organization, minus the total elective deferrals made by the employer on the participant's behalf in prior years.

If a participant qualifies for the 15-year rule, his or her elective deferrals can be as high as $20,500 for 2013 and 2014 ($17,500 + $3,000).

Designated Roth Contributions

Effective January 1, 2006, 403(b) plans may contain a designated Roth contribution program (or Roth 403(b)).

In a Roth 403(b), participants may elect to treat their salary deferrals as designated Roth (after-tax) contributions. Roth 403(b) contributions must be

1 specifically designated as Roth contributions,

2 made to separate accounts and separately tracked within the plan,

3 made on an after-tax basis, and

4 limited, to where the combined total of pre-tax salary deferrals and Roth after-tax contributions does not exceed the annual limit on salary deferrals.

Participant Eligibility

The salary deferral portion of a 403(b) plan is subject to the "universal availability" rule, which says that all employees must be permitted to make salary deferrals, unless they are considered "excludible." Excludible employees include

- those who have made a one-time, irrevocable election not to make salary deferrals,

- employees whose contributions would total $200 or less annually,

- employees who are students performing services described in section 3121(b)(10)

- those who are participants in an eligible 457(b) governmental plan, 401(k) plan, or another 403(b) plan;

- non-resident aliens; and

- certain students and employees who normally work less than 20 hours per week.

If a 403(b) plan also provides for employer contributions, the plan may require employees to complete up to two years of service before becoming entitled to receive those contributions. If the plan imposes two years of service for employer contribution eligibility, a participant's benefit may not be subject to a vesting schedule, meaning each participant must have an immediate nonforfeitable right to 100 percent of his/her accrued benefit attributable to employer contributions under the plan.

If the plan imposes a year of service requirement to be eligible to receive employer contributions, each participant's accrued benefit may be subject to a risk of forfeiture according to the plan's vesting schedule, if one applies.

Sponsoring Employer Characteristics

An employer is allowed to have an IRC Sec. 403(b) plan if it is a

- public school, college or university,
- church,
- public hospital, or
- tax-exempt entity under IRC Sec. 501(c)(3).

IRC Sec. 457(b) Plans

457(b) plans are a type of nonqualified deferred compensation plan for state and local governmental units, certain educational organizations, and certain tax-exempt entities. 457(b) plans operate much like a 401(k) plan or a 403(b) plan, and allow employees of sponsoring organizations to delay taxation on salary that they contribute to the plan. Employers may also make contributions to the 457(b) plan on behalf of participants, but such amounts are considered compensation deferred by the participant. 457(b) plan contributions remain tax deferred until distributed from the plan. Assets held in 457(b) plans maintained by governmental employers (but not those maintained by tax-exempt entities) are eligible for roll over to IRAs or other retirement plans such as 401(k) and 403(b) plans.

Trust Requirements for Governmental Plans

All amounts deferred under a 457(b) plan maintained by a governmental employer must be held in trust for the exclusive benefit of the participants (IRC Sec. 457(b)).

An employer can meet this requirement by establishing a trust account for the plan. Alternatively, custodial accounts and/or annuity contracts may also satisfy the trust requirement, provided they meet the criteria under IRC Sec. 401(f) and Notice 98-8.

Sponsoring Employer Characteristics

IRC Sec. 457(b) plans may only be offered by the following types of employers:

- state and local governments, and any political subdivision, agency or instrumentality thereof;
- nongovernmental, tax-exempt entities under IRC Sec. 501; and
- tax-exempt rural electric cooperatives.

Cities, county or state hospitals, local police and fire departments, county governments, state universities and colleges, and public elementary and secondary schools are common examples of governmental employers that maintain 457(b) plans.

Typical tax-exempt entities that maintain 457(b) plans include charitable organizations, nonprofit civic leagues, chambers of commerce, and labor unions. It is important to note that in order for a qualifying tax-exempt entity to maintain a 457(b) plan, it must limit participation to a select group of upper management or highly compensated employees.

Churches are not considered eligible employers for purposes of establishing a 457(b) plan (IRC Sec. 457(e)(13)). However, certain church-related hospitals, colleges, and universities are eligible to establish 457(b) plans.

Eligible Participants

Governmental employers that sponsor 457(b) plans must limit participation to only those individuals who perform service for the employer (including independent contractors). Tax-exempt employers not only must limit participation to only those employees who perform service for the employer, but must further limit participation to highly paid employees, or a select group of upper management. The industry refers to this type of plan as a "top-hat" plan. This operational difference between governmental and tax-exempt employers exists because tax-exempt employers are not automatically exempt from the requirements of Title I of the Employee Retirement Income Security Act of 1974 (ERISA), as are governmental employers. Tax-exempt employers under IRC Sec. 501(c) can only become exempt from the additional administrative requirements of Title I of ERISA by offering their IRC Sec. 457(b) plans as "top-hat" plans.

Contributions

There are four different types of contributions that can be made under an IRC Sec. 457(b) plan: employee salary deferrals, catch-up contributions (two options), and employer contributions and, beginning January 1, 2011, designated Roth contributions.

Employee Salary Deferrals

457(b) participants may make employee salary deferrals for a year up to the lesser of "includible compensation" or $17,500 for 2013 and 2014 (IRC Sec. 457(b)(2)). The dollar amount may increase in future years pursuant to cost-of-living increases.

Catch-Up Contributions

457(b) participants have two options for making catch-up contributions to the plan. The first option is the special catch-up contribution, which is unique to IRC Sec. 457(b) plans (IRC Sec. 457(b)(3)). In the three years prior to the year a participant reaches normal retirement age (as defined by the plan), eligible participants may contribute up to the lesser of

- twice the annual salary deferral limit, or
- the sum of the current year salary deferral limit, plus the unused portion of prior years' limits.

The second catch-contribution option allows participants who are age 50 or older to defer an additional $5,500 for 2013 and 2014. This dollar amount may be increased in future years for cost-of-living adjustments.

A participant may not use both the age-50 catch up contribution option and the final-three-years catch-up contribution option in the same year. If a participant is eligible for both for a year, then the catch-up contribution limit is the greater of

- the age-50 catch-up contribution, or
- the final-three-year catch-up contribution.

Contributions made to other non-457(b) plans (i.e., 401(k) 403(b), salary deferral simplified employee pension (SEP) and savings incentive match plans for employees (SIMPLE) plans do not have to be aggregated to determine whether the annual contribution limits have been exceeded (IRC Sec. 457(b)).

Although IRC Sec. 457 does not explicitly address employer contributions as IRC Sec. 401(k) does, employers offering IRC Sec. 457(b) plans may make contributions on behalf of their employees. Regardless of who makes the contributions, the amount is deemed to be an employee contribution. Therefore, any contributions made by an employer on behalf of an employee reduces, dollar-for-dollar, the amount that the employee may defer into the plan.

EXAMPLE

Todd, a 30-year-old employee with the State of Illinois, who participates in the 457(b) plan, receives an employer-provided contribution of $5,000 for 2014. Since the annual deferral limit for 457(b) plans is $17,500, inclusive of both employee and employer contributions, Todd may not defer more than $12,500 for 2014.

As a result of the Small Business Jobs and Credit Act of 2010, sponsors of governmental 457(b) plans are permitted (but are not required) to have designated Roth contribution programs and permit in-plan Roth conversions in their plans, effective January 1, 2011. Roth 457(b) contributions must be

1 specifically designated as Roth contributions,

2 made to separate accounts and separately tracked within the plan,

3 made on an after-tax basis, and

4 limited, to where the combined total of pre-tax salary deferrals and designated Roth contributions does not exceed the annual limit on salary deferrals.

Ineligible IRC Sec. 457(f) Plans

Another flavor of 457 plan is the 457(f) plan, otherwise known as an ineligible plan. Ineligible 457(f) plans are relatively uncommon, and are ineligible for roll over to IRAs or other eligible retirement plans. For these reasons, a detailed discussion of 457(f) plans is beyond the scope of this book. However, the following paragraphs provide a brief synopsis of this plan type for the reader's edification.

- 457(f) plans are nonqualified deferred compensation plans available to state and local governmental employers, as well as tax-exempt employers.

- They are called ineligible plans because they fail to meet one or more of the requirements to be considered an "eligible" 457(b) plan, either intentionally, or unintentionally.

- Typically, there are no deferral limits under a 457(f) plan; however, a participant's assets must be subject to a "substantial risk of forfeiture," which must be conditioned upon future performance of substantial services.

- Plan assets become taxable to the participant when they are no longer subject to a substantial risk of forfeiture.

Some common types of 457(f) arrangements include arrangements for

- coaches, and

- presidents and upper management of tax-exempt organizations.

Thrift Savings Plan

A Thrift Savings Plan (TSP) is a retirement savings and investment plan available to government employees covered under either the Federal Employees' Retirement System (FERS) or the Civil Service Retirement System (CSRS). Starting on October 9, 2001, eligibility for benefits under the TSP was extended to members of the uniformed services, including the Ready Reserve. The regulations for these plans are found under Title 5 of the Code of Federal Regulations, Parts 1600-1690.

Although TSPs offer slightly different benefits depending on which program an employee or member of the uniformed services is participating in (FERS, CSRS, or military), they operate similarly to an IRC Sec. 401(k) plan. For example, they are defined contribution salary deferral programs, with annual deferral limits that mirror the limits allowed under an IRC Sec. 401(k) plan ($17,500 for 2013 and 2014), including the ability to make catch-up contributions for those age 50 and above. For that matter, many of the other rules that apply to IRC Sec. 401(k) plans, such as withdrawal restrictions, spousal protection regarding loans and withdrawals, and the ability to take in-service distributions for hardship, and the ability to roll pre-tax assets into a TSP from either an IRA or another type of qualified retirement plan also apply to TSPs. More information on these programs is available at www.tsp.gov.

Common Plan Design Strategies

Depending on the type of plan and plan document used to establish a retirement plan, the employer may have the flexibility to be able to incorporate some or all of the following plan design strategies.

401(k) Plan Automatic Enrollment

In a 401(k) plan, an affirmative deferral election has been the standard deferral model for years. This model requires the participant to execute a written election to defer receipt of a certain amount or percentage of pay. The employer then contributes the deferred amount to the 401(k) plan.

Over the last several years, an automatic enrollment model (also sometimes referred to as an "auto deferral" or "negative election" plan) has gained popularity with plan sponsors (Treas. Reg. 1.401(k)-1(a)(3)(ii)). In this model, the employer withholds a predetermined percentage of pay if an eligible participant fails to elect not to defer into the plan. The plan sponsor must give each eligible participant a notice that explains the automatic deferral arrangement, his or her right to elect not to have deferrals automatically made to the plan, and how the person may alter the amount of contributions, if desired. Following receipt of the notice, the plan sponsor must give each eligible employee a reasonable period of time to make a deferral election, and, ongoing, opportunity to change his or her election. Including an automatic enrollment feature has been an effective way for many employers to increase participation in their 401(k) plans.

In 1998, the Internal Revenue Service (IRS) issued a ruling clarifying that automatic enrollment in 401(k) plans is permissible for newly hired employees (Revenue Ruling 98-30). The IRS issued a second ruling (Revenue Ruling 2000-8) stating that automatic enrollment also is permissible for current employees who have not already enrolled in the plan. In 2004, the IRS published a general information letter that clarified two previously ambiguous points. The letter stated that (1) the amount deducted from the employee's pay and contributed to the plan can be any amount that is permissible under the plan up to the annual contribution limits under IRC Sec. 402(g), and (2) the plan can automatically increase the employee's contribution over time, such as after each pay raise. Again, the IRS emphasized that employees must be fully informed of these plan provisions, and they must have the option to change the amount of their contribution, or to stop contributing to the plan altogether.

1 the amount deducted from the employee's pay and contributed to the plan can be any amount that is permissible under the plan up to the annual contribution limits under IRC Sec. 402(g), and

2 the plan can automatically increase the employee's contribution over time, such as after each pay raise. Again, the IRS emphasized that employees must be fully informed of these plan provisions, and they must have the option to change the amount of their contribution, or to stop contributing to the plan altogether.

For plan years beginning on or after January 1, 2008, 401(k) plans can be designed or amended to include automatic enrollment safe harbors which allow plans to automatically satisfy the 401(k) nondiscrimination and top-heavy requirements. The automatic enrollment safe harbor provisions require:

- the automatic deferral contributions cannot exceed 10%, and must be at least 3% during the initial plan year, increasing to 4% during the second plan year, increasing to 5% during the third plan year, and increasing to 6% during any subsequent plan years,

- an employer-provided contribution in the form of either a matching contribution or nonelective contribution,

- the employer contribution must vest at least as rapidly under a two-year cliff,

- employer contributions are subject to the withdrawal rules applicable to elective contributions, and

- a notice be provided to each eligible employee explaining the employee's rights and obligation.

In Notice 2009-65, the IRS provides two sample amendments that sponsors of 401(k) plans can use to add automatic enrollment features to their plans.

Automatic Deferral Increases

In addition to an automatic enrollment feature, another new design strategy in a 401(k) plan is the scheduling of automatic deferral increases, usually to coincide with pay increases. In this model, participants commit in advance to allocating a portion of their future salary increases toward retirement savings. Typically, the increase is for a set amount (e.g., one or two percent of pay).

Vesting

The minimum vesting standards for plans are designed to ensure that participants will vest (i.e., own) their accrued benefit within a certain time period. Generally, the plan's vesting schedule must satisfy the legal requirements under one of two minimum schedules: "cliff" vesting or "graded" vesting.

Employer matching contributions in a 401(k) plan must vest under either a three-year cliff or six-year graded schedule. Effective for plan years after December 31, 2006, all employer contributions must also vest under either a three-year cliff or six-year graded schedule. Also, employee salary deferrals and safe harbor 401(k) contributions for participants are always 100 percent vested.

Three-Year Cliff Schedule

Under the three-year cliff vesting schedule, employees must be 100 percent vested once they complete three years of service. Prior to completing the third year of service, the vesting percentage can be zero percent.

Six-Year Graded Schedule

Under the six-year graded vesting schedule, employees must be 100 percent vested once they have completed six years of service. Prior to completing six years of service, participants must vest according to a minimum vesting percentage as outlined next.

Two years of service – 20 percent vested

Three years of service – 40 percent vested

Four years of service – 60 percent vested

Five years of service – 80 percent vested

Six years of service – 100 percent vested

Hours of Service vs. Elapsed Time

There are two methods for measuring service with an employer for plan eligibility purposes—the hours of service method and the elapsed time method. Under the hours of service method, the employer must count hours, and a year of service is a 12-month period during which the employee works a requisite number of hours for an employer. An employer cannot require more than 1,000 hours (IRC. Sec. 410(a)(3)(a)).

Under the elapsed time method, the employer is not required to count hours. An employee will be credited with a year of service under the elapsed time method if he or she is still employed on the first anniversary of his or her initial employment date (Treas. Reg. 1.410(a)-7(c)(2)(i)).

Statutory vs. Class Exclusions

Under the terms of the plan document, an employer may exclude certain individuals from participating in the plan. There are two types of exclusions: statutory and class.

Statutory Exclusions

According to IRC Sec. 410(b)(3), statutory exclusions include:
- those who do not meet a minimum age requirement (21 is the maximum age),
- those who do not satisfy a years of service requirement,
- union employees (as long as retirement benefits were the subject of good-faith bargaining), and
- nonresident aliens who receive no earned income.

Class Exclusions

Under a class exclusion, an employer may define a group of employees for exclusion from participation as long as the plan can meet minimum coverage rules under IRC Sec. 410(b). Note that a plan may not exclude part-time employees from participation as a class exclusion.

Last Day Requirement

An employer may impose a "last day" requirement in order for an individual to be eligible to receive a contribution. The last day requirement simply means the plan participant must be employed on the last day of the plan year in order to share in any employer contributions. A last day requirement may not apply to safe harbor 401(k) plans.

Loans

Having the ability to take a nontaxable loan from the plan is an appealing feature, but one that increases the complexity of plan administration. Among the many requirements that must be satisfied so that a loan is not considered a taxable distribution is the limit on the maximum amount. The maximum amount of a participant loan may not exceed half the participant's vested account balance up to $50,000 (IRC Sec. 72(p)(2)(A)). There are many questions to answer when designing the plan's loan program, such as, will participants be allowed to have more than one outstanding loan, how will loan fees be handled (e.g., charged against the participant's account), and from what money sources will the loan be taken? The IRS cites failure to satisfy plan loan provisions as one of the top 10 plan failures found in its voluntary correction program.

In-Service and Hardship Distributions

Employers can design their 401(k)/profit sharing plans to allow participants to take all or a portion of their plan assets while they are still employed. This is called an "in-service" distribution provision. Different contribution types are often subject to different in-service distribution rules. For example, employee salary deferrals are subject to the most restrictive in-service distributions rules (i.e., generally limited to situations of hardship or attainment of age 59½.) The rules related to in-service distributions of employer-provided contributions and rollover contributions are usually more liberal. In-service distributions, other than those taken as a result of hardship, are generally eligible for rollover. For 2007 and later plan years, employers may include an in-service distribution option in their defined benefit plans, beginning at age 62.

Rollovers

When designing a plan, an employer can decide whether it will allow rollovers from other eligible plans and IRAs to its retirement plan. Having the ability to roll over plan assets from their old employers' plans into their new employers' plans has great appeal to job changers—and there are a lot of them. According to the Bureau of Labor Statistics, an individual holds an average of 10.2 jobs from ages 18 to 38.

Self-Direction of Investments

An employer can retain the responsibility for investing the plan's assets, or allow participants to self-direct all or a portion of their plan assets. Self-direction of investments is one of the requirements that an employer must meet if it chooses to take advantage of ERISA Sec. 404(c) fiduciary protection. Under the provisions of ERISA Sec. 404(c), if a plan, such as a profit sharing, 401(k) or money purchase pension plan, gives its participants

1 the ability to exercise control over the assets in their individual accounts,

2 the ability to invest plan assets in a broad range of investment alternatives, and

3 sufficient information about investment options under the plan, thereby enabling them to make informed investment decisions, then the employer will not be held responsible for the participants' investment decisions.

The employer would retain the fiduciary responsibility for prudently selecting and monitoring the investment alternatives contained in the broad range of investments, however.

Under the new ERISA 404(a)(5) rules, effective for plan years beginning after October 31, 2011, a plan will satisfy the information requirements of ERISA 404(c) if plan participants receive:

- an explanation that the plan is a 404(c) plan and, therefore, the fiduciaries may not have liability for losses resulting from the participants' investment choices

- the information required under the new participant disclosure regulations required under ERISA 404(a)

Furthermore, if a plan offers stock of the sponsoring employer as an investment alternative, the plan sponsor must provide participants with a description of the procedures established to provide for the confidentiality of information regarding holding and voting those securities, including contact information for the responsible fiduciary.

Fiduciary Advisers

"Fiduciary Advisers" may provide investment advice to participants in an "eligible investment advice arrangement", and plan sponsors may reduce their fiduciary liability if certain monitoring and disclosure rules are followed (effective 2007). The Pension Protection Act of 2006 (PPA-06) created a statutory prohibited transaction exemption for "fiduciary advisers" who deliver investment advice as part of an "eligible investment advice arrangement." On October 25, 2011, the Department of Labor (DOL) issued final regulations relating to the provision of investment advice to individual account plan participants and beneficiaries, and IRA owners. The regulation is designed to provide guidance on the statutory exemption enacted in PPA-06 for investment advice to participants in participant-directed individual account plans and in individual retirement accounts (IRAs) through a level-fee or computer-based advice model. These final rules take effect December 27, 2011, replacing proposed rules the DOL had previously issued on March 2, 2010, which had replaced final (but never applicable) DOL regulations that were withdrawn on November 20, 2009. Meeting the requirements of the prohibited transaction exemption reduces the overall plan liability for a plan sponsor because the plan sponsor is not responsible for the specific investment advice given by the fiduciary adviser. The plan sponsor is still responsible for the prudent selection and monitoring of the available investments under the plan and the fiduciary adviser. The next section outlines the fiduciary adviser and eligible investment advice arrangement requirements.

Who May Be A Fiduciary Adviser?

Under PPA-06, and subsequent Department of Labor guidance, a fiduciary adviser is defined as a person who is a fiduciary of the plan by reason of the provision of investment advice to participants or beneficiaries, and who is also

- registered as an investment adviser under the Investment Advisers Act of 1940 or under State laws;

- a bank, a similar financial institution supervised by the United States or a State, or a savings association (as defined under the Federal Deposit Insurance Act), but only if the advice is provided through a trust department that is subject to periodic examination and review by Federal or State banking authorities;

- an insurance company qualified to do business under State law;

- registered as a broker or dealer under the Securities Exchange Act of 1934;

- an affiliate of any of the preceding; or

- an employee, agent or registered representative of any of the preceding who satisfies the requirements of applicable insurance, banking and securities laws relating to the provision of advice.

- any person who develops the computer model, or markets the computer model or investment advice program (An election pursuant to the regulations can be made to treat one individual as the FA in this situation.)

Eligible Investment Advice Arrangement

In order to meet the prohibited transaction exemption, the fiduciary adviser must meet several requirements. The exemption is available only if the investment advice offering of the fiduciary adviser is part of an eligible investment advice arrangement. To be an eligible investment advice arrangement the program must be

- a level-fee arrangement;

- a computer model arrangement; or

- a combination of the above.

Level Fee Requirements

The level-fee arrangement must meet all of the following criteria.

1 Any investment advice is based on generally accepted investment theories that take into account the historic risks and returns of different asset classes over defined periods of time. Advice may also take into account additional considerations.

2 Any investment advice takes into account investment management and other fees and expenses.

3 To the extent furnished, take into account requested information relating to age, time horizons (e.g., life expectancy, investment options, other assets or sources of income, and investment preferences of the participant or beneficiary.

4 No FA (including any employee, agent, or registered representative thereof) receives from any party (including an affiliate of the FA), directly or indirectly, any fee or other compensation that is based in whole or in part on a participant's or beneficiary's selection of an investment option. Note: The commentary to the regulations indicates that the level-fee requirement under the relief only applies to an FA and does not extend to affiliates of the fiduciary adviser unless the affiliate also is a provider of investment advice (see FAB 2007-1).

Consequently, even though an affiliate of a FA may receive fees that vary depending on investment options selected, any provision of financial or economic incentives by an affiliate (or any other party) to a FA or any individual employed by such FA (e.g., an employee providing advice on its behalf or an individual responsible for supervising such an employee) to favor certain investments would be impermissible.

Computer Model Requirements

Computer model advice must meet all of the following criteria.

1. Based on generally accepted investment theories that take into account the historic risks and returns of different asset classes over defined periods of time. Advice may also take into account additional considerations.
2. Take into account investment management and other fees and expenses.
3. Appropriately weight the factors used in estimating future returns of the investment options
4. To the extent furnished, take into account requested information relating to age, time horizons (e.g., life expectancy, retirement age), risk tolerance, current investments in designated investment options, other assets or sources of income, and investment preferences. Advice may also take into account additional considerations.
5. Utilize appropriate objective criteria to provide asset allocation portfolios comprised of investment options available under the plan.
6. Avoid investment recommendations that
   - Inappropriately favor investment options offered by the FA or a person with a material affiliation or material contractual relationship with the FA over other investment options, if any, available under the plan; =
   - Inappropriately favor investment options that may generate greater income for the FA or a person with a material affiliation or material contractual relationship with the FA; or
   - Inappropriately distinguish among investment options within a single asset class on the basis of a factor that cannot confidently be expected to persist in the future.
7. Take into account all designated investment options available under the plan (including qualifying employer securities, and properly disclosed target date or target risk funds, and excluding properly disclosed retirement income annuity options) without giving inappropriate weight to any investment option. The computer model can also exclude any investments excluded at the election of the participant.

Other Requirements

Additionally, the investment advice program must meet several other requirements to qualify for the prohibited transaction exemption.

1. The eligible investment advice arrangement must be authorized by a plan fiduciary who is not the fiduciary adviser.
2. Every year the investment advice program must be audited by a qualified

independent auditor to verify that it meets the requirements. The auditor is required to issue a written report to the plan fiduciary that authorized the arrangement. **For a retirement plan**, within 60 days of the completed audit, the independent auditor must issue a written report to the FA and to each fiduciary that authorized the use of the EIAA. **For an IRA**, within 30 days of receipt of the auditor's report, the FA must furnish a copy of the report to the IRA beneficiary or make such report available on its web site. If the report reveals noncompliance with the regulations, the FA must send a copy of the report to the DOL. In both cases the report must indentify the

  (1) FA,
  (2) type of arrangement,
  (3) eligible investment advice expert and date of the computer model, certification (if applicable), and
  (4) findings of the auditor.

3 Before the initial investment advice is given, the fiduciary adviser must give written notification to plan participants or beneficiaries, which includes information regarding

- the role of any related party in the development of the investment advice program or the selection of investment options under the plan;

- past performance and rates of return for each investment option offered under the plan;

- any fees and compensation of the FA or affiliate as a result of the provision of advice; sale, acquisition or holding of a security or property pursuant to the advice; any rollover or other distribution; or investment of distributed assets in any security or property pursuant to the advice

- any material affiliation or contractual relationship of the fiduciary adviser or affiliates in the security or other property involved in the investment transaction;

- the manner and under what circumstances any participant or beneficiary information will be used or disclosed;

- the types of services provided by the fiduciary adviser regarding the provision of investment advice;

- the adviser's status as a fiduciary of the plan in connection with the provision of the advice; and

- the ability of the recipient of the advice to separately arrange for advice by another adviser that could have no material affiliation with and receive no fees or other compensation in connection with the security or other property.

The notification must be written in a way that can to be understood by the average plan participant, and is sufficiently accurate and comprehensive to inform the participants and beneficiaries of the required information. The DOL has developed a model form for the required disclosures of fees and other compensation. Additionally, the fiduciary adviser must maintain all of the information required to be disclosed in the notification, deliver the notice to participants at least annually, provide a revised notice to participants timely when any material change occurs, and upon request at no charge.

4 The fiduciary adviser must provide disclosures as required by all applicable securities laws.

5 The plan participant must provide the sole direction to effect the transaction.

6 The compensation received by the fiduciary adviser must be reasonable.

7 Any transaction must be at least as favorable to the plan as an arm's length transaction would be.

8 Finally, the fiduciary adviser must maintain records necessary to prove compliance with the requirements of the fiduciary adviser's eligible investment advice arrangement for six years after the provision of advice to plan participants and beneficiaries.

Qualified Default Investment Alternatives

ERISA 404(c) protection is expanded to include "qualified default investment alternatives" (QDIA) if certain notice and disclosure requirements are satisfied (effective 2007). Prior to PPA-06, the rules for selecting and monitoring default investments were vague at best. Traditionally, many plans defaulted to a stable value or money market fund. Generally, participants were not informed of the defaults, nor were the default funds subject to ongoing plan sponsor review or scrutiny.

PPA-06 addressed many of the outstanding issues with respect to ERISA 404(c) coverage and the use of default investments within a plan. Section 624 of PPA-06 added a new Section 404(c)(5) to ERISA. In general, as long as certain disclosure and notice requirements are satisfied, the participant's contributions may be placed in default investment options and the plan will retain ERISA 404(c) protection.

PPA-06 mandates various requirements regarding default investment options. These requirements include the following.

1 The dollars must be invested in "qualified default investment alternatives (defined below).

2 Participants must have opportunity to direct their investments into other options.

3 A notice must be provided at least 30 days before the date of plan eligibility, or at least 30 days before the initial investment in a QDIA, and then at least 30 days before each subsequent plan year. The notice must be in a form deemed to be understandable by the average participant, and must contain the following information, a description of

- when the participant's assets may be invested in the defaults;
- the default, including investment objectives, risk and return characteristics, and fees and expenses;
- the participant's rights to direct assets out of the default without fees or penalties; and
- where the participant can obtain investment information concerning other investment options within the plan.

4 All account statements, proxies, prospectuses, etc., received by the employer must be forwarded to the participant.

5 Participants must be able to transfer from the default without penalty.

6 Participants must be afforded opportunity to invest in a broad range of investment alternatives.

7 Fees and expenses may not exceed the limits on such amounts that plans can impose on participants who opt out of the plan or decide to direct their investments.

Under the DOL final regulations, four types of investments are permitted as QDIAs.

The first option is a "life-cycle" or "target-retirement-date" fund or model portfolio that applies generally accepted investment theories, is diversified so as to minimize the risk of large losses, and is designed to provide varying degrees of long-term appreciation and capital preservation through a mix of equity and fixed income exposures based on the participant's age, target retirement date or life expectancy. Such products and portfolios must change their asset allocations and associated risk levels over time with the objective of becoming more conservative with increasing age. Asset allocation decisions for such products and portfolios are not required to take into account risk tolerances, investments or other preferences of an individual participant. For plans that use target date funds, the DOL has issued proposed regulations that, when finalized, will require plans to give employees more information about their target date fund and the changes to the percentage of stocks and bonds held in the fund as investors approach the target date.

A second option is a "balanced" fund or model portfolio similar to the first option, except that it must be consistent with a target level of risk appropriate for participants of the plan as a whole. Asset allocation decisions for such products and portfolios are not required to take into account the age, risk tolerances, investments or other preferences of an individual participant.

A third option is a "managed account," where participants' dollars are allocated based on age, target retirement date or life expectancy among the existing fund options in the plan by an investment management service that applies generally accepted investment theories, allocates the assets of a participant's individual account to achieve varying degrees of long-term appreciation and capital preservation through a mix of equity and fixed income exposures. Such portfolios must be diversified so as to minimize the risk of large losses and change their asset allocations and associated risk levels for an individual account over time with the objective of becoming more conservative with increasing age. Asset allocation decisions are not required to take into account risk tolerances, investments or other preferences of an individual participant.

A fourth, albeit limited, option is a capital preservation product. However, a plan may only use a capital preservation product as a QDIA for the first 120 days of an employee's participation. At the end of the 120-day period, the plan fiduciary must redirect the participant's investment in the capital preservation product to another QDIA. The DOL included this type of product for two reasons:

1 because it realized that some plan sponsors may find it desirable to reduce investment risks for all or part of their workforce following employees' initial enrollment in the plan; and

2 to allow employees in automatic enrollment plans a reasonable amount of time following the end of the applicable 90-day withdrawal period to transfer assets to another QDIA.

Transition Rule for Certain Stable Value Products

A transition rule applies to plans that adopted certain stable value products with a guaranteed interest rate as their default investment. The final rules grandfather these arrangements by providing relief for contributions invested in the default stable value investment on or before December 24, 2007. The transition rule does not apply to future contributions to stable value products.

Proposed Regulations

On November 29, 2010, the DOL issued proposed rules that would, if finalized, amend the QDIA regulations and participant-level disclosure regulations to require plan sponsors to provide more information to participants and beneficiaries with respect to target date funds if they are used as default investment alternatives. As of November 2013, the industry was still awaiting finalized regulations. The proposed rule would amend these two regulations to ensure that all participants and beneficiaries (whether or not defaulted into a target date fund) in participant-directed individual account plans receive comprehensive information needed to evaluate target date funds and how specific these funds may meet their investment objectives, including the following details:

1 A narrative explanation of how the target date fund's asset allocation will change over time, and the point in time when it will reach its most conservative position;

2 A graphical illustration of how the target date fund's asset allocation will change over time, and

3 For a target date fund that refers to a particular date (e.g., "Retirement 2050 Fund"), an explanation of the relevance of the date.

In addition, the Department of Labor (DOL) issued guidelines addressing the selection and monitoring of default investment options that would be deemed "qualified default investment alternatives," for the purpose of extending ERISA 404(c) protection. With the provisions of PPA-06 and the DOL guidelines, plan sponsors have greater clarity with respect to the use of default investments.

Target Date Tips

In late February 2013, the Department of Labor released on its web site (irs.gov) a three-page document entitled "Target Date Retirement Funds—Tips for ERISA Plan Fiduciaries," designed to assist plan fiduciaries in selecting and monitoring TDFs and other investment options in 401(k) and similar participant-directed individual account plans. The document highlights eight key considerations for plan sponsors when considering TDFs for their plans. The eight key considerations include the following:

- Establish a process for comparing and selecting TDFs
- Establish a process for the periodic review of selected TDFs
- Understand the fund's investments
- Review the fund's fees and investment expenses
- Inquire about whether a custom or non-proprietary target date fund would be a better fit for your plan
- Develop effective employee communications
- Take advantage of available sources of information to evaluate the TDF and recommendations you received regarding the TDF selection
- Document the process

In light of these regulations, many plan sponsors are beginning to review their default investment election practices and give consideration to automatic enrollment features. Traditionally, many employers simply defaulted to stable value or money market options. Plan sponsors should now review these decisions in light of the default investment regulations.

In addition, the regulations are clear that the default investment selection process is not a one-time event. Plan sponsors must periodically review their default election decisions to ensure their choices remain appropriate, and that performance and fees remain competitive. The DOL notes in the regulations, "… that fees and expenses would be an important consideration in selecting among the [default investment election] alternatives."

Plan advisers should take steps to ensure plan sponsors are aware of the default investment requirements and, at minimum, review the plan's default investments in light of the requirements. The expansion of ERISA 404(c) coverage to default investments is a positive development that advisers can use as a talking point with current and prospective retirement plan clients.

Investment Policy Statement

An investment policy statement for a plan is a written document that details how plan fiduciaries who are responsible for plan investments will make investment management decisions. ERISA does not require a plan to have a written investment policy statement, but the Department of Labor endorses the use of a written investment policy (DOL Reg. 2509.94-2). The only thing worse than not having an investment policy statement, is having one to which the plan fiduciaries do not adhere.

Heightened Disclosure Requirements

The Department of Labor (DOL) has flooded the industry with new service provider and plan sponsor fee disclosure rules for retirement plans. The new fee disclosure rules present a great opportunity to talk to your plan sponsor clients and prospects.

Fee disclosure can be segmented into three primary components. Each component has a unique focus and purpose; however, a certain amount of overlap exists. The three elements include the following.

Form 5500 Schedule C Disclosures
(effective for 2009 and later plan years)

- Plans with more than 100 participants must report amounts paid to service providers.
- Service providers with more than $5,000 of compensation are reported on the Schedule C of Form 5500 (the annual information return).
- Fees, commissions, and other charges through self-directed brokerage windows must be reported.
- TPA fees are disclosed separately, even if they are paid indirectly as part of a bundled product.

The Department of Labor has issued two sets of FAQs on the Schedule C requirements to help service providers and plan sponsors comply with the new requirements.

Plan Fee Disclosure
[ERISA Sec. 408(b)(2) regulations effective July 1, 2012.

- Service providers must disclose to plan fiduciaries of defined benefit and defined contribution plans the specific services they provide along with the direct and indirect compensation received of $1,000 or more.
- These disclosures are required before contracts with service providers are executed and before any contract is renewed.
- Contract termination fees and charges will be subject to new scrutiny.

Participant-Level Disclosure Requirements
[ERISA Sec. 404(a)(5) regulations are applicable for plan years beginning on or after November 1, 2011, subject to a "transitional rule."

- Plan sponsors of participant-directed defined contribution plans must report plan- and investment-related fees to participants and beneficiaries.

- Investment information must include one-, five- and 10-year investment returns. The DOL has issued a model disclosure form.

- Participants must be alerted to potential fees such as qualified domestic relations order (QDRO) determination fees, loan and/or distribution fees.

- Participants must receive quarterly fee reporting that discloses the actual (noninvestment-related) amount taken from the account in the prior quarter.

- Transitional Rule: Initial annual notices were required to be provided by the later of 60 days after the first day of the first plan year beginning on or after November 1, 2011; or 60 days after the effective date of the plan service provider disclosure rules (i.e., August 30, 2012 for calendar year plans). Initial quarterly statements were due no later than 45 days after the end of the quarter in which the initial annual disclosure is required (i.e., by November 14, 2012 for calendar year plans).

- Six month delay for second year disclosure: On Monday July 22, 2013, the Employee Benefits Security Administration (EBSA) division of the Department of Labor announced, in Field Assistance Bulletin (FAB) 2013-02, plan sponsors of participant-directed defined contribution plans will have an additional six months to provide participants with plan-related and investment-related information as required pursuant to DOL Reg. 2550.404a-5 (i.e., the final participant fee disclosure regulations).The six-month delay effectively allows plan sponsors to re-set the delivery deadline for such disclosures going forward.

Example:
Dean's Discs provided initial participant fee disclosures to participants of its participant-directed 401(k) plan on August 25, 2012. Prior to FAB-2013-02, Dean's Discs would have been required to provide the second annual disclosure by August 25, 2013. However, under FAB 2013-02, Dean's Discs may delay providing the second annual disclosure until February 25, 2014 — 18 months after distribution of the initial disclosures. The third and subsequent years' annual participant disclosures would need to be provided no later than the February 25 deadline following the end of each respective year, thereby accomplishing the one-time reset of the timing of the disclosures.

Plan sponsors who already provided the 2013 disclosures by August 30, 2013, may choose to apply the same 18-month delay to next year's disclosures (i.e., provide the 2014 disclosures no later than 18 months after August 30, 2013).

Plan Type	DOL Reg. 2550.408b-2	DOL Reg. 2550.404a-5	Form 5500, Schedule C
Who	Service provider to plan sponsor	Plan sponsor to participants and beneficiaries	Plan sponsors to IRS and DOL
Applicablity Date	04/01/2012	Plan years beginning on or after 11/01/2011; transitional rule* applied	2009 and later plan years
Plans Affected	DC and DB plans regardless of size	All participant-directed DC plans	DC, DB and welfare benfit plans with 100 or more participants
Guidelines	Disclose receipt of direct and indirect compensation of $1,000 or more	Disclose certain plan and investment-related information to participants and beneficiaries	Report direct and indirect compensation of $5,000 or more paid to service providers

*Transitional Rule: Initial annual notices were required to be provided by the later of 60 days after the first day of the first plan year beginning on or after November 1, 2011; or 60 days after the effective date of the plan service provider disclosure rules (i.e., May 31, 2012 for calendar year plans). Initial quarterly statements were due no later than 45 days after the end of the quarter in which the initial annual disclosure is required (i.e., by August 14, 2012 for calendar years plans).

Financial Professional Considerations

Fees and Investment Selection

As a result of these rule changes, participants will be receiving a glut of information on fees and expenses. Obviously, fees are an important consideration when making investment choices. However, fees are not the only consideration when making investment decisions. Work with participants to help them understand the factors (e.g., risk, time horizon, asset class and asset class allocation, etc), in addition to fees, that are part of good investment decision making.

Post-Fee Disclosure Next Steps

Fee disclosure is not an end onto itself. The DOL intends the fee disclosure requirements to help plan fiduciaries make better overall decisions with respect to the plan and its service providers.

Ask your plan sponsor clients the following key questions.

- "Have you incorporated the new fee disclosure requirements into your overall fiduciary oversight policy?"
- "Have you reviewed your ERISA liability containment strategy to reflect the new fee disclosure requirements?"

Fee disclosure is complex. The new requirements are great opportunities to provide value by helping clients understand a subtle and sometimes sensitive subject.

In keeping with the fee disclosure compliance theme, the Employee Benefits Security Administration (EBSA), the branch of the Department of Labor (DOL) that protects the rights of participants and beneficiaries in workplace retirement plans subject to the Employee Retirement Income Security Act of 1974 (ERISA), has implemented the Fiduciary Service Provider Compensation Project for fiscal year (FY) 2013.

Under this project, the EBSA will continue to investigate retirement plan consultants, financial advisors and other service providers regarding the receipt of possible improper or undisclosed compensation from the plans they service. This project complements the EBSA's regulatory and reporting initiatives intended to ensure that plan fiduciaries and participants receive comprehensive disclosures about service provider compensation and conflicts of interest. Through this initiative, the EBSA will also conduct criminal investigations of cases dealing with potential fraud, kickbacks, and embezzlement involving advisors to plans and participants.

IRS Correction Programs

Despite their best efforts, plan sponsors may find their qualified retirement plans fail to comply with all of the IRS' requirements. To address these situations, the IRS created the Employee Plans Compliance Resolution System (EPCRS) as a way to permit plan sponsors to correct plan qualification failures that could jeopardize the qualified status of their plans and, thereby, allow them to continue to provide their employees with retirement benefits on a tax-favored basis. The components of EPCRS are the Self-Correction Program (SCP), the Voluntary Correction Program (VCP), and the Audit Closing Agreement Program (Audit CAP). The IRS has updated the EPCRS in Revenue Procedure (Rev. Proc.) 2013-12, which modifies and supersedes the previous governing guidance in Rev. Proc. 2008-50. Significant changes to the ERCRS include, but are not limited to, the following:

- Expanded corrections for 403(b) plan failures

- Revised submission procedures for the VCP

- Rules for plans subject to IRC Sec. 436 benefit restrictions for certain underfunded defined benefit plans

- Changes to safe harbor correction methods and fee structures

Rev. Proc. 2013-12 is generally effective April 1, 2013. For 403(b) plan failures that occurred prior to January 1, 2009, plans must use the definitions in Rev. Proc. 2008-50 to determine which failures may be resolved under EPCRS.

Practice Management Application

Financial professionals who assist employers with designing their ideal retirement plan must begin by knowing each client's overall objectives for adopting a plan. From there, a financial professional can suggest various plan design strategies. The following chart provides examples of specific employer objectives and suggested plan design strategies.

Employer Objective	Plan Design Strategy
Maximize owner's contributions	• Allocate contributions using an integrated formula • Use stringent eligibility rules (e.g., two years of service, age 21, 1,000 hours of service required annually, last day of employment required for contribution) For owner-only businesses, consider a solo or individual (k) plan.
Provide a valuable employee benefit and maximize employee participation	• Use liberal eligibility rules (e.g., no age or service requirements) • Provide matching contributions to encourage participation • Consider an automatic enrollment and auto increase feature • Allow rollovers from other retirement plans • Allow catch-up contributions • Allow Roth 401(k) contributions
Flexibility in plan contributions	• Elect a discretionary matching contribution formula • Elect discretionary employer profit sharing contributions • Consider an automatic enrollment and auto increase feature • Allow catch-up contributions • Allow Roth 401(k) contributions
Minimize IRS testing requirements	• Consider a 401(k) safe harbor or a safe harbor automatic enrollment arrangement • Do not require 1,000 hours of service and/or employment on the last day of the year for plan contribution eligibility.
Minimize the employer's liability	• Allow participants to self direct their investments and take advantage of ERISA 404(c). • Conduct an annual plan review. • Create an Investment Policy Statement. • Use qualified default investments. • Use fiduciary advisers.

Plan Type	SIMPLE IRA	SEP
Employer Eligibility	100 or fewer employees who earned $5,000 or more SIMPLE IRA plan must be the only plan of the employer Most employers, including sole proprietorships, S and C corporations, partnerships, nonprofit organizations and governmental entities	Any employer, including sole proprietorships, S and C corporations, partnerships, nonprofit organizations and governmental entities If SAR-SEP, 25 or fewer eligible employees, with at least 50% electing to participate; no new plans after 1996
Contribution or Benefit Limits	Salary deferrals: 100% of compensation up to $12,000 for 2013 and 2014 Mandatory employer contribution: 100% match on deferrals up to 3% of compensation; or 2% nonelective contribution	Participant limit: Lesser of 25% of compensation or $51,000 for 2013 and $52,000 for 2014 Employer deduction: 25% of compensation of all participants If SAR-SEP, elective salary deferrals of 100% of compensation up to $17,500 for 2013 and 2014 Compensation cap of $255,000 for 2013 and $260,000 for 2014
Catch Up	For age 50 and over, $2,500 in 2013 and 2014	If SAR-SEP, for age 50 and over, $5,500 for 2013 and 2014
Vesting	Immediate	Immediate
Deadline to Establish	Generally, not later than Oct. 1 for current year contribution Should be established early in the year to take advantage of salary deferral option	Business's tax-filing deadline, including extensions
Contribution Deadline	Salary deferrals must be deposited as soon as they can be segregated from the employer's general assets and not later than 30 days after the end of the month deferred; 7-day safe harbor rule applies Matching and nonelective contributions: business's tax-filing deadline, including extensions	Business's tax-filing deadline, including extensions If SAR-SEP, as soon as administratively feasible, and not later than 15 business days after the end of the month of deferral

Plan Type	Profit Sharing	Money Purchase Pension
Employer Eligibility	Any employer, including sole proprietorships, S and C corporations, partnerships, nonprofit organizations, and governmental entities	Any employer, including sole proprietorships, S and C corporations, partnerships, nonprofit organizations, and governmental entities
Contribution or Benefit Limits	Employer deduction: up to 25% of compensation of all participants Participant: Lesser of 100% of compensation or $51,000 for 2013 and $52,000 for 2014	Mandatory contribution as specified by plan Employer deduction: up to 25% of compensation of all participants Participant limit: Lesser of 100% of compensation or $51,000 for 2013 and $52,000 for 2014
Catch Up	Not applicable	Not applicable
Vesting	According to plan terms May apply 3-year cliff or 6-year graded schedule	According to plan terms. May apply 3-year cliff or 6-year graded schedule
Deadline to Establish	Business' tax year end	Business' tax year end
Contribution Deadline	Business's tax-filing deadline, including extensions	Earlier of business's tax-filing deadline, including extensions, or minimum funding deadline (Sept. 15 for calendar-year plans)

Plan Type	401(k)	Standard Safe Harbor 401(k)
Employer Eligibility	Most employers, including sole proprietorships, S and C corporations, partnerships, and nonprofit organizations. Governmental entities may not establish 401(k) plans	Most employers, including sole proprietorships S and C corporations, partnerships, and nonprofit organizations. Governmental entities may not establish 401(k) plans
Contribution or Benefit Limits	Elective salary deferrals: 100% of compensation up to $17,500 for 2013 and 2014 Employer deduction: up to 25% of compensation of all participants Participant limit: Lesser of 100% of compensation or $51,000 for 2013 and $52,000 for 2014	Salary deferrals: 100% of compensation up to $17,500 for 2013 and 2014 Required employer contribution: either matching or nonelective. Basic match formula: 100% match on first 3% of compensation deferred, plus 50% of the next 2% deferred Enhanced formula: no less than what the basic formula would be at each deferral rate Nonelective contribution: no less than 3%of compensation
Catch Up	For age 50 and over, $5,500 for 2013 and 2014	For age 50 and over, $5,500 for 2013 and 2014
Vesting	Salary deferrals: Immediate Employer contribution: According to plan terms. May apply 3-year cliff or 6-year graded schedule	Immediate for salary deferrals and safe harbor contributions
Deadline to Establish	Business's tax year end Should be established early in the year to take advantage of salary deferral	Generally, prior to the beginning of the plan year in order to satisfy notice requirements Exceptions apply for existing profit sharing plans
Contribution Deadline	Employer contributions: Business's tax-filing deadline including extensions For small plans (i.e., plans with fewer than 100 participants), salary deferrals must be deposited within 7 business days of being withheld for safe harbor. For large plans, salary deferrals must be deposited as soon as administratively feasible, and not later than 15 business days after the end of the month deferred	Employer contributions: Business's tax-filing deadline, including extensions For small plans (i.e., plans with fewer than 100 participants), salary deferrals must be deposited within 7 business days of being withheld for safe harbor. For large plans, salary deferrals must be deposited as soon as administratively feasible, and not later than 15 business days after the end of the month deferred

Plan Type	Automatic Enrollment Safe Harbor	Defined Benefit
Employer Eligibility	Available for 401(k), 403(b) and governmental 457(b) plans	Any employer including sole proprietorships, S and C corporations, partnerships, nonprofit organizations, and governmental entities Those interested in benefiting older, more highly compensated employees
Contribution or Benefit Limits	Mandatory contributions Automatic salary deferrals cannot exceed 10%, and must be at least 3% during the initial plan year, increasing to 4% during the second plan year, 5% during the third plan year, and 6% during any subsequent plan year. Required employer contribution: either matching or nonelective A matching contribution equal to 100% of deferrals up to 1% of compensation, plus a matching contribution equal to 50% of deferrals between 1 and 6% of compensation; OR a 3% nonelective contribution	Annual benefit limit of 100% of average compensation of three highest years, up to $205,000 for 2013 and $210,00 for 2014
Catch Up	For age 50 and over, $5,500 for 2013 and 2014	Not applicable
Vesting	Salary deferrals: Immediate Employer contribution: maximum 2 years	According to plan terms May apply 5-year cliff or 7-year graded schedule
Deadline to Establish	Generally, prior to the beginning of the plan year in order to satisfy notice requirements.	Business's tax year end
Contribution Deadline	Employer contributions: Business's tax-filing deadline, including extensions For small plans (i.e., plans with fewer than 100 participants), salary deferrals must be deposited within 7 days of being withheld for safe harbor. For large plans, salary deferrals must be deposited as soon as administratively feasible, and not later than 15 business days after the end of the month deferred	Earlier of business's tax-filing deadline, including extensions, or minimum funding deadline (Sept. 15 for calendar-year plans)

Plan Type	403(b)	457(b)
Employer Eligibility	Only certain employers: Tax-exempt charitable organizations, public school systems, hospitals	Only certain employers: State and local governmental entities, educational organizations and tax-exempt entities Tax-exempt entities must limit participation to a select group of upper management employees Churches may not establish 457 plans
Contribution or Benefit Limits	Salary deferrals: 100% of compensation up to $17,500 for 2013 and 2014 Participant limit: Lesser of 100% of compensation or $51,000 for 2013 and $52,000 for 2014	100% of compensation up to $17,500 in 2013 and 2014
Catch Up	For age 50 and over, $5,500 for 2013 and 2014 For those with 15 years or more of service at qualifying institution up to an additional $3,000 elective salary deferral per year ($15,000 max lifetime). Prior year contributions may limit this amount	For age 50 and over, $5,500 for 2013 and 2014 In the 3 years prior to the year a participant reaches normal retirement age, he/she may contribute the lesser of: 1) twice the basic annual limit ((e.g., $17,500 x 2 = $35,000 for 2014); or 2) the basic annual limit plus the unused portion (if any) of basic annual limits in prior years
Vesting	Salary deferrals: Immediate Employer contribution: According to plan terms May apply 3-year cliff or 6-year graded schedule	Not applicable
Deadline to Establish	Business's tax year end Should be established early in the year to take advantage of salary deferral	Business's tax year end Should be established early in the year to take advantage of salary deferral
Contribution Deadline	For small plans (i.e., plans with fewer than 100 participants), salary deferrals must be deposited within 7 business days of being withheld for safe harbor. For large plans, salary deferrals must be deposited as soon as administratively feasible, and not later than 15 business days after the end of the month deferred Employer contributions: Business's tax-filing deadline, including extensions	For small plans (i.e., plans with fewer than 100 participants), salary deferrals must be deposited within 7 business days of being withheld for safe harbor. For large plans, salary deferrals must be deposited as soon as administratively feasible, and not later than 15 business days after the end of the month deferred

Retirement Plan Limitations 2007-2014

	2014	2013	2012	2011
Elective Deferral Limit (401(k), 403(b), Roth 401(k), SARSEP)	$17,500	$17,500	$17,000	$16,500
Catch-Up Contribution Limit	$5,500	$5,500	$5,500	$5,500
Annual Defined Benefit Limit	$210,000	$205,000	$200,000	$195,000
Annual DC Contribution Limit	$52,000	$51,000	$50,000	$49,000
Annual Compensation Limit	$260,000	$255,000	$250,000	$245,000
457 Deferral Limit	$17,500	$17,500	$17,000	$16,500
Highly Compensated Dollar Threshold	$115,000	$115,000	$115,000	$110,000
SIMPLE Contribution Limit	$12,000	$12,000	$11,500	$11,500
SIMPLE Catch-Up Contributions	$2,500	$2,500	$2,500	$2,500
SEP Coverage Minimum Comp.	$550	$550	$550	$550
SEP Compensation Limit	$260,000	$255,000	$250,000	$245,000
Social Security Taxable Wage Base	$117,000	$113,700	$110,100	$106,800
Top-Heavy Key Employee Comp.	$170,000	$165,000	$165,000	$160,000
Traditional or Roth IRA Contribution Limit	$5,500	$5,500	$5,000	$5,000
Traditional or Roth IRA Catch Up Contribution	$1,000	$1,000	$1,000	$1,000

(cont.)

2010	2009	2008	2007
$16,500	$16,500	$15,500	$15,500
$5,500	$5,500	$5,000	$5,000
$195,000	$195,000	$185,000	$180,000
$49,000	$49,000	$46,000	$45,000
$245,000	$245,000	$230,000	$225,000
$16,500	$16,500	$15,500	$15,500
$110,000	$110,000	$105,000	$100,000
$11,500	$11,500	$10,500	$10,500
$2,500	$2,500	$2,500	$2,500
$550	$550	$500	$500
$245,000	$245,000	$225,000	$220,000
$106,800	$106,800	$97,500	$94,200
$160,000	$160,000	$145,000	$140,000
$5,000	$5,000	$4,000	$4,000
$1,000	$1,000	$1,000	$1,000

Chapter Review Questions

Feedback for the review questions can be found at the end of the chapter.

1 In 2014, what is the maximum amount of compensation that can be considered
when calculating a participant's accrued benefit in a defined benefit plan?

    A $180,000
    B $210,000
    C $260,000
    D $280,000

2 What type of defined benefit plan is funded exclusively by the purchase of life
insurance contracts or fixed annuity contracts?

    A 401(k) plan
    B Target Benefit Plan
    C 412(e) plans
    D 457 plans

3 Which type of contribution allocation method uses cross-testing to allow plan
sponsors to contribute at a higher rate for a select group of participants?

    A New comparability
    B Flat dollar
    C Pro rata
    D Integrated

4 If Tom, age 35, has $55,000 of compensation and defers $17,500 to his 401(k) plan,
what would be his annual additions limit for 2014?

    A $17,500
    B $52,000
    C $55,000
    D $67,000

5 In addition to the compensation paid to employees and the overall IRC Section 404
deduction limit, what additional information would you consider in order to determine
the maximum tax deductible contribution a plan sponsor could make to a defined
contribution plan?

    A Allocation formula
    B Investment fees paid by the plan
    C Salary deferrals
    D Qualified Roth contributions

Chapter Review Questions Feedback

1 In 2014, what is the maximum amount of compensation that can be considered when calculating a participant's accrued benefit in a defined benefit plan?

> A $180,000
> B $210,000
> C $260,000
> D $280,000

>> A *Incorrect, pursuant to IRC Section 401 (a)(17), the maximum amount is $260,000.*

>> B *Incorrect, pursuant to IRC Section 401 (a)(17), the maximum amount is $260,000.*

>> C *Correct, pursuant to IRC Section 401(a)(17).* Chapter 2 Page 20

>> D *Incorrect, pursuant to IRC Section 401 (a)(17), the maximum amount is $260,000.*

2 What type of defined benefit plan is funded exclusively by the purchase of life insurance contracts or fixed annuity contracts?

> A 401(k) plan
> B Target Benefit Plan
> C 412(e) plans
> D 457 plans

>> A *Incorrect, a 401(k) plan is a cash or deferred arrangement; and not a type of defined benefit plan.*

>> B *Incorrect, a target benefit plan is a type of defined contribution plan, and not a type of defined benefit plan.*

>> C *Correct, pursuant to IRC Section 412(e), 412(e) plans may only be funded through the purchase of life insurance or fixed annuity contracts.* Chapter 2 Page 22

>> D *Incorrect, 457 plans are a type of nonqualified deferred compensation plan; and not a type of defined benefit plan.*

3 Which type of contribution allocation method uses cross-testing to allow plan sponsors to contribute at a higher rate for a select group of participants?

> A New comparability
> B Flat dollar
> C Pro rata
> D Integrated

>> A *Correct, a new comparability allocation methods allow employers to contribute to a select group of employees at a higher rate than for other groups through a testing method called cross-testing.* Chapter 2 Page 28

B *Incorrect, because the contribution for each participant is the same dollar value.*

C *Incorrect, because each participant's contribution is based on the same percentage of his/her compensation.*

D *Incorrect, because each participant's contribution is based on his/her compensation, taking into consideration the plan's integration level.*

4 If Tom, age 35, has $55,000 of compensation and defers $17,500 to his 401(k) plan, what would be his annual additions limit for 2014?

    A $17,500
    B $52,000
    C $55,000
    D $67,000

A *Incorrect, this would represent his IRC Sec. 402(g) employee salary deferral limit alone.*

B *Correct, pursuant to IRC. Section 415, a participant's annual additions limit is the lesser of 100% of compensation or $52,000.* Chapter 2 Page 40

C *Incorrect, because the annual additions limit is capped at $52,000 for participants under age 50.*

D *Incorrect, the annual additions limit is capped at $52,000.*

5 In addition to the compensation paid to employees and the overall IRC Section 404 deduction limit, what additional information would you consider in order to determine the maximum tax deductible contribution a plan sponsor could make to a defined contribution plan?

    A Allocation formula
    B Investment fees paid by the plan
    C Salary deferrals
    D Qualified Roth contributions

A *Correct, the plan sponsor must follow the plan's contribution allocation formula but in no event could the contribution exceed 25% of total employee compensation.* Chapter 2 Page 30

B *Inorrect, because these items are not a type of deductible employer contribution.*

C *Incorrect, because salary deferrals are not employer contributions for deduction purposes.*

D *Incorrect, because qualified Roth contributions are not employer contributions for deduction purposes.*

CHAPTER 3

Understanding IRAs, Roth IRAs, SEP, SARSEP, and SIMPLE IRA Plans

Chapter Goal

Upon completion of this chapter the reader will understand the various features of traditional IRAs, Roth IRAs, and IRA-based retirement plans, and be able to determine the appropriateness of an IRA-based plan for an employer.

Learning Objectives

✓ List the two basic contribution eligibility rules for traditional IRAs.

✓ Differentiate between the contribution and conversion eligibility rules for Roth IRAs.

✓ Identify the differences between a Simplified Employee Pension (SEP) plan and a Savings incentive Match Plan for Employees (SIMPLE) IRA plan.

✓ Apply the contribution formulas and limits for traditional and Roth IRAs, and SEP, SARSEP and SIMPLE IRA plans.

Traditional IRAs

Congress created individual retirement arrangements (IRAs) in 1975, pursuant to the Employee Retirement Income Security Act of 1974, for two primary reasons: to provide a means of saving for retirement for workers not covered by an employer plan, and to serve as a tax-deferred vehicle for rollover purposes.

A traditional IRA is either an individual retirement account or annuity (IRC Sec. 408(a) and (b)). An IRA is a personal retirement savings plan that offers the IRA owner the ability to save for retirement on a tax-deferred basis. IRA assets are not taxed until distributed.

Contributions

In order to be eligible to contribute to an IRA, the individual must be under age 70½ during the entire year, and have earned income or compensation (IRC Sec. 219(f)(1)). Compensation for IRA contribution eligibility is wages, salaries, tips, professional fees, bonuses, and other amounts the individual receives for providing personal services (IRS Publication 590). The IRS treats as compensation any amount shown in box 1 of Form W-2 (wages, tips, other compensation) for the year for which the contribution is made, provided that amount is reduced by any amount shown in box 11 of Form W-2 (nonqualified plans) (Revenue Procedure 91-18). Other amounts treated as compensation include commissions, self-employment income, alimony, and nontaxable combat pay.

The IRA contribution deadline is no later than individual's tax return due date, without consideration of filing extensions (IRC Sec. 219(f)(3)). For example, most IRA owners have a calendar year tax year, which means their IRA contribution deadline is April 15.

Contribution Limits

IRA owners may contribute 100 percent of their earned income up to a set annual dollar limit to their IRAs. Individuals who turn age 50 or older during the year may make additional "catch-up" contributions. The annual dollar limit and catch-up amounts are outlined below.

Year	Basic Annual Limit	Additional Catch-Up Amount for Age 50 and Over
2012	$5,000	$1,000
2013	$5,500	$1,000
2014	$5,500	$1,000

Important Note: The maximum amount as outlined that may be contributed by an individual to his or her Roth and Traditional IRA is an aggregate limit that applies to all traditional IRA and Roth IRA contributions made for the year (IRC Sec. 408A(c)(2)(B)).

Eligibility for Tax Deduction

Not all individuals who are eligible to contribute to an IRA will be able to deduct the contribution on their federal income tax returns. If the IRA owner or his or her spouse (if applicable) are covered by an employer-sponsored retirement plan for the year, then the deductible amount of the contribution may be reduced or eliminated, based on the IRA owner's tax filing status and modified adjusted gross income (MAGI). IRA owners may use the following charts to help them determine the deductibility of their 2014 IRA contributions. The definition of spouse now includes same-sex individuals, as well as opposite-sex individuals, who are legally married under state law, regardless of the couple's current state of residence.

IRA Owner Covered by an Employer Plan 2014

If your filing status is	And your modified adjusted gross income is	Then you
Single or head of household[1]	$60,000 or less	Can take a **full** deduction
	More than $60,000 but less than $70,000	Can take a **partial** deduction
	$70,000 or more	**Cannot** take a deduction
Married filing jointly or qualifying widow(er)[2]	$96,000 or less	Can take a **full** deduction
	More than $96,000 but less than $116,000	Can take a **partial** deduction
	$116,000 or more	**Cannot** take a deduction
Married filing separately[3]	Less than $10,000	Can take a **partial** deduction
	$10,000 or more	**Cannot** take a deduction

[1] 2013 phase-out range is $59,000 - $69,000
[2] 2013 phase-out range is $95,000 - $115,000
[3] 2013 phase-out range is $0 - $10,000

Married IRA Owner Not Covered by an Employer Plan (But Spouse Is) 2014

If your filing status is	And your modified adjusted gross income is	Then you
Married filing jointly with a spouse who is covered by a plan at work[1]	$181,000 or less	Can take a **full** deduction
	More than $181,000 but less than $191,000	Can take a **partial** deduction
	$191,000 or more	**Cannot** take a deduction
Married filing separately with a spouse who is covered by a plan at work[2]	Less than $10,000	Can take a **partial** deduction
	$10,000 or more	**Cannot** take a deduction

[1] 2013 phase-out range is $178,000 - $188,000 [2] 2013 phase-out range is $0 -$10,000

What is Modified Adjusted Gross Income?

Modified adjusted gross income (MAGI) is adjusted gross income from Form 1040, without considering any of the following amounts:

- IRA deduction,
- Student loan interest deduction,
- Tuition and fees deduction,
- Domestic production activities deduction,
- Foreign earned income exclusion,
- Foreign housing exclusion or deduction,
- Exclusion of qualified savings bond interest shown on Form 8815, and
- Exclusion of employer-provided adoption benefits show on Form 8839.

General Maximum Deductible Contribution Formula

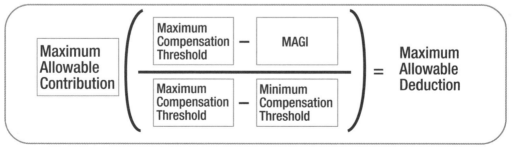

Filing Status	2014 Compensation Thresholds for Reduced Deduction
Married, filing jointly	$96,000 - $116,000[1]
Single	$60,000 - $70,000[2]
Married, filing separately	$0 - $10,000[3]
Not covered by employer plan, but spouse is	$181,000 - $191,000[4]

[1] 2013 range is $95,000 - $115,000
[2] 2013 range is $59,000 - $69,000
[3] 2013 range is $0 - $10,000
[4] 2013 range is $178,000 - $188,000

EXAMPLE:

Mary, age 44, is married, and filing a joint tax return. The couple's MAGI is $100,000. She participates in her 401(k) plan at work. She would calculate her 2014 maximum deductible contribution as follows.

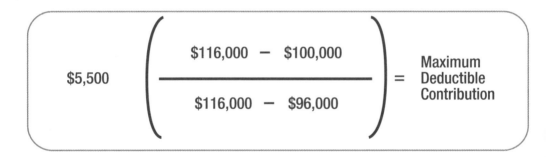

$$\$5,500 \left(\frac{\$116,000 - \$100,000}{\$116,000 - \$96,000} \right) = \text{Maximum Deductible Contribution}$$

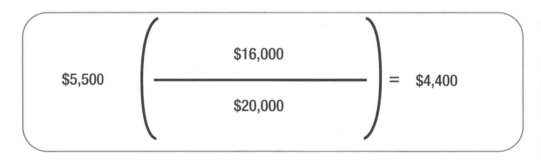

$$\$5,500 \left(\frac{\$16,000}{\$20,000} \right) = \$4,400$$

Taxpayer Characteristics

IRA households generally are headed by middle-aged individuals who are married with moderate household incomes. These investors are more likely to hold mutual funds, especially long-term mutual funds, in their IRA portfolios than any other type of investment. The Investment Company Institute's 2012 IRA Survey found that 20% of IRA owners have more than one IRA.

Roth IRAs

The Roth IRA, the nondeductible alternative to traditional IRAs, was officially made available to taxpayers in 1998 (although taxpayers have had the ability to make nondeductible traditional IRA contributions since 1987). Contributions to a Roth IRA are not tax deductible, and distributions are potentially tax and penalty-free if certain requirements are met (IRC Sec. 408A).

If a Roth IRA distribution meets the following requirements, it is considered "qualified," and may be taken free of tax and penalty.

1 The distribution is made after five years, beginning with the first taxable year for which the Roth IRA owner made a contribution.

2 The distribution is made on or after the Roth IRA owner reaches age 59½; or after the Roth IRA owner becomes disabled; or to the Roth IRA owner's beneficiary after death; or to purchase a first home (up to a $10,000 lifetime limit).

For more details on Roth IRA distributions, see Chapter 11, Retirement Income and Taxation Issues.

Contributions

In order to be eligible to contribute to a Roth IRA, the individual must have earned income or compensation, and his or her modified adjusted gross income must fall within a specified range (IRC Sec. 408A). There is no age restriction for making Roth IRA contributions.

Compensation for Roth IRA contribution eligibility is wages, salaries, tips, professional fees, bonuses, and other amounts the individual receives for providing personal services (IRS Publication 590 and Treas. Reg. 1.408A-4, Q&A 4). The IRS treats as compensation any amount shown in box 1 of Form W-2 (Wages, tips, other compensation) for the year for which the contribution is made, provided that amount is reduced by any amount shown in box 11 of Form W-2 (Nonqualified plans) (Revenue Procedure 91-18). Other amounts treated as compensation include commissions, self-employment income, alimony, and nontaxable combat pay.

The Roth IRA contribution deadline is no later than individual's tax return due date, without consideration of filing extensions (Treas. Reg. 1.408A-3, (Q&A 2)). For example, most Roth IRA owners have a calendar year tax year, which means their Roth IRA contribution deadline is April 15.

Contribution Limits

Roth IRA owners may contribute 100 percent of their earned income up to a set annual dollar limit to their Roth IRAs. Individuals who turn age 50 or older during the year may make additional "catch-up" contributions. The annual dollar limit and catch-up amounts are outlined below.

Year	Basic Annual Limit	Additional Catch-Up Amount for Age 50 and Over
2012	$5,000	$1,000
2013	$5,500	$1,000
2014	$5,500	$1,000

Important Note: The maximum amount as outlined that may be contributed by an individual to his or her Roth and Traditional IRAs is an aggregate limit that applies to all traditional IRA and Roth IRA contributions made for the year (IRC Sec. 408A(c)(2)(B)).

Contribution Eligibility

Not all individuals will be eligible to contribute to a Roth IRA. Contribution eligibility may be reduced or eliminated, based on the Roth IRA owner's tax filing status and modified adjusted gross income. Roth IRA owners may use the following charts to help them determine their ability to make 2014 Roth IRA contributions.

Roth Contribution Eligibility 2014

If your filing status is	And your modified adjusted gross income is	Then you
Single or head of household [1]	$114,000 or less	Can make a **full** contribution
	More than $114,000 but less than $129,000	Can make a **partial** contribution
	$129,000 or more	**Cannot** make a contribution
Married filing jointly or qualifying widow(er) [2]	$181,000 or less	Can make a **full** contribution
	More than $181,000 but less than $191,000	Can make a **partial** contribution
	$191,000 or more	**Cannot** make a contribution
Married filing separately [3]	Less than $10,000	Can make a **partial** contribution
	$10,000 or more	**Cannot** make a contribution

[1] 2013 phase-out range is $112,000 - $127,000 [2] 2013 phase-out range is $178,000 - $188,000
[3] 2013 phase-out range is $0 - $10,000

General Maximum Contribution Formula

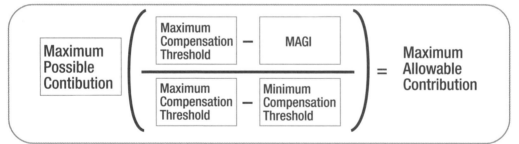

$$\text{Maximum Possible Contibution} \left(\frac{\text{Maximum Compensation Threshold} - \text{MAGI}}{\text{Maximum Compensation Threshold} - \text{Minimum Compensation Threshold}} \right) = \text{Maximum Allowable Contribution}$$

Filing Status	Compensation Range for Reduced Roth IRA Contribution
Married, filing jointly	$181,000 - $191,000
Single	$114,000 - $129,000
Married, filing separately	$0 - $10,000 [3]

[1] 2013 phase-out range is $178,000 - $188,000 [2] 2013 phase-out range is $112,000 - $127,000
[3] 2013 phase-out range is $0 - $10,000

Sloan, age 57, is married, and filing a joint tax return. The couple's MAGI is $182,000. He would calculate his 2014 maximum Roth IRA contribution as follows.

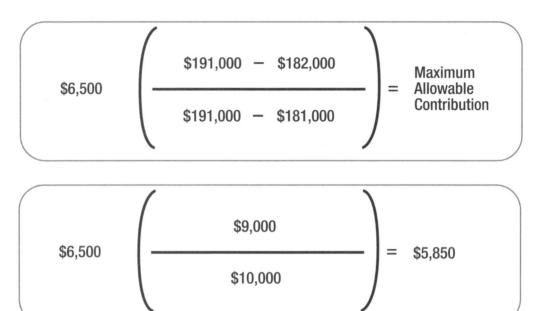

$$\$6,500 \left(\frac{\$191,000 - \$182,000}{\$191,000 - \$181,000} \right) = \text{Maximum Allowable Contribution}$$

$$\$6,500 \left(\frac{\$9,000}{\$10,000} \right) = \$5,850$$

Roth IRA Conversions Frequently Asked Questions

Traditional IRA owners (as of 1998) and plan participants in defined contribution and 403(b) plans (as of 2008) have had the option to convert their retirement assets to Roth IRAs if they meet certain criteria. Prior to 2010, individuals could convert to a Roth IRA as long as their modified adjusted gross income (MAGI) did not exceed $100,000 and they were not a married individual filing a separate tax return. For 2010, and for subsequent years, Roth IRA conversion eligibility is greatly liberalized. Anyone with a traditional, simplified employee pension (SEP), or savings incentive match plan for employees (SIMPLE) IRA, or a defined contribution or 403(b) plan can convert all or a portion of these assets to a Roth IRA. The following are the top 20 most frequently asked Roth conversion questions.

Q1 What changes occurred in 2010 for Roth conversions?

In 2010, significant changes to Roth IRA conversions took effect that may benefit taxpayers. First, the $100,000 modified adjusted gross income (MAGI) limit for conversion eligibility was eliminated. Second, the joint filing requirement for married individuals was eliminated, and third, individuals who converted assets to Roth IRAs in 2010 could choose to spread the taxable amount of the conversion—pro rata—over 2011 and 2012. Alternatively, they could choose to include the taxable amount as income for 2010. (Note: Individuals who convert before and after 2010 must include the taxable amount of the conversion in income in the year of the conversion.)

Q2 I don't qualify for a regular Roth IRA contribution, but I understand I am eligible to convert to a Roth. What are the advantages of having a pool of Roth assets?

Taxpayers may want to consider creating a pool of Roth assets if they would like

- A source of tax free income in retirement,
- To avoid mandatory distributions during their lifetime,
- To accumulate, potentially, tax-free assets for beneficiaries.

Even taxpayers who do not qualify for a regular Roth IRA, deductible traditional IRA or Roth 401(k) can create a pool of Roth IRA assets through a conversion. Anyone under age 70½ with earned income can make nondeductible Traditional IRA contributions of 100 percent of income up to $5,500 (or $6,500 if they are age 50 or older). Investors can fund a traditional IRA with nondeductible contributions, and then convert the traditional IRA to a Roth IRA.

Q3 If a child inherits a traditional IRA, can he/she convert it to a Roth IRA?

An inherited IRA is not eligible for conversion to a Roth unless the beneficiary is the spouse of the deceased IRA owner.   In that case, the spouse beneficiary can elect to treat the inherited traditional IRA as his/her own and convert it to his/her own Roth IRA.

In contrast, nonspouse beneficiaries of qualified plan (e.g., 401(k)) assets may complete a conversion of the inherited assets to an inherited Roth IRA (IRS Notice 2008-30, Q&A 7, IRC Sec. 402(c)(11) and IRS Publication 590).

Q4 If an individual completed a 2010 conversion, how did he/she elect and apply the special 2011 and 2012 tax split?

For individuals who converted amounts between January 1, 2010 and December 31, 2010, they could elect to spread the taxable amount of their conversions ratably over 2011 and 2012. Taxpayers made the tax-spread election on Form 8606 in Part II.

Q5 What is IRS Form 8606, who files it and what is its purpose?

IRS Form 8606, Nondeductible IRAs, has multiple uses. Taxpayers file the form with the IRS to report the following transactions.

- Nondeductible contributions made to traditional IRAs

- Distributions from non-Roth IRAs (i.e., traditional, simplified employee pension (SEP) or SIMPLE IRAs) that hold nondeductible contributions

- Distributions from Roth IRAs

- Conversions from non-Roth IRAs to Roth IRAs

Taxpayers file Form 8606 as an attachment to their IRS Form 1040, 1040A or 1040NR tax form. If the individual is not required to file a version of Form 1040 for the year, but is required to file Form 8606, he/she must submit Form 8606 directly to the IRS by the Form 1040 due date.

A $50 failure-to-file penalty applies if an individual fails to submit Form 8606 to report nondeductible contributions (unless reasonable cause can be shown).

An individual is not required to file Form 8606 to report a conversion that was entirely recharacterized or distributions from Roth or traditional IRAs that were returned with any related earnings by the due date of the individual's tax return.

Link to the IRS Form 8606: http://www.irs.gov/pub/irs-pdf/f8606.pdf

Q6 What are "after tax" IRA contributions?

After-tax or nondeductible IRA contributions consist of the following:

- Annual traditional IRA contributions for which the individual does not take a deduction on his/her IRS Form 1040;

- Rollovers of after-tax dollars from a 401(k) plan to a traditional IRA; and

- Rollovers and transfers of nondeductible amounts from another traditional IRA.

Q7 When and how does a taxpayer determine the ratio of pre-tax to after-tax dollars in an IRA-to-Roth IRA conversion?

The ratio is determined by using Form 8606. The taxpayer uses the total basis in all his/her non-Roth IRAs as of 12/31 of the year as the numerator, and the total value of all his/her non-Roth IRAs as of 12/31 plus any distributions or conversions done during the year as the denominator (i.e., he/she would take the total value of all his/her non-Roth IRAs, and add back in any distributions or conversions done during the year.) This is the individual's "8606 ratio." The taxpayer would then apply his/her 8606 ratio to the total amount of distributions converted (also to any other distributions during the year) to determine the nontaxable amount. The taxpayer reports the conversion on the appropriate IRS Form 1040 by including the total amount of the conversion on line 15a of IRS Form 1040 and the taxable portion on line 15b (or lines 11a and 11b for Form 1040A).

Ellie made a 2013 nondeductible contribution to her traditional IRA on February 10, 2014. Her total basis, as reported on her Form 8606 was $10,000. The total value of all her non-Roth IRAs as of 12/31/13 is $50,000. On August 17, 2013, she took a $2,000 distribution from her SEP IRA. She converted $10,000 from her traditional IRA to a Roth IRA on December 29, 2013. Ellie is curious to see what the overall tax implications of her 2013 IRA transactions will be. She uses IRS Form 8606 to find her answer.

$$\frac{\text{Total Basis in All Non-Roth IRAs as of 12/31*}}{\text{Total Value of All Non-Roth IRAs as of 12/31**}} \times \frac{\text{Conversion}}{\text{Amount}} = \frac{\text{Nontaxable Portion}}{\text{of Conversion}}$$

* Do not include nondeductible contributions made from January 1-April 15 *for the prior year.*
**Add back in outstanding rollovers, distributions and conversions taken during the year.

$$\frac{\$10,000}{\$62,000} \times \$10,000 = \$1,610$$

$$0.161 \text{ (8606 Ratio)} \times \$10,000 = \$1,610$$

Form **8606**

Department of the Treasury
Internal Revenue Service (99)

Nondeductible IRAs

▶ Information about Form 8606 and its separate instructions is at *www.irs.gov/form8606.*
▶ Attach to Form 1040, Form 1040A, or Form 1040NR.

OMB No. 1545-0074

2013

Attachment
Sequence No. **48**

Name. If married, file a separate form for each spouse required to file Form 8606. See instructions. | Your social security number

**Fill in Your Address Only
If You Are Filing This
Form by Itself and Not
With Your Tax Return**

Home address (number and street, or P.O. box if mail is not delivered to your home) | Apt. no.

City, town or post office, state, and ZIP code. If you have a foreign address, also complete the spaces below (see instructions).

Foreign country name | Foreign province/state/county | Foreign postal code

---

Part I | **Nondeductible Contributions to Traditional IRAs and Distributions From Traditional, SEP, and SIMPLE IRAs**

Complete this part only if one or more of the following apply.

- You made nondeductible contributions to a traditional IRA for 2013.
- You took distributions from a traditional, SEP, or SIMPLE IRA in 2013 **and** you made nondeductible contributions to a traditional IRA in 2013 or an earlier year. For this purpose, a distribution does not include a rollover, qualified charitable distributions, one-time distribution to fund an HSA, conversion, recharacterization, or return of certain contributions.
- You converted part, but not all, of your traditional, SEP, and SIMPLE IRAs to Roth IRAs in 2013 (excluding any portion you recharacterized) **and** you made nondeductible contributions to a traditional IRA in 2013 or an earlier year.

1	Enter your nondeductible contributions to traditional IRAs for 2013, including those made for 2013 from January 1, 2014, through April 15, 2014 (see instructions)	**1**	
2	Enter your total basis in traditional IRAs (see instructions)	**2**	
3	Add lines 1 and 2	**3**	

> In 2013, did you take a distribution from traditional, SEP, or SIMPLE IRAs, or make a Roth IRA conversion? — **No** ▶ Enter the amount from line 3 on line 14. Do not complete the rest of Part I.
> — **Yes** ▶ Go to line 4.

4	Enter those contributions included on line 1 that were made from January 1, 2014, through April 15, 2014	**4**	
5	Subtract line 4 from line 3	**5**	
6	Enter the value of **all** your traditional, SEP, and SIMPLE IRAs as of December 31, 2013, plus any outstanding rollovers	**6**	
7	Enter your distributions from traditional, SEP, and SIMPLE IRAs in 2013. **Do not** include rollovers, qualified charitable distributions, a one-time distribution to fund an HSA, conversions to a Roth IRA, certain returned contributions, or recharacterizations of traditional IRA contributions (see instructions)	**7**	
8	Enter the net amount you converted from traditional, SEP, and SIMPLE IRAs to Roth IRAs in 2013. **Do not** include amounts converted that you later recharacterized (see instructions). Also enter this amount on line 16	**8**	
9	Add lines 6, 7, and 8	**9**	
10	Divide line 5 by line 9. Enter the result as a decimal rounded to at least 3 places. If the result is 1.000 or more, enter "1.000"	**10** × .	
11	Multiply line 8 by line 10. This is the nontaxable portion of the amount you converted to Roth IRAs. Also enter this amount on line 17	**11**	
12	Multiply line 7 by line 10. This is the nontaxable portion of your distributions that you did not convert to a Roth IRA	**12**	
13	Add lines 11 and 12. This is the nontaxable portion of all your distributions	**13**	
14	Subtract line 13 from line 3. This is **your total basis in traditional IRAs for 2013 and earlier years**	**14**	
15	**Taxable amount.** Subtract line 12 from line 7. If more than zero, also include this amount on Form 1040, line 15b; Form 1040A, line 11b; or Form 1040NR, line 16b	**15**	

Note. You may be subject to an additional 10% tax on the amount on line 15 if you were under age 59½ at the time of the distribution (see instructions).

For Privacy Act and Paperwork Reduction Act Notice, see separate instructions. Cat. No. 63966F Form **8606** (2013)

| **Part II** | **2013 Conversions From Traditional, SEP, or SIMPLE IRAs to Roth IRAs** |

Complete this part if you converted part or all of your traditional, SEP, and SIMPLE IRAs to a Roth IRA in 2013 (excluding any portion you recharacterized).

16	If you completed Part I, enter the amount from line 8. Otherwise, enter the net amount you converted from traditional, SEP, and SIMPLE IRAs to Roth IRAs in 2013. **Do not** include amounts you later recharacterized back to traditional, SEP, or SIMPLE IRAs in 2013 or 2014 (see instructions)	16	
17	If you completed Part I, enter the amount from line 11. Otherwise, enter your basis in the amount on line 16 (see instructions)	17	
18	**Taxable amount.** Subtract line 17 from line 16. Also include this amount on Form 1040, line 15b; Form 1040A, line 11b; or Form 1040NR, line 16b	18	

| **Part III** | **Distributions From Roth IRAs** |

Complete this part only if you took a distribution from a Roth IRA in 2013. For this purpose, a distribution does not include a rollover, qualified charitable distributions, a one-time distribution to fund an HSA, recharacterization, or return of certain contributions (see instructions).

19	Enter your total nonqualified distributions from Roth IRAs in 2013, including any qualified first-time homebuyer distributions (see instructions)	19	
20	Qualified first-time homebuyer expenses (see instructions). **Do not** enter more than $10,000 . .	20	
21	Subtract line 20 from line 19. If zero or less, enter -0- and skip lines 22 through 25	21	
22	Enter your basis in Roth IRA contributions (see instructions)	22	
23	Subtract line 22 from line 21. If zero or less, enter -0- and skip lines 24 and 25. If more than zero, you may be subject to an additional tax (see instructions)	23	
24	Enter your basis in conversions from traditional, SEP, and SIMPLE IRAs and rollovers from qualified retirement plans to a Roth IRA (see instructions)	24	
25	**Taxable amount.** Subtract line 24 from line 23. If more than zero, also include this amount on Form 1040, line 15b; Form 1040A, line 11b; or Form 1040NR, line 16b	25	

Sign Here Only If You Are Filing This Form by Itself and Not With Your Tax Return

Under penalties of perjury, I declare that I have examined this form, including accompanying attachments, and to the best of my knowledge and belief, it is true, correct, and complete. Declaration of preparer (other than taxpayer) is based on all information of which preparer has any knowledge.

| Your signature | | Date | |

Paid Preparer Use Only	Print/Type preparer's name	Preparer's signature	Date	Check ☐ if self-employed	PTIN
	Firm's name ▶			Firm's EIN ▶	
	Firm's address ▶			Phone no.	

Form **8606** (2013)

Q8 When calculating a person's "8606 ratio," what retirement accounts are included?

An individual includes all of his/her non-Roth IRAs for which they are the direct owner, including traditional IRAs, SEP IRAs, and SIMPLE IRAs.

Retirement accounts not considered include

- Inherited traditional, SEP or SIMPLE IRAs (unless a spouse beneficiary has elected to treat the inherited IRA as his or her own)[1] ;
- Defined contribution employer-sponsored plans;
- Defined benefit employer-sponsored plans;
- 403(b) plans;
- 457 plans;
- Nonqualified plans; and
- Annuities (unless they are IR annuities).

Q9 When completing a 401(k)-to-Roth IRA conversion, how is the conversion tax liability determined and reported?

The plan participant includes the amount of any pre-tax assets converted in his or her taxable income for the year. If the both pre-tax and after-tax assets are converted, then the plan administrator must apply the standard qualified plan "basis recovery rules" as outlined in IRS Publication 575, Pension and Annuity Income, and report the taxable amount on IRS Form 1099-R. The tax consequences will depend on whether the distribution comes from pre-1987 amounts. Pre-1987 amounts can be recovered tax-free. Post-1986 after-tax contributions must follow the basis recovery rules. The plan participant reports the conversion on the appropriate IRS Form 1040 by including the total amount of the conversion on line 16a of IRS Form 1040 and the taxable portion on line 16b (or lines 12a and 12b for Form 1040A). Conversions for 2010 and later years are also reported on Form 8606.

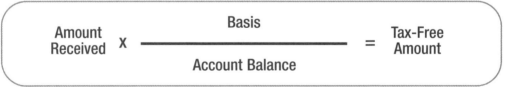

$$\text{Amount Received} \times \frac{\text{Basis}}{\text{Account Balance}} = \text{Tax-Free Amount}$$

Use the following formula to figure the tax-free amount of the distribution.

For this purpose, your account balance includes only amounts to which you have a nonforfeitable right (a right that cannot be taken away).

[1] See IRS Publication 590 for reasoning

Ann Brown received a $50,000 distribution from her retirement plan. She had $10,000 invested (basis) in the plan. Her account balance was $100,000. She can exclude $5,000 of the $50,000 distribution, figured as follows:

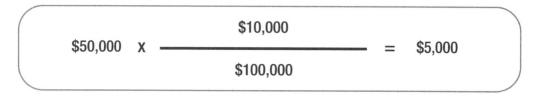

$$\$50,000 \quad X \quad \frac{\$10,000}{\$100,000} \quad = \quad \$5,000$$

Defined Contribution Plan

Under a defined contribution plan, your contributions (and income allocable to them) may be treated as a seperate contract for figuring the taxable part of any distribution. A defined contribution plan is a plan in which you have an individual account. Your benefits are based only on the amount contributed to the account and the income, expenses, etc., allocated to the account.

EXAMPLE

Ryan participates in a defined contribution plan that treats employee contributions and earnings allocable to them as a seperate contract. He received a non-annuity distribution of $5,000 before his annuity starting date. He had made after-tax contributions of $10,000. The earnings allocable to his contributions were $2,500. His employer also contributed $10,000. The earnings allocable to the employer contributions were $2,500.

To determine the tax-free amount of Ryan's distribution use the same formula shown above. However, because employee contributions are treated as a separate contract, the account balance would be the total of Ryans' contributions and allocable earnings.

Thus, the tax-free amount would be $5,000 x ($10,000/$12,500) =$4,000. The taxable amount would be $1,000 ($5,000 - $4,000).

Q10 Is it possible to do a direct conversion of just 401(k) after-tax contributions to a Roth IRA and, if so, how will the conversion be treated for tax purposes?

Some 401(k) plans will allow in-service distributions of after-tax contributions, which would allow a participant to directly convert the after-tax contributions and associated earnings to a Roth IRA. If the plan document so permits, it may be possible to request a conversion of after-tax contributions; the tax consequences will depend on whether the converted amount comes from pre-1987 or post-1986 after-tax amounts. Pre-1987 amounts can be recovered tax-free. Post-1986 after-tax contributions are subject to basis recovery rules. In this case, the tax obligation is determined by the amount of earnings associated with the after-tax dollars converted from the plan. The pre-tax contributions and earnings in the 401(k) plan are not a factor because the after-tax contributions and their earnings are considered held under a separate contract. In a direct 401(k)-to-Roth IRA (custodian-to-custodian) conversion, any assets held in the individual's IRAs that he/she may have do not factor into the conversion tax liability.

Q11 How are contributions to a Roth IRA treated for tax purposes when distributed?

The IRS has prescribed a distribution hierarchy for Roth IRA assets. Contributions are always taken first; conversions (if any) are second in order by year of contribution, with converted pre-tax assets taken first and converted after-tax assets taken second. Earnings are considered distributed last. Contributions are always distributed tax and penalty free. Converted pre-tax assets are distributed tax and penalty free as long as they have been held in the account for five years. If not, a 10 percent would apply to the distribution. Converted after-tax assets are always distributed tax and penalty free. Earnings are distributed tax and penalty free if the Roth IRA has existed for five years and the distribution is done on or after age 59½, or following death, disability or first-time home purchase. Otherwise the earnings would be taxable and subject to penalty unless a penalty exception applies. The following table summarizes the Roth IRA distribution ordering rules.

Ordering Rules	Qualified Distribution	Nonqualified Distribution	
		Client Has a Penalty Exception	Client Does Not Have a Penalty Exception
1 Contributory Dollars	No tax; No penalty	No tax; No penalty	No tax; No penalty
2 Taxable Conversion Dollars (Client paid taxes at the time of the conversion)	No tax; No penalty	No tax; No penalty	No tax; Subject to penalty if within 5 years of the conversion*
3 Nontaxable Conversion Dollars	No tax; No penalty	No tax; No penalty	No tax; No penalty
4 Earnings	No tax; No penalty	Subject to tax; No penalty	Subject to tax; Subject to penalty

*Roth IRA conversions have their own "five-year clocks" based on the year of conversion. If a Roth IRA owner takes a distribution of conversion dollars within five years of the conversion, the Roth IRA owner could be subject to a penalty.

Q12 A parent converts money to a Roth IRA and dies before the Roth has existed for five years. The beneficiary (his daughter) elects to take required minimum distributions (RMDs) over her life expectancy. What tax treatment applies to the Roth IRA distributions for the beneficiary?

Contributory dollars are always distributed on a tax and penalty free basis. Conversion dollars are always distributed on a tax free basis and, because the beneficiary has a penalty exception (death), will be penalty free as well, regardless of the amount of time held. Any distributed earnings would come out penalty free at any time, but, if taken before the Roth IRA has existed for five years, would be subject to taxation until the five-year period has expired. The amount of time the Roth IRA was held by the deceased would count towards the five-year period for determining taxability. (Treas. Reg. 1.408A-6, Q&A 7)

Q13 I have an inherited traditional IRA. Can I convert it to a Roth IRA?

An inherited IRA is not eligible for conversion to a Roth unless the beneficiary is the spouse of the deceased IRA owner. In that case, the spouse beneficiary can elect to treat the inherited traditional IRA as his/her own and convert it to his/her own Roth IRA.

Q14 The value of my Roth IRA dropped significantly after I converted it. I understand that I am still liable for the taxes on the original conversion amount. Is there any way to reduce my tax bill?

In this circumstance, the individual may want to consider a recharacterization and a subsequent re-conversion. A recharacterization allows the taxpayer to undo a conversion and eliminate his/her tax liability. To accomplish a recharacterization, the taxpayer must transfer the converted amount, along with any gains or losses, back to an IRA. For those who file their tax returns on time for the year that they convert, they can recharacterize unwanted conversions without tax or penalty up to October 15 of the year following the year of conversion. It may be necessary to file an amended tax return. Following a recharacterization, an individual can reconvert the same amount after satisfying a required waiting period, which is the longer of 30 days after the recharacterization or, January 1 of the year following the conversion.

Q15 If a traditional IRA owner or 401(k) plan participant converts assets to a Roth IRA and later determines he/she is ineligible for the Roth IRA, or simply does not want the conversion, may the individual "undo" the conversion?

Yes, in both cases, the individual would be able to "recharacterize" or undo the unwanted conversion as long as it is done within the IRS-specified timeframe (Treasury Regulation 1.408A-4, Q&A 1 and Notice 2008-30, Q&A 5). A recharacterization allows an individual to undo a conversion and eliminate the associated tax liability by moving the assets, plus gains or losses, back to a traditional IRA (even in the case of a qualified plan-to-Roth IRA conversion).

Taxpayers who file their federal income taxes on time for a given year may recharacterize an unwanted conversion without tax or penalty up to October 15th of the year following the year of conversion. The individual may be required to file an amended tax return to reflect the transaction. Following a recharacterization, an individual can reconvert the same amount after he/she has satisfied the required waiting period, which is the later of 30 days after the recharacterization or January 1 of the year following the conversion.

Q16 What estate planning benefits do Roth IRAs offer?

There are several.

- Roth IRA owners are never required to distribute the assets while alive— so Roth IRAs may be an ideal arrangement for accumulating substantial—potentially tax-free—assets for heirs.

- Any distributions of inherited Roth assets to a beneficiary [either Roth IRA or Roth 401(k)] are tax-free as long as the original owner satisfied a five-year participation period. If the original owner dies before the five-year period has expired, the beneficiary would have to pay income taxes on any earnings taken from the Roth until the 5-year period has elapsed. The period of time that the decedent held the Roth would count towards the 5-year period. There would be no early withdrawal penalty as death is an exception.

- Although Roth IRAs are included when determining a decedent's taxable estate and, consequently, could be subject to estate tax (depending on the size of the accountholder's estate), Roth assets are not subject to income tax after the accountholder's death if the five-tax-year holding period has been satisfied.

- When a regular IRA is converted to a Roth IRA, the accountholder's taxable estate is reduced by the income taxes paid as a result of the conversion.

Q17 Will a conversion affect the taxability of Social Security benefits?

Because any pre-tax assets that are converted are includible in the individual's taxable income, a conversion may affect the taxability of any Social Security benefits received. There is a set formula to determine whether Social Security Benefits will be taxable to a recipient for a particular tax year. Please refer to IRS Publication 915, www.irs.gov/pub/irs-pdf/p915.pdf, for complete details. In general, to determine taxability of Social Security benefits, the recipient must

- Take 50% of his/her Social Security benefit and add it to all other income, including taxable pension and retirement income.

- He/she then compares the amount to the "base amount" ($32,000 for those who are married, filing jointly; and $25,000 for single filers).

- If the income exceeds the base amount, then Social Security benefits are likely subject to taxation by including a percentage of the benefit in ordinary income for the year—anywhere from 50% to 85% of the benefit.

Q18 When an individual converts a Roth IR annuity (or annuity contract within a traditional IRA), how is the annuity contract valued for conversion taxation purposes?

Generally speaking, when an individual converts an annuity contract, the amount includible in gross income is the fair market value (FMV) of the contract on the date the annuity contract is converted to the Roth IRA. The rules for determining FMV for conversion purposes for IR annuity contracts, or annuity contracts within IR accounts, are found in Treasury Decision 9418, and Treas. Regs. 1.408A-4, Q&A 14. The good news is—the insurance carriers offering the annuity contracts are responsible for properly determining the FMV of converted annuity contracts, and reporting the amount on IRS Form 1099-R to the taxpayer and IRS.

http://edocket.access.gpo.gov/cfr_2009/aprqtr/pdf/26cfr1.408A-4.pdf

Q19 When does it make sense for a person to convert to a Roth IRA?

That is a difficult question that each investor can only answer after considering his/her overall tax situation and consulting with his/her tax professional. Generally speaking, however, an individual should think twice about completing a conversion if any of the following are true.

- The added income from the conversion would cause a reduction in other tax deductions.

- The individual does not have sufficient assets outside of the IRA to pay for taxes on the conversion.

- The individual expects to be in a lower income tax bracket in retirement.

- The added income from the conversion would cause Social Security benefits to be taxable.

- The added income from the conversion would increase the premium amount for Medicare Part B coverage.

Q20 Can a 401(k) or 403(b) plan participant convert assets within the company's plan to a qualified Roth account?

Yes, as a result of the Small Business Jobs and Credit Act of 2010, 401(k) and 403(b) plans that offer a Roth contribution feature can allow in-plan conversions of non Roth assets, effective September 27, 2010. Plan sponsors may, but are not required to, implement this option. Plan sponsors can allow in-plan conversions immediately if they wish, and will be allowed to amend their plans at a later date under retroactive amendment guidance.

Participants may only complete in-plan conversions to designated Roth accounts if the plan 1) offers a designated Roth contribution feature; and 2) allows for in-plan conversions. Prior to January 1, 2013, the rules also required a participant to meet a distribution triggering event under the terms of the plan (e.g., attaining age 59½). The American Taxpayer Relief Act of 2012 eliminated this requirement. In-plan conversions must be completed as a direct rollover within the plan to a designated Roth account. Participants who complete in-plan conversions must include the taxable portion of their conversions in income for the year under the standard conversion tax rules. However, a special two-year income inclusion option is available for amounts converted in-plan during 2010 (i.e., half of the taxable amount is included in income in 2011 and half is included in 2012.)

If plan sponsors want to offer in-plan conversions, they should review their plan documents to determine what amendments may be necessary (e.g., adding an in-plan conversion option, adding a designated Roth contribution feature). Beginning January 1, 2011, governmental 457(b) plans will be allowed to add Roth contribution and in-plan conversion features.

Simplified Employee Pension Plans

A Simplified Employee Pension (SEP) plan allows employers to make contributions to traditional IRAs established for each of their employees without getting into the complex qualified plan rules. Contributions to a SEP plan are not mandatory for any given year, so employers can determine from year to year whether a contribution will be made.

Contribution Formulas

Contributions to SEP plans are discretionary. If a SEP contribution is made, the contribution must be made according to a nondiscriminatory allocation formula. The most common formula used is a formula which allocates contributions based on a percentage of each participant's compensation, but there are several others, as described in the following paragraphs. The actual formula that must be used is dependent upon the plan document that governs the SEP plan.

Pro Rata

An allocation formula that provides eligible participants with a contribution based on the same percentage of compensation is known as a pro rata formula.

Flat Dollar

A plan sponsor who uses a flat dollar contribution formula in its SEP plan must contribute the same dollar amount to each eligible employee.

An integrated allocation formula allows a plan sponsor to provide higher contributions for eligible participants who earn amounts over a set threshold, as long as the "permitted disparity rules" of IRC Sec. 401(l) are satisfied. Integrated plans are also known as "Social Security-based" or "permitted disparity" plans. The permitted disparity rules allow plan sponsors to give eligible participants who earn compensation above the "integration level," which is typically the Social Security Taxable Wage Base ($113,700 for 2013 and $117,000 for 2014), an additional contribution. This additional contribution is equal to the lesser of

- two times the base contribution percentage, or

- the base contribution percentage plus the "permitted disparity factor."

If the plan sponsor sets the integration level at the Social Security Taxable Wage Base, then the permitted disparity factor equals 5.7 percent. Note that the plan sponsor may set the integration level at an amount lower than the Social Security Taxable Wage Base. If this is done, however, the plan sponsor must then reduce the permitted disparity factor according to the following table.

EXAMPLE:

Founders, Inc. maintains an integrated SEP plan for its employees. The integration level is the taxable wage base (i.e., $113,700 for 2013 and $117,000 for 2014). For 2014, Founders, Inc. will make a 6% contribution (i.e., the base contribution) up to the taxable wage base for all eligible participants. For those participants with compensation above the taxable wage base, Founders, Inc. will make an 11.7% contribution (which is the lesser of twice the base contribution [12%] or the base contribution plus 5.7% [11.7%]).

Contribution Limits

In addition to contributions being limited by the terms of the plan document, there are also statutory limits that apply to SEP plan contributions. These limits include the compensation cap, the IRC Sec. 402(h)(2) limit, and the employer's IRC Sec. 404 limit for deductibility of plan contributions. A brief discussion of each of these limits follows.

Compensation Cap

The amount of compensation that can be considered when calculating a participant's contributions according to the plan's allocation formula is limited under IRC Sec. 401(a)(17). The limit for 2013 is $255,000 and for 2014 is $260,000. This amount may be indexed periodically for cost-of-living increases.

EXAMPLE

Mark Smith, a participant in the DATA SEP plan, has annual compensation of

$270,000. For 2014, Mark's employer decides to make a 10% pro rata contribution to the plan. How large will Mark's contribution be?

ANSWER

Even though 10% of $270,000 would be $27,000, Mark's contribution will be $26,000 because only the maximum compensation amount of $260,000 can be considered when making plan contributions for 2014.

IRC Sec. 402(h)(2) Limit (Annual Additions)

The maximum dollar amount that can be contributed to a SEP plan on behalf of an individual participant is the lesser of

- 25 percent of compensation, or
- the applicable dollar amount; $51,000 for 2013 and $52,000 for 2014

EXAMPLE

Judy Nelson, a participant in the Bolt Company SEP plan, has annual compensation of $225,000. For the 2014 tax year, the Bolt Company makes a 25%, pro rata contribution to the plan. How large will Judy's contribution be?

ANSWER

Even though 25% of $225,000 is $56,250, Judy may receive a maximum contribution of only $52,000 in order to stay within the annual additions limit for 2014.

IRC Sec. 404 Deductibility Limit

Employers with SEP plans may receive tax deductions for contributions up to the prescribed limits under IRC Sec. 404(h)(1)(C). An employer may only receive a tax deduction for contributions up to 25 percent of eligible payroll (i.e., the total compensation of all eligible participants in the plan).

EXAMPLE

Jesse Jones is to receive a contribution equal to 30% of his compensation. Will his employer be able to deduct such a large contribution?

ANSWER

If, when Jesse's contribution is added to the contributions made to all the other eligible participants in the plan, the total of all contributions do not exceed 25% of total eligible compensation, then the employer will be able to deduct a contribution of 30% of compensation made on Jesse's behalf.

Participant Eligibility

An employer can limit participation in a SEP plan as long as the plan satisfies the participation requirements set forth in the IRC. 408(k)(2).

Age Requirement

Under minimum participation rules, the age requirement that an employer may impose through the terms of the SEP plan for participation eligibility can be no greater than age 21 (IRC Sec. 408(k)(2)(A)).

Service Requirement

A plan sponsor may require employees to complete a specified amount of service (at least three of the immediately preceding five years) before becoming eligible to participate in a SEP plan (IRC Sec. 408(k)(2)(B)).

Compensation Requirement

The SEP plan may limit participation to employees who have received at least $550 for 2013 and 2014 in compensation from the employer for the year.

Exclusions

A plan sponsor may exclude from coverage employees covered under a collective bargaining agreement and/or nonresident aliens with no U.S. earned income.

Multiple Plans

A plan sponsor could maintain another qualified plan in addition to the SEP plan. However, contributions to the SEP plan will reduce the contribution amount to the other plan. In other words, the two plans will be treated as a single plan for determining the deduction limit. Also, there would only be one annual additions limit for each individual participant.

Sponsoring Employer Characteristics

The employer most likely to sponsor a SEP plan is one that is employee-oriented, and wants to help participants save for retirement, but desires the flexibility of discretionary contributions from year to year, and the simplicity of using an IRA-based plan.

SARSEP Plans

A Salary Reduction SEP (SARSEP) plan is a SEP plan which includes a salary deferral arrangement. An employer who established a SARSEP plan prior to 1997 may continue to maintain this type of plan. However, no new plans may be established after 1996.

Contribution Formula

SARSEP plans allow participants to make salary deferrals. A SARSEP may be paired with a regular SEP plan if employer contributions are desired.

Contribution Limits

The annual deferral limit under IRC Sec. 402(g)(1) for SARSEP is the lesser of 100 percent of compensation or $17,500 for 2013 and 2014, plus catch-up contributions. This limit is an individual limit, not a plan limit. Therefore, if an individual participates in two or more plans that are subject to the annual deferral limit, all annual deferrals must be added together for the purpose of determining whether the limit has been exceeded (except those deferrals made to 457 plans.)

EXAMPLE

Ann White, age 47, works part time for a company that offers a SARSEP in which she is eligible to participate. Her annual salary is $12,000. How much of her salary may she defer to her employer's SARSEP plan for 2014?

ANSWER

If Ann only participates in this employer's plan, she could defer up to $12,000, as long as the plan itself does not cap the maximum deferral at a lesser amount. However, if Ann participates in another employer's 401(k) plan for the year, she must aggregate the salary deferrals, and contribute no more than the maximum amount of $17,500 between the two plans for 2014.

Catch-Up Contribution for Participants Age 50 or Older

In the year a SARSEP participant turns age 50, and thereafter, catch-up contributions may be allowed under a SARSEP. A catch-up contribution allows participants who have already reached their annual deferral limit, a plan-imposed limit, or a statutory limit to contribute an additional amount as a salary deferral contribution. For 2014, the maximum additional amount is $5,500. As with conventional salary deferral amounts, catch-up contributions are not considered when determining deductibility limits for employers. Catch-up contributions also do not count toward a participant's annual additions limit (explained later).

EXAMPLE

If Tom turns 50 years old on December 1, 2014, and his plan allows participants to make catch-up contributions, how much may he contribute to his SARSEP as a deferral if he earns $50,000 in eligible compensation?

Tom may elect to defer up to $23,000 of his compensation to his SARSEP plan for 2014 (i.e., as a $17,500 standard salary deferral, and $5,500 as a catch-up contribution).

IRC Sec. 402(h)(2) Limit (Annual Additions)

The maximum dollar amount that can be contributed to a SARSEP on behalf of an individual participant is the lesser of

- 25 percent of compensation, or
- the applicable dollar amount; $51,000 for 2013 and $52,000 for 2014

This includes all salary deferrals and employer contributions. Catch-up contributions, however, do not count toward this limit.

IRC Sec. 404 Deductibility Limit

Employers with SEP plans may receive tax deductions for contributions up to the prescribed limits under IRC Sec. 404(h)(1)(C). Unlike SEP contributions made by the employer, SARSEP deferrals are not considered when determining whether an employer has exceeded his or her deductibility limit for plan contributions. An employer may only receive a tax deduction for contributions up to 25 percent of eligible payroll (i.e., the total compensation of all eligible participants in the plan).

Participant Eligibility

An employer can limit participation in a SARSEP plan as long as the plan satisfies the participation requirements set forth in the IRC. 408(k).

Age Requirement

Under minimum participation rules, the age requirement that an employer may impose through the terms of the SEP for participation eligibility can be no greater than age 21 (IRC Sec. 408(k)(2)(A)).

Service Requirement

A plan sponsor may require employees to complete a specified amount of service (at least three of the immediately preceding five years) before becoming eligible to participate in a SARSEP plan (IRC Sec. 408(k)(2)(B)).

Compensation Requirement

The SARSEP plan may limit participation to employees who have received at least $550 for 2013 and 2014 in compensation from the employer for the year.

A plan sponsor may exclude from coverage employees covered under a collective bargaining agreement and/or nonresident aliens with no U.S. earned income.

Sponsoring Employer Characteristics

Employer eligibility requirements to maintain a SARSEP plan are quite restrictive.

1 No new SARSEP plans are allowed to be established as of January 1, 1997.

2 Only employers with 25 or fewer eligible employees may maintain SARSEP plans (IRC Sec. 408(k)(6)(B)).

3 At least 50 percent of eligible employees must elect to defer into the SARSEP plan (IRC Sec. 408(k)(6)(A)(ii)).

4 Highly compensated employees must meet the actual deferral percentage (ADP) testing requirements for SARSEP plans.

Savings Incentive Match Plan for Employees

A Savings Incentive Match Plan for Employees (SIMPLE) plan allows small employers who have 100 or fewer employees to offer a retirement plan to their employees without the complicated nondiscrimination testing and reporting required for qualified retirement plans (IRC Sec. 408(p)).

Contribution Formula

An employer must either make a matching contribution to each employee's deferrals on a dollar for dollar basis up to three percent of the employee's compensation, or a nonelective contribution of two percent of compensation on behalf of each eligible employee's compensation. As an alternative to the three-percent match stated above, an employer could choose to match a percentage less than three percent, but the percentage must be at least one percent. This option is only available for two years during a five-year period.

Contribution Limits

The maximum contribution to a SIMPLE IRA plan depends upon the contribution formula, annual compensation cap (for employer nonelective contributions), and employer deductibility limit.

Annual Deferral Limit

The annual deferral limit under IRC Sec. 408(p)(2)(A)(ii) is $12,000 for 2013 and 2014. This limit is an individual limit, not a plan limit. Therefore, if an individual participates in two or more plans that are subject to the annual deferral limit, all annual deferrals must be added together for the purpose of determining whether the limit has been exceeded (except those deferrals made to 457 plans.)

EXAMPLE

Sidney Sanders, age 43, works part-time for a company that offers a SIMPLE IRA plan, in which she is eligible to participate. Her annual salary is $50,000. How much of his salary may he defer to his employer's SIMPLE IRA plan for 2014?

ANSWER

If Sidney only participates in this employer's SIMPLE IRA plan, he could defer up to $12,000. However, if Sidney participates in another employer's plan (e.g., a 401(k) plan) for the year, he must aggregate the salary deferrals, and contribute no more than the maximum amount of $17,500 between the two plans, with no more than $12,000 being contributed to the SIMPLE IRA plan.

Catch-Up Contribution for Participants Age 50 or Older

In the year a SIMPLE IRA participant turns age 50, and thereafter, catch-up contributions may be allowed under the plan. A catch-up contribution allows participants who have already reached their annual deferral limit, a plan-imposed limit, or a statutory limit to contribute an additional amount as a salary deferral contribution. For 2013 and 2014, the maximum catch-up contribution is $2,500. As with conventional salary deferral amounts, catch-up contributions are not considered when determining deductibility limits for employers.

EXAMPLE

Jake turns 50 years old on December 20, 2014, and his plan allows participants to make catch-up contributions. How much may he contribute to his SIMPLE IRA plan as a salary deferral if he earns $40,000 in eligible compensation?

ANSWER

Jake may elect to defer up to $14,500 of his compensation to his SIMPLE IRA plan for 2014 (i.e., $12,000 as a standard salary deferral, and $2,500 as a catch-up contribution).

Maximum Deductible Contributions

Typically, an employer will be allowed to deduct the employer contributions as determined by the contribution formula chosen. Also deferrals are not considered when determining whether an employer has exceeded his or her deductibility limit.

Compensation Cap

For SIMPLE IRA plans, the compensation cap is only of concern if the employer chooses to make a nonelective contribution (in lieu of a matching contribution). The amount of compensation that can be considered when calculating an employer two-percent nonelective contribution to a SIMPLE IRA plan is limited under IRC Sec. 401(a)(17). The limit for 2013 is $255,000 and is $260,000 for 2014. This amount may be indexed periodically for cost-of-living increases.

Participant Eligibility

Service Requirement

A plan sponsor may require employees to receive at least $5,000 in compensation from the employer during any two preceding years, and be reasonably expected to earn $5,000 in the current year before becoming eligible to participate in a SIMPLE IRA plan (IRC Sec. 408(p)(4)(A)). Employers may impose less restrictive requirements.

Exclusions

A plan sponsor may exclude from coverage employees covered under a collective bargaining agreement and/or nonresident aliens with no U.S. earned income.

Exclusive Plan Rule

Generally, employers can maintain more than one retirement plan at the same time and make contributions to both as long as certain limits are not exceeded. However, under a SIMPLE IRA plan, an employer cannot make contributions to the SIMPLE IRA in the same year the employer maintains a qualified plan in which the same employees receive contributions or accrue benefits (IRC Sec. 408(p)(2)(D)).

Sponsoring Employer Characteristics

Employers that sponsor SIMPLE IRA plans for employees may only have 100 or fewer employees. Typically, they are employers that want to encourage their workers to take on some personal responsibility for preparing for retirement through making employee salary deferrals, but are willing to guarantee an annual contribution to their employees.

Practice Management Application

- Clients with multiple IRA types (i.e., traditional, SEP, and rollover) are often surprised to learn they can combine them into one traditional IRA, which may be referred to as a "Super" IRA. After participating in a SIMPLE IRA plan for two years, participants can transfer or roll over their SIMPLE IRAs to the same Super IRA that holds their SEP, traditional IRA, and rollover contributions.

- A Super IRA is simply a traditional IRA that holds multiple types of IRA contributions. The most compelling reasons to consolidate include the following:

  - increased buying power, which allows for more sophisticated investment strategies;
  - fee consolidation and reduction;
  - beneficiary organization and consolidation;
  - consistent service;
  - streamlined paperwork; and
  - simplified retirement income planning.

- A Roth IRA owner cannot transfer or roll over a Roth IRA to a Super IRA, but he or she can consolidate multiple Roth IRAs in a Super Roth IRA.

- Many Roth IRA dollars can be accessed tax and/or penalty free—even if they are not considered "qualified" distributions.

- IRS Publications 590 and 560 cover traditional IRA, rollover, SEP and SIMPLE IRA plan rules. They are good resources, and can be viewed and downloaded from the IRS' web site (www.IRS.gov).

Feedback for the review questions can be found at the end of the chapter.

1 In order to contribute to a traditional IRA, an individual must be under age 70 ½ and have what type of income?

    A Interest and dividend income
    B Wages, tips and other compensation
    C Deferred compensation
    D All of the above

2 Based on the following facts, what would be Alicia's maximum IRA contribution for 2014?

    Tax filing status: Single   Age: 42
    Earned income: $135,000   No other retirement savings plan

    A She cannot make a 2014 contribution
    B $5,500
    C $6,500
    D $17,000

3 What is the deadline for making contributions to a Traditional IRA?

    A No later than individual's tax return due date not including extensions
    B No later than individual's tax return due date including extensions
    C No later than 12/31 of the IRA owner's tax year
    D There is no contribution deadline

4 Given the following facts, what would be the maximum deductible contribution an employer could make?

    Plan type: SEP
    Tax year: Calendar year 2014
    Employer's compensation: $150,000
    Total compensation paid to all participants: $500,000

    A $37,500
    B $50,000
    C $125,000
    D $150,000

5 When distributed, Roth IRA annual contributions are

    A Subject to tax and penalty if taken within five years of contribution
    B Not subject to tax or penalty
    C Subject only to tax
    D Subject only to penalty

Chapter Review Questions Feedback

1   In order to contribute to a traditional IRA, an individual must be under age 70 ½ and have what type of income?

   A Interest and dividend income
   B Wages, tips and other compensation
   C Deferred compensation
   D All of the above

   A *Incorrect, income must be earned income, which excludes interest and dividend income.*

   B *Correct, pursuant to Revenue Procedure 91-18, earned income for IRA contribution purposes includes wages, tips and other compensation as reported on IRS Form W-2, reduced by compensation deferred to a nonqualified plan.* Chapter 3 Page 85

   C *Incorrect, pursuant to Revenue Procedure 91-18, earned income does not include deferred compensation.*

   D *Incorrect, interest and dividend income, and deferred compensation do not qualify as earned income for IRA contribution purposes.*

2   Based on the following facts, what would be Alicia's maximum IRA contribution for 2014?

   Tax filing status: Single   Age: 42
   Earned income: $135,000   No other retirement savings plan

   A She cannot make a 2014 contribution
   B $5,500
   C $6,500
   D $17,500

   A *Incorrect, Alicia meets the requirements to make a traditional IRA contribution (i.e., she has earned income and is under age 70 ½); the contribution may not be deductible, however.*

   B *Correct, pursuant to IRC Sec. 219, $5,500 is the maximum traditional IRA contribution for an individual under age 50.* Chapter 3 Page 85

   C *Incorrect, $6,500 is the maximum traditional IRA contribution for an individual age 50 or older.*

   D *Incorrect, $17,500 represents an individual's salary deferral limit to a 401(k), 403(b) or 457(b) plan under IRC Sec. 402(g).*

3 What is the deadline for making contributions to a Traditional IRA?

    A No later than individual's tax return due date not including extensions
    B No later than individual's tax return due date including extensions
    C No later than 12/31 of the IRA owner's tax year
    D There is no contribution deadline

    A *Correct, pursuant to IRC Sec. 219(f)(3), the IRA contribution deadline is no later than the individual's tax return due date, without consideration of filing extensions.* Chapter 3 Page 85

    B *Incorrect, pursuant to IRC Sec. 219(f)(3), tax filing extensions cannot be considered when determining the individual's IRA contribution deadline.*

    C *Incorrect, the contribution deadline is related to the individual's tax filing deadline.*

    D *Incorrect, in order to be credited for a particular tax year, the contribution must be made by the individual's tax return due date for the year.*

4 Given the following facts, what would be the maximum deductible contribution an employer could make?

    Plan type: SEP
    Tax year: Calendar year 2014
    Employer's compensation: $150,000
    Total compensation paid to all participants: $500,000

    A $37,500
    B $50,000
    C $125,000
    D $150,000

    A *Incorrect, $37,500 would be the employer's maximum contribution for himself/herself.*

    B *Incorrect, $50,000 would represent the maximum individual contribution any one participant could receive.*

    C *Correct, the maximum deductible contribution would be 25% of the total compensation paid to all participants.* Chapter 3 Page 106

    D *Incorrect, the maximum deductible contribution would be 25% of the total compensation paid to all participants.*

5 When distributed, Roth IRA annual contributions are

> A Subject to tax and penalty if taken within five years of contribution
> B Not subject to tax or penalty
> C Subject only to tax
> D Subject only to penalty

A *Incorrect, only earnings in a Roth IRA are potentially subject to tax and penalty if taken with five years of contribution.*

B **Correct, because of distribution ordering rules, Roth IRA annual contributions are deemed distributed first and are not subject to tax or penalty.** Chapter 3 Page 100

C *Incorrect, because Roth IRA annual contributions are taxed when made to the Roth IRA they are not taxable upon distribution.*

D *Incorrect, a penalty would only apply potentially to Roth IRA earnings and conversion amounts taken within five years of conversion.*

CHAPTER 4

Standard Access to Retirement Plan Assets: Distribution Triggering Events

Chapter Goal

Upon completion of this chapter, the reader will understand the various circumstances, also known as "triggering events," under which retirement plan participants may begin receiving distributions of their retirement plan benefits. This knowledge is important not only to ensure compliance with rules and regulations that govern retirement plan distributions, but to empower financial professionals to help clients who are establishing retirement plans make appropriate decisions regarding distribution provisions from a plan-design perspective, and to help clients who are facing a plan distribution decision to choose the ideal distribution option.

Learning Objectives

✓ Identify the six most common distribution triggering events for conventional retirement plans.

✓ Define the "on demand" distribution concept that applies to IRAs and IRA-based retirement plans.

✓ Apply the unique rules that affect 401(k), 403(b) and 457(b) governmental plan participants with respect to the availability of distributions.

Distribution Triggering Events in General

A "triggering event" is a milestone or occurrence that a retirement plan participant must experience to be eligible to receive a distribution of assets from a retirement plan. The most common triggering events include

- attainment of a normal retirement age or early retirement age,
- severance of employment,
- plan termination,
- disability,
- divorce, or
- death

The terms of the plan document will define the distribution triggering events that allow participants to take distribution of some or all of their plan balances. That is why it is important to review the distribution section of the plan document or the summary plan description for the plan in order to know precisely which triggering events apply.

Although some plans allow for so-called "in-service" distributions, these distributions are not covered in this chapter, but, rather, are covered in *Chapter 5 Accessing Retirement Assets While Working.*

Plan participants must begin taking minimum payments from their retirement plans by their "required beginning date." The rules surrounding these required minimum distributions are explained in *Chapter 9 Required Minimum Distributions.*

Triggering Events Do Not Apply to IRAs

Before discussing individual triggering events, it is important to note that IRA owners, and participants in simplified employee pension (SEP) and savings incentive match plans for employees (SIMPLE) IRA plans need not experience a triggering event in order to take a distribution of assets from their plans. This is because IRAs and IRA-based plans are considered "payable on demand." Consequently, IRA owners, SEP, and SIMPLE IRA plan participants may take distributions from their IRAs or plans at any time, for any reason. However, although they may be able to take distributions at any time, they must be aware the distributions may be taxable and may be subject to an early distribution penalty tax. In order for a distribution to be penalty-free, the distribution recipient must be eligible for an exception to the early distribution penalty tax. These penalty exceptions are addressed in more detail in *Chapter 11 Retirement Income and Taxation Issues.*

Traditional IRA, SEP and SIMPLE IRA owners are required to take required minimum distributions after attaining age 70 1/2 (IRC Sec. 401(a)(9)). See Chapter 9 Required Minimum Distributions for details.

Common Triggering Events for Qualified Retirement Plans

The following paragraphs describe the most common distribution triggering events present in conventional retirement plans. Remember that the terms of the governing plan document will dictate which of the available distribution triggering events apply to a particular plan.

Attainment of Normal Retirement Age

The definition of normal retirement age for a plan is contained in the plan document. For defined benefit plans, the most common normal retirement age is age 65. Historically, age 65 was also the most common normal retirement age for defined contribution plans such as 401(k) and profit sharing plans. However, in recent years, the trend for defined contribution plans has been for the sponsoring employer to set normal retirement age at age 59 ½, which coincides with the age at which individuals may take distributions from qualified retirement plans (or IRAs) without incurring an early distribution penalty tax.

Attainment of Early Retirement Age

As with normal retirement age, the definition of early retirement age (if one applies) is included in the plan document. For example, for defined benefit plans, early retirement age may be defined as age 55 with at least 10 years of service. Because of the way benefits are generally calculated in a defined benefit plan, taking advantage of an early retirement age benefit usually entails a reduction in the benefit for which the participant would have been eligible had he or she worked until normal retirement age.

With a defined contribution plan, an early retirement age (if applicable) is also defined in the plan document; however, an early retirement age provision in a defined contribution plan is less likely to include a years of service requirement. Furthermore, because a defined contribution plan's retirement benefit is not guaranteed as it is with a defined benefit plan, and is based solely on the participant's cumulative balance at retirement, taking advantage of an early retirement provision does not reduce a participant's benefit per se, although, obviously, the longer a person saves, the greater his or her benefit will typically be in a defined contribution plan. As with defined benefit plans, age 55 is the most commonly chosen early retirement age in a defined contribution plan, perhaps because separation from service after attaining age 55 is an exception to the early distribution penalty tax (IRC Sec. 72(t)(2)(A)(v)).

Severance From Employment

Prior to the passage of the Economic Growth and Tax Relief Reconciliation Act of 2001 (EGTRRA), a "separation from service" was a distribution triggering event linked to the point at which a worker left employment with a particular employer. Effective in 2002, EGTRRA replaced separation from service, with "severance from employment" as a triggering event, with the hope that the new terminology and its modified definition would eliminate some of the operational complications that had developed under the separation from service definition, and an associated employment conundrum referred to as the "same-desk rule."

The definition of separation from service became inextricably linked to the same-desk rule. In general, the same-desk rule stated that an employee did not incur a separation from service (and, therefore, did not have a distribution triggering event) if he or she continued doing the same job but for a new employer that had purchased or otherwise acquired the business from the former employer.

In the case of a "corporate sale," where substantially all of the assets of a trade or business were sold by one corporation to another corporation, IRC Sec. 401(k)(10) allowed for an exception to the same-desk rule. However, this exception did not apply if less than 85 percent of the assets were sold, or if the buyer or seller was a partnership or limited liability company.

For 2002 and later years, a separation from service occurs when a common law employment relationship with an employer maintaining a plan has been severed. In other words, a severance of employment occurs when a participant ceases to be employed by the employer that maintains the retirement plan. In some cases, this is quite easy to determine, for example, in the situation where a person terminates employment, and moves to another state to work for a completely unrelated employer, a severance of employment has clearly occurred. However, it is not always that easy to determine whether there has been a severance from employment. Determining whether a common law employment relationship has been severed may involve looking at several factors, including the following. Is the new employer part of the same controlled group of employers as the original employer? If so, employees do not experience a severance from employment. Or, have the participants gone to work for an unrelated employer that has adopted the existing retirement plan of the old employer? If yes, the employees have not experienced a severance from employment for distribution purposes. Was the retirement plan "spun off" from the old employer, with a new employer being substituted as the plan sponsor? If yes, no severance from employment has happened.

Issues with applying the severance of employment rules come up most frequently in cases of mergers and acquisitions, and, unfortunately, issues relating to retirement plan distributions are often overlooked in the course of these types of business transactions.

Plan Termination

Although the IRS requires an employer that establishes a qualified retirement plan to do so with the intent that the plan will be continued indefinitely, an employer may terminate a plan at its discretion.

A plan is not fully terminated unless the following occur:

- the date of termination is established;
- benefits and liabilities under the plan are determined as of the date of plan termination; and
- all assets are distributed "as soon as administratively feasible.

As soon as administratively feasible is determined only after considering all the facts and circumstances of a specific case, but generally, the IRS has indicted that as soon as administratively feasible means within one year after the date of plan termination.

It is also possible under certain conditions for a plan to be considered partially terminated. Generally, partial terminations are deemed to occur when there is a significant reduction in the number of individuals covered by the plan. The determination of whether a partial termination has occurred is based on the facts and circumstances of the specific case.

When a qualified retirement plan is terminated, or deemed partially terminated, all affected participants become fully vested in their account balances upon the date of plan termination or partial plan termination.

Disability

The definition of disability in a retirement plan for distribution purposes is often closely linked to the definition of disability found in IRC Sec. 72(m)(7), which states the following.

> ... an individual shall be considered to be disabled if he is unable to engage in any substantial gainful activity by reason of any medically determinable physical or mental impairment which can be expected to result in death or to be of long-continued and indefinite duration. An individual shall not be considered to be disabled unless he furnishes proof of the existence thereof in such form and manner as the Secretary may require.

Most plan documents will also leave the determination of whether a person satisfies the requirements for being considered disabled up to the plan's administrator (who, in most cases, is the sponsoring employer).

Divorce

When a participant in a qualified retirement plan divorces or legally separates, a judge will issue a domestic relations order. A domestic relations order is a judgment, decree, or order that is made pursuant to state domestic relations law (including community property law), and that relates to the provision of child support, alimony payments, or marital property rights for the benefit of a spouse, former spouse, child, or other dependent of a participant. The definition of spouse now includes same-sex individuals, as well as opposite-sex individuals, who are legally married under state law, regardless of the couple's state of residence.

A qualified domestic relations order (QDRO) is a domestic relations order that creates or recognizes the existence of an "alternate payee's" right to receive, or assigns to an alternate payee the right to receive, all or a portion of the benefits payable with respect to a participant under a retirement plan, and that includes certain information and meets certain other requirements (ERISA Sec. 206(d)(3)(B)(i) and IRC Sec. 414(p)(1)(A)). An alternate payee is a spouse, former spouse, child, or other dependent of a participant who is identified by a QDRO.

A QDRO must contain certain specific information, such as the name and last known mailing address of the participant and each alternate payee, and the amount or percentage of the participant's benefits to be paid to each alternate payee. However, QDROs are limited to amounts and forms of benefits available under the plan.

When a spouse or former spouse receives benefits from a retirement plan under a QDRO, he or she receives them as if he or she were a plan participant, with one exception. A distribution from a qualified plan under a QDRO is not subject to the early distribution penalty tax, even if the recipient is under age 59 ½. However, if a QDRO recipient rolls a distribution over to an IRA, any distributions from the IRA taken prior to attaining age 59 ½ are subject to the early distribution penalty tax.

Plan assets paid to an ex-spouse are taxable to the ex-spouse, unless the ex-spouse makes a qualified rollover of the assets to an IRA or other eligible retirement plan. In contrast, in cases where plan assets are paid to a child or a dependent pursuant to a QDRO, the assets are taxable to the plan participant, and the assets are ineligible for rollover.

Death

A qualified retirement plan must provide that, in the event of the plan participant's death, plan benefits become payable to the beneficiaries.

Required Minimum Distributions

The IRS requires plan participants to begin taking distributions from their plans after attaining age 70½ or, if still employed and not a five-percent owner of the company, after retirement. Please see Chapter 9 Required Minimum Distributions for more details.

Distribution Triggering Events for 401(k) Plan Salary Deferrals

Typically, employee salary deferrals in a 401(k) plan may not be distributed prior to

- attainment of age 59½,
- severance from employment,
- death,
- disability,
- plan termination, or
- hardship.

Regarding hardship distributions of employee salary deferrals, the plan may limit the amount of the distribution to the lesser of the participant's employee salary deferrals, plus the following pre-1989 amounts: earnings on deferrals, qualified nonelective contributions (QNECs) and qualified matching contributions (QMACs). More details regarding hardship distributions of salary deferrals are provided in *Chapter 5 Accessing Retirement Assets While Working.*

Distribution Triggering Events for 403(b) Plans

Distribution triggering events for 403(b) plans are similar to those that apply to 401(k) plans, including plan termination, which, prior to 2009, was not considered a distribution triggering event for 403(b) plans.

403(b) plan distribution restrictions are based on the type of contribution and whether the 403(b) is an annuity contract or a custodial account, as explained in the following paragraphs.

403(b) Annuity Contracts

The unique distribution restrictions that apply to 403(b) annuity contracts are found in IRC Sec. 403(b)(11). Generally, 403(b) plan participants with 403(b) annuity contracts may withdraw their employee salary deferrals only upon

- employer termination of the plan,
- attainment of age 59½,
- severance from employment,
- death,
- disability, or
- hardship

Additionally, the following distribution rules apply.

- Distribution restrictions do not apply to pre-1989 balances in 403(b) annuity contracts.

- Distribution restrictions do not apply to employer-provided contributions in 403(b) annuity contracts. However, pursuant to the final 403(b) regulations, for annuity contracts issued on or after January 1, 2009, plans may not distribute employer contributions prior to the completion of a fixed number of years, the attainment of a stated age, or upon the occurence of some other identified event (such as the occurence of a financial need, including a need to buy a home).

- Hardship withdrawals of employee salary deferrals in 403(b) annuity contracts may not include earnings.

403(b) Custodial Accounts

The unique distribution restrictions that apply to 403(b) custodial accounts are found in IRC Sec. 403(b)(7). Generally, 403(b) plan participants with 403(b) custodial accounts may withdraw their balances (regardless of the type of contribution) only upon

- employer termination of the plan,
- attainment of age 59½,
- severance from employment,
- death,
- disability, or
- hardship.

Moreover, hardship distributions of employee salary deferrals in a 403(b) custodial account may be made from salary deferrals, and pre-1989 earnings on pre-1989 deferrals.

Distribution Triggering Events for 457(b) Plans

Because 457(b) governmental plans are a type of nonqualified deferred compensation plan, they are subject to different distribution triggering events than, say, 401(k) plans. According to Treasury Regulation 1.457-6, 457(b) plan participants may only access their plan assets upon

- reaching age 70½,

- severing employment,

- experiencing an unforeseeable emergency,

- qualifying for a one-time cash-out if the account balance is $5,000 or less, and there have been no employee contributions for at least two years,

- plan termination, or

- divorce, pursuant to a qualified domestic relations order.

Of course, the terms of the governing plan document will dictate which of the available distribution triggering events apply to a particular 457(b) plan.

Age 70½ Distributions

A 457(b) plan must satisfy minimum distribution requirements similar to those that apply to 401(k) plans (IRC Sec 457(d)(2) and IRC Sec. 401(a)(9)). Consequently, lifetime distributions to a participant must begin no later than the individual's required beginning date, which is April 1 of the calendar year following the later of

- the calendar year in which the participant attains age 70½; or

- the calendar year in which the participant retires (if the plan allows the delay).

Severing Employment

An employee has a severance from employment if the he or she dies, retires, or otherwise leaves employment. Severance from employment could include an early retirement provision as defined by the plan document. For independent contractors, a separate definition of severance from employment applies. In general, an independent contractor incurs a severance from employment when his or her contract with the eligible employer expires, and the contract will not be renewed.

Unforeseeable Emergencies

A 457(b) plan may allow participants to take distributions if they face an "unforeseeable emergency." Treasury regulations define an unforeseeable emergency as a severe financial hardship of the participant or beneficiary resulting from an illness or accident of the participant or beneficiary, the participant's or beneficiary's spouse, or the participant's or beneficiary's dependent; loss of the participant's or beneficiary's property due to casualty (including the need to rebuild a home following damage to a home not otherwise covered by homeowner's insurance, (e.g., as a result of a natural disaster); or other similar extraordinary and unforeseeable circumstances arising as a result of events beyond the control of the participant or the beneficiary. The definition of spouse now includes same-sex individuals, as well as opposite-sex individuals, who are legally married under state law, regardless of the couple's state of residence.

For example, the imminent foreclosure of or eviction from the participant's primary residence may constitute an unforeseeable emergency. In addition, the need to pay for medical expenses, including nonrefundable deductibles, as well as for the cost of prescription drug medication, may constitute an unforeseeable emergency. Finally, the need to pay for the funeral expenses of a spouse or a dependent may also constitute an unforeseeable emergency. Typically, the purchase of a home and the payment of college tuition are not considered unforeseeable emergencies. IRS Revenue Ruling 2010-27 contains examples of certain expenses that may be eligible for an unforeseeable emergency distribution from a 457(b) plan.

Cash-Out Provision

Similar to 401(k) plans, 457(b) plans may include small balance "cash-out" provisions. If the participant's total account balance, excluding rollover contributions, is $5,000 or less, and no amount has been contributed to or on behalf of the participant in the two-year period preceding the date of distribution; and no prior cash-out has occurred, then the plan may permit a distribution of the account balance. If a governmental plan provides for an involuntary distribution, the plan must provide for the automatic rollover of distributions greater than $1,000.

Practice Management

- Review the distribution section of the plan document or the summary plan description for the plan in order to know precisely which triggering events apply. Each plan is unique.

- Sometimes the distribution forms are incomplete or out-of-date, and may not reference all of the distribution triggering events.

- IRAs and IRA-based retirement plans are payable on demand; therefore, owners need not wait for a trigger to take distributions.

- Severance from employment as a distribution triggering event can be tricky to determine sometimes. Generally, a severance of employment for distribution purposes occurs when a participant ceases to be employed by the employer that maintains the retirement plan.

- Following a plan termination, generally, the IRS requires the employer to pay out plan assets within a year of the date of termination.

- Keep in mind that a plan participant or IRA owner who takes a distribution prior to attaining age 59½ may be subject to a 10 percent early distribution penalty tax, unless a penalty exception applies. The early distribution penalty tax does not apply to distributions from 457 plans, nor does it apply to distributions taken from a qualified retirement plan pursuant to a QDRO.

Chapter Review Questions

Feedback for the review questions can be found at the end of the chapter.

1 For what reason is age 55 the most commonly chosen early retirement age in defined contribution plans?

    A It is an IRS requirement.

    B Because attaining age 55 is a requirement to receive a lump sum distribution in order to qualify for certain tax benefits.

    C Because age 55 is the earliest that a plan participant can complete a direct rollover of an eligible rollover amount to an IRA.

    D Because separation from service after attaining age 55 is an exception to the early distribution penalty tax.

2 All of the following could be considered an alternate payee under a qualified domestic relations order, *EXCEPT*?

    A Spouse

    B Former spouse

    C Child

    D Trust

3 In what plan type would a participant be able to take a distribution of salary defer rals upon reaching age 59 ½?

    A 401(k)

    B 403(b)

    C Governmental 457(b)

    D A and B

4 With respect to an IRA, what does the phrase "payable on demand" mean?

    A No distribution triggering event is required, the recipient includes the distribution in taxable income for the year, and may be required to pay an early distribution penalty tax

    B A distribution triggering event is required, and taxes and penalties are waived

    C A distribution may be taken after attaining age 59 ½ at any time and for any reason without tax and penalty

    D A distribution may only be taken in the case of hardship, the distribution is taxed at a flat rate of 10%, and hardship is an exception to any penalties

5 If a plan participant wanted to know the distribution triggering events for his/her retirement plan, what documentation should he/she review?

    A Annual IRS Form 5500 filings for the plan

    B Treasury regulations

    C The plan document

    D Internal Revenue Code

Chapter Review Questions Feedback

1 For what reason is age 55 the most commonly chosen early retirement age in defined contribution plans?

    A It is an IRS requirement.

    B Because attaining age 55 is a requirement to receive a lump sum distribution in order to qualify for certain tax benefits.

    C Because age 55 is the earliest that a plan participant can complete a direct rollover of an eligible rollover amount to an IRA.

    D Because separation from service after attaining age 55 is an exception to the early distribution penalty tax.

    A *Incorrect, the IRS does require a plan to have an early retirement provision, nor does it prescribe a specific age if the plan includes an early retirement provision.*

    B *Incorrect, attaining age 59 ½ is a requirement for receiving a lump distribution in order to qualify for certain tax benefits.*

    C *Incorrect, there is no age restriction associated with the ability to complete a direct rollover of an eligible rollover amount.*

    D *Correct, plans with an early retirement provision often set the early retirement age at 55 so that participants may take their plan balances without an additional 10% early distribution penalty tax.* Chapter 4 Page 120

2 All of the following could be considered an alternate payee under a qualified domestic relations order, *EXCEPT*?

    A Spouse

    B Former spouse

    C Child

    D Trust

    A *Incorrect, pursuant to IRC Sec. 414(p) a spouse can be identified as an alternate payee in a QDRO.*

    B *Incorrect, pursuant to IRC Sec. 414(p), a former spouse can be identified as an alternate payee in a QDRO.*

C *Incorrect, pursuant to IRC Sec. 414(p), a child can be identified as an alternate payee in a QDRO.*

D *Correct, pursuant to IRC Sec. 414(p)(1)(A), only a spouse, former spouse or child may be listed as an alternate payee in a QDRO.* Chapter 4 Page 123

3 In what plan type would a participant be able to take a distribution of salary deferrals upon reaching age 59 ½?

    A 401(k)

    B 403(b)

    C Governmental 457(b)

    D A and B

A *Incorrect, in addition to a 401(k) plan, participants in a 403(b) plan may be able to withdraw their salary deferrals upon reaching age 59 ½.*

B *Incorrect, in addition to a 403(b) plan, participants in a 401(k) plan may be able to withdraw their salary deferrals upon reaching age 59 ½.*

C *Incorrect, pursuant to Treasury Regulation 1.457-6, participants in governmental 457(b) plans would not be able to withdraw salary deferrals upon reaching age 59 ½.*

D *Correct, both 401(k) and 403(b) plan participants may be able to withdraw their salary deferrals upon reaching age 59 ½.* Chapter 4 Page 124

4 With respect to an IRA, what does the phrase "payable on demand" mean?

    A No distribution triggering event is required, the recipient includes the distribution in taxable income for the year, and may be required to pay an early distribution penalty tax

    B A distribution triggering event is required, and taxes and penalties are waived

    C A distribution may be taken after attaining age 59 ½ at any time and for any reason without tax and penalty

    D A distribution may only be taken in the case of hardship, the distribution is taxed at a flat rate of 10%, and hardship is an exception to any penalties

A *Correct, IRA owners may take distributions from their IRAs at any time for any reason; they will be required to include the amount in their taxable income for the year, plus pay an early distribution penalty tax if the distribution occurs before age 59 ½ without a penalty exception.* Chapter 4 Page 119

B *Incorrect, IRA owners may take distributions from their IRAs at any time for any reason, they will be required to include the amount in their taxable income for the year, plus pay an early distribution penalty tax if the distribution occurs before age 59 ½ without a penalty exception.*

C *Incorrect, IRA owners may take distributions from their IRAs at any time for any reason—even before attaining age 59 ½; however, they will be required to include the amount in their taxable income for the year, plus pay an early distribution penalty tax if the distribution occurs before age 59 ½ without a penalty exception.*

D   *Incorrect, IRA owners may take distributions from their IRAs at any time for any reason; however, they will be required to include the amount in their taxable income for the year, plus pay an early distribution penalty tax if the distribution occurs before age 59 ½ without a penalty exception.*

5 **If a plan participant wanted to know the distribution triggering events for his/her retirement plan, what documentation should he/she review?**

   A Annual IRS Form 5500 filings for the plan
   B Treasury regulations
   C The plan document
   D Internal Revenue Code

   A   *Incorrect, the IRS Form 5500 is used to report plan financial information, and does not identify specific distribution triggering events for a plan.*

   B   *Incorrect, Treasury regulations provide general distribution guidelines but not the specific triggering events for a particular plan.*

   C   *Correct, the employer identifies the applicable distribution triggering events for its plan in the governing plan documents.* Chapter 4 Page 120

   D   *Incorrect, applicable Internal Revenue Code sections provide the general legal framework for retirement plan distributions, but not the specific triggering events for a particular plan.*

CHAPTER 5

Accessing Retirement Plan Assets While Working

Chapter Goal

Chapter 4 focused on how participants may gain access to their retirement plan assets in general, and covered the most common types of distribution triggering events that allow a person to distribute assets from their retirement plans. In general, once a triggering event has occurred, a distribution may be taken from a qualified plan. However, it is possible, if a plan document allows and certain requirements are met, for plan participants to take distributions while they are still working. These distributions are sometimes referred to as "in-service" distributions. According to the Plan Sponsor Council of Americas's 56th Annual Survey, 81% of defined contribution plans offer some type of in-service distribution option.

Upon completion of this chapter the reader will understand the various circumstances under which participants may receive in-service distributions from retirement plans. The reader will learn how IRAs and qualified retirement plans differ with respect to in-service distributions, which plans allow for in-service distributions, and which ones do not, and special rules that apply to salary deferrals and employer contributions. A good understanding of in-service distribution rules can help financial professionals facilitate client rollovers prior to retirement, and can help financial professionals sell more plans to clients who are concerned about giving participants access to contributions prior to normal retirement age.

Learning Objectives

✓ Identify situations in which an employee would be able to take an in-service distribution.

✓ Distinguish the four major types of retirement plans that allow for nonhardship in-service distributions.

✓ Differentiate between the restrictions on in-service distributions of employer-provided contributions vs. salary deferral amounts.

✓ Recognize the differences between hardship and in-service distributions from a tax and penalty perspective.

IRA-Based Plans

As was mentioned in the Chapter 4, it is possible to access Savings Incentive Match Plans for Employees (SIMPLE) IRA and Simplified Employee Pension (SEP) plan assets at any time, for any reason, so in-service distributions are very common with IRA-based plans. However, unless a person has an exception to the early distribution penalty tax, not only will the distribution recipient pay income taxes on the amount he or she withdraws, the individual will also be required to pay an early distribution penalty tax if he or she is under age 59½. Exceptions to the early distribution penalty for IRA-based plans include the following (IRC Sec. 72(t)).

- Attainment of age 59½
- Unreimbursed medical expenses representing more than 7.5 percent of adjusted gross income
- Distributions to unemployed individuals receiving unemployment payments for at least 12 weeks to cover health insurance premiums
- Disability (within the meaning under IRC Sec. 72(m)(7))
- Death
- Substantially equal periodic payments for life or life expectancy
- The cost of unreimbursed qualified higher education expenses
- The cost of buying, building, or rebuilding a first home (lifetime limit of $10,000)
- IRS levy on the IRA
- Qualified reservist distribution for an individual who is called to active duty for longer than 179 days after September 11, 2001
- Conversion to a Roth IRA
- Federally-qualifying disaster-related distributions

The early distribution penalty tax is generally 10 percent. However, for SIMPLE IRA distributions taken within the first two years of participation, the penalty tax is increased to 25 percent (IRC Sec. 72(t)(6)).

Money Purchase and Target Benefit Pension Plans Cannot Allow In-Service Distributions

Unlike other qualified retirement plans, which may allow for in-service withdrawals, depending on the terms of the plan document, money purchase and target benefit pension plans may not allow distributions prior to normal or early retirement age, death, disability, severance from employment, or termination of the plan.

Defined Benefit Plans May Allow In-Service Distributions

Effective for plan distributions in the 2007 plan year and later years, the Pension Protection Act of 2006 (PPA-06) allows defined benefit plans to include an in-service distribution option. A defined benefit plan may be amended to allow in-service distributions to participants beginning at age 62.

Profit Sharing Plans May Allow In-Service Distributions of Employer-Provided Contributions

The circumstances under which a profit sharing plan will allow for in-service withdrawals of employer-provided contributions (including matching contributions in 401(k) plans) may vary widely based on provisions found in the plan document. Generally, in order to take an in-service distribution from a profit sharing plan, the plan document must allow for the disbursement, and the funds must be held in the plan for two years if the number of years of plan participation for the worker is fewer than five years. This rule is sometimes referred to as the "two-year bake" rule. Once a participant has participated in a profit sharing plan for five-years or longer, he or she may take out up to the full balance of his or her account if the plan document so allows. An employer may also choose to limit in-service distributions of employer-provided contributions to situations of hardship. When that is the case, the employer may waive the two-year-bake rule.

Salary Deferrals Not Distributable Before Age 59½ Without Hardship

In-service distributions of salary deferrals in a 401(k) plan are more restricted than in-service distributions of other types of plan assets. In general, employee salary deferrals may not be distributed prior to severance from employment, death, disability, plan termination, attainment of age 59½, or hardship (IRC Sec. 401(k)(2)(B)(i)).

Hardship distributions of employee salary deferrals are not subject to the two-year bake rule as discussed previously, but the plan must limit the amount of the distribution to the lesser of the amount needed to cover the hardship or "the maximum distributable amount." The maximum distributable amount is the participant's employee salary deferrals (minus amounts previously distributed on account of hardship), plus the following pre-1989 amounts if the plan so permits: earnings on deferrals, qualified nonelective contributions (QNECs) plus earnings, and qualified matching contributions (QMACs) plus earnings.

The rules on hardship distributions of salary deferrals are found in 1.401(k)-1(d) of the

Treasury regulations. To satisfy the regulations relating to a hardship, an in-service distribution of salary deferral amounts must be for the purpose of covering an immediate and heavy financial need (i.e., the "events test"), and must not exceed the amount that is necessary to satisfy the financial need (the "needs test"). However, the amount required to satisfy the financial need may include any amounts necessary to pay any taxes or penalties that are expected to result from the distribution. The regulations provide two different standards for determining whether the events and needs tests for a hardship are satisfied: the general standard (also called the facts-and-circumstances standard) and the safe harbor standard. Most plan documents incorporate the safe harbor standard.

What Is Considered "An Immediate and Heavy Financial Need?"

In general, determining whether an employee has an immediate and heavy financial need is based on all relevant facts and circumstances. A financial need may be immediate and heavy even if it was reasonably foreseeable or voluntarily incurred by the employee. However, the purchase of luxury items such as boats or televisions, generally, would be excluded from the definition of hardship.

Under Treasury Regulation 1.401(k)-1(d)(3)(iii)(B), some distribution reasons are deemed to automatically qualify for hardship. A distribution is deemed to be on account of an immediate and heavy financial need of the employee if the distribution is for

- medical expenses that would be deductible (determined without regard to whether the expenses exceed 7.5 percent of adjusted gross income);
- the purchase of a principal residence (excluding mortgage payments);
- payments of tuition, related educational expenses and room and board expenses, for up to the next 12 months of post-secondary education for the employee, employee's spouse, the employee's children, or certain other dependents;
- payments to prevent the eviction of the employee from his or her principal residence, or foreclosure on that residence;
- payments for burial or funeral expenses for the employee's deceased parent, spouse, children or certain other dependents;
- expenses for the repair of damage to the employee's principal residence that qualify for the casualty deduction, without regard to whether the loss exceeds 10 percent of adjusted gross income.

With the enactment of the Pension Protection Act of 2006 (PPA-06), the availability of hardship distributions to plan participants was extended to include events that cause financial hardship to a beneficiary of the plan participant even if the beneficiary is not the spouse or dependent.

Alternative Financial Means Must Be Exhausted First

In general, a 401(k) participant must have exhausted all other financial options to cover his or her financial hardship before taking a hardship distribution of salary deferrals from his or her plan. Assets that must be considered before taking a hardship distribution of salary deferral amounts include assets of the employee's spouse and minor children that are reasonably available to the employee (e.g., a vacation home owned by the employee and the employee's spouse, whether as community property, joint tenants, tenants by the entirety, or tenants in common). However, assets held in an irrevocable trust are generally not considered "available" to a plan participant.

The IRS requires a participant to first exhaust all other distribution and loan options from the plan before allowing him or her to take a hardship distribution of employee salary deferrals (Treas. Reg. 1.401(k)-1(d)(3)(iv)(B)).

A distribution is deemed necessary for the purpose of using other available resources first if a plan participant satisfies each of the following requirements.

- The participant obtains all other currently available distributions under the plan (including nontaxable loans), and from all other plans maintained by the employer.
- Under the terms of the plan or an otherwise legally enforceable agreement, the participant is prohibited from making salary deferrals to the plan and all other plans maintained by the employer for at least six months after receipt of the hardship distribution.

However, an employee need not take an action, such as taking a loan if the effect of such an action would further increase his or her financial hardship.

Hardship Distributions Not Eligible for Rollover

Although it was possible for plan participants to roll over hardship distributions prior to 2002, participants no longer have this option. Therefore, a person should be absolutely certain that he or she needs a distribution for hardship purposes because once it is distributed, it may not be rolled over to avoid taxation. Also, a hardship distribution is not automatically exempt from the 10 percent early distribution penalty tax; the waiver of the penalty depends on the reason for distribution. (See "Early Distribution Penalty Tax for Qualified Plans" next.)

Service Member In-Service Distributions

Effective January 1, 2009, as a result of the Heroes Earnings Assistance and Tax Relief Act of 2008 (HEART Act), eligible service members may take in-service distributions of their 401(k), 403(b) and/or 457(b) elective deferrals and/or after-tax contributions. The HEART Act allows plan sponsors to consider certain employees who are on active duty for at least 30 days in the uniformed services as "severed from employment" for purposes of being able to take a plan distribution. The term uniformed services means the Armed Forces, the Army National Guard and the Air National Guard when engaged in active duty for training, inactive duty training, or full-time National Guard duty, the commissioned corps of the Public Health Service, and any other category of persons designated by the President in time of war or national emergency (IRC Sec. 3401(h)(2)(a)).

Are there any restrictions to service member in-service distributions? Yes, following the distribution, the individual would be prohibited from making elective deferrals or employee after-tax contributions to the plan for a six-month period.

Early Distribution Penalty Tax for Qualified Plans

Distributions from qualified retirement plans are subject to a 10 percent early distribution penalty tax unless an exception to the penalty applies (IRC Sec. 72(t)). While many of the exceptions are the same as those that apply to distributions from IRAs, there are some differences. With qualified retirement plans, the 10 percent early distribution penalty tax will not apply if distributions are made in any of the following circumstances.

- Attainment of age 59½

- Death

- Disability

- Substantially equal periodic payments for life or life expectancy beginning after separation from service

- Separation from service if the separation occurs during or after the calendar year in which the participant reaches age 55

- Qualified domestic relations orders (QDROs)

- Deductible medical expenses (without regard to whether the employee itemizes deductions)

- To reduce excess salary deferrals, excess contributions or excess aggregate contributions under a 401(k) plan, if timely distributed

- IRS Levy

- Dividends paid with respect to certain stock held by an employee stock ownership plan (ESOP)

- Qualified reservist distribution (for 401(k) or 403(b) salary deferrals)

- Pension plan distributions to public safety employees who leave employment after age 50

- PS-58 costs, if the taxable cost of life insurance is reported annually by a participant

- Certain permissible withdrawals of default contributions from eligible automatic contribution arrangements

Qualified Reservists and Public Safety Employees

The Pension Protection Act of 2006 (PPA-06) added two additional exceptions to the 10 percent early distribution penalty tax for qualified plans. The first penalty exception is provided for qualified reservist distributions. This penalty exception is available for an individual who is called to active duty for longer than 179 days and takes a distribution from IRA contributions, or 401(k) or 403(b) plan salary deferrals during the active duty period. The Heros Earnings Assistance and Relief Tax Act of 2008 made this exception permanent for active duty periods beginning after September 11, 2001.

The second penalty exception is available for distributions from a governmental defined benefit plan to police, firefighters or emergency medical employees of a state or political subdivision, and other public safety employees after separation from service following the attainment of age 50.

Access to Rollover Account

Plans generally allow liberal access to amounts rolled over to a qualified retirement plan as compared to amounts that were contributed to the plan. This makes sense given that rollover accounts in qualified plans are funded with assets that were eligible to be distributed from another plan in the first place. However, plans may restrict access to rollover accounts, so it is important to refer to a plan document to be sure what rules apply to distributions of rollover contributions.

403(b) Plans and In-Service Distributions

403(b) plan distribution restrictions are based on the type of contribution and whether the 403(b) is an annuity contract or a custodial account, as explained in the following paragraphs.

The unique distribution restrictions that apply to 403(b) annuity contracts are found in IRC Sec. 403(b)(11). Generally, 403(b) plan participants with 403(b) annuity contracts may withdraw their employee salary deferrals only upon

- attainment of age 59½ ,
- severance from employment,

- death,

- disability, or

- hardship.

Additionally, the following distribution rules apply.

- Distribution restrictions do not apply to pre-1989 balances in 403(b) annuity contracts.

- Distribution restrictions do not apply to employer-provided contributions in 403(b) annuity contracts. However, pursuant to the final 403(b) regulations, for annuity contracts issued on or after January 1, 2009, plans may not distribute employer contributions prior to the completion of a fixed number of years, the attainment of a stated age, or upon the occurrence of some other identified event (such as the occurrence of a financial need, including a need to buy a home).

- Hardship withdrawals of employee salary deferrals in 403(b) annuity contracts may not include earnings.

The unique distribution restrictions that apply to 403(b) custodial accounts are found in IRC Sec. 403(b)(7). Generally, 403(b) plan participants with 403(b) custodial accounts may withdraw their balances (regardless of the type of contribution) only upon

- attainment of age 59½,

- severance from employment,

- death,

- disability, or

- hardship.

Moreover, hardship distributions of employee salary deferrals in a 403(b) custodial account may be made from salary deferrals, and pre-1989 earnings on pre-1989 deferrals.

90-24 Transfer Changes

A "90-24" transfer is a movement of money between 403(b) accounts or contracts made pursuant to IRS Revenue Ruling 90-24 at the direction of the participant. Unrestricted 90-24 transfers were eliminated as of September 24, 2007, except for 403(b) contacts and accounts received in a valid transfer on or before that date (these are referred to as "grandfathered" contracts and accounts). 403(b) contacts and accounts received in a transfer after September 24, 2007, must be "affiliated" with an employer's 403(b) plan that satisfies final rules as of January 1, 2009. (Affiliated means the transfer is to a contract or account offered by an approved provider of the plan, or a provider with an information sharing arrangement with the plan.) Consequently, as of January 1, 2009, nongrandfathered, unaffiliated 403(b) contracts or accounts may cease to be valid 403(b) arrangements, and may become taxable to their owners, *unless the contracts or accounts follow the IRS relief measures outlined next, which are outlined in Revenue Procedure 2007-71.*

Relief for Contracts Issued Before 2009

Current employees' contracts or accounts issued after December 31, 2004, and before January 1, 2009, that have not received contributions on or after January 1, 2005, nonetheless will be deemed compliant with the final rules, and will preserve their tax-deferred status, if the employer or provider makes a "reasonable good faith effort" to include these contracts or accounts in the plan (not required on contracts or accounts that ceased to receive contributions before January 1, 2005). A reasonable good faith effort means either

1 the employer collects available information on the providers of the contracts or accounts, and notifies them of the name and contact information of the person in charge of administering the employer's plan for purposes of coordinating an information sharing agreement; or

2 the provider, before making any distribution or loan from the account or contract, contacts the employer in an effort to exchange required information.

For former employees and beneficiaries, contracts or accounts that ceased to receive contributions before January 1, 2009, will not be disqualified merely because they are not part of a written plan as long as the provider, pursuant to a loan request from the former employee or beneficiary, makes a reasonable effort to determine loan eligibility by contacting the former employer.

(Reasonable effort does not mean merely relying on information provided by the former employee or beneficiary. However, if the employer is no longer in existence, the provider may rely on the former employee's or beneficiary's say-so that he/she is not a current employee, assuming the information provided is reasonable under a standard facts and circumstances test.)

Contracts or accounts issued in a 90-24 transfer between September 24, 2007 and January 1, 2009, that are not issued by an approved provider of the employee's plan, nor subject to an information sharing agreement, may be at risk of disqualification. However, a contract or account that was re-exchanged for a contract or account from an approved provider before July 1, 2009, or for a contract or account with an information sharing agreement in place before July 1, 2009, will retain its qualified status (Revenue Procedure 2007-71).

New Transfer Rules

Going forward, 403(b) plan sponsors must limit 90-24 transfers to "same-plan" transfers (i.e., where transfers occur only among the approved investment providers within the plan); to "plan-to-plan" transfers (i.e., where the transferring participant is an employee or former employee of the employer maintaining the receiving 403(b) plan); or to purchase permissive service credits or to make a repayment of a cash out in.

457(b) Plans and In-Service Distributions

Participants in 457(b) plans may generally receive in-service distributions in two scenarios, one is in the case of an "unforeseeable emergency," and the other is what is often referred to as a "de minimis" distribution.

Unforeseeable Emergency

To qualify to take a distribution for an unforeseeable emergency under a 457(b) plan, the plan must contain the provision, and the participant must be experiencing a severe financial hardship (Treas. Reg. 1.457-6(c)(2)). This hardship may include

- an illness or accident of the participant or beneficiary, the participant's or beneficiary's spouse, or the participant's or beneficiary's dependent;
- loss of the participant's or beneficiary's property due to casualty (including the need to rebuild a home following damage to a home not otherwise covered by homeowner's insurance, [e.g., as a result of a natural disaster]); or
- other similar extraordinary and unforeseeable circumstances arising as a result of events beyond the control of the participant or the beneficiary.

At first sight, an unforeseeable emergency may seem quite similar to a 401(k) plan hardship, and there are some similarities. For example, the imminent foreclosure of or eviction from the participant's primary residence may constitute an unforeseeable emergency. In addition, the need to pay for medical expenses, including non-refundable deductibles, as well as for the cost of prescription drug medication, may constitute an unforeseeable emergency. Finally, the need to pay for the funeral expenses of a spouse or a dependent may also constitute an unforeseeable emergency. However, an unforeseeable emergency does not encompass as many financial hardship situations as a typical hardship provision in a 401(k) plan. For example, sending a child to college or purchasing a home may constitute a financial hardship with respect to a 401(k) plan, but because these two events are foreseeable, they do not constitute an unforeseeable emergency for 457(b) plan purposes.

- Distributions for unforeseeable emergencies are not allowed if the hardship can be relieved through reimbursement or compensation by insurance or from other sources;

- by liquidation of assets (to the extent that the liquidation does not cause severe financial hardship); or

- by stopping deferrals or contributions to the plan.

De Minimis Distributions

IRC Sec. 457(b) plans may also allow in-service withdrawals of small balances (Treas. Reg. 1.457-6(e)). If the participant's total account balance, excluding rollover contributions, is $5,000 or less; no amount has been contributed to or on behalf of the participant in the two-year period preceding the date of distribution; and no prior cash-out has occurred, then the plan may permit a distribution of the account balance. If a plan provides for an involuntary distribution, the plan must provide for the automatic rollover of distributions greater than $1,000.

Practice Management Application

- From a plan design standpoint, giving participants access to some or all of their account balances while employed is a plan feature popular with many participants.

- Whether an in-service distribution option exists is dependent upon plan language. In order to help a participant determine the availability of in-service distributions, a financial professional has several options. He or she could 1) go to the benefits web site (if available, and with the help of the plan participant) to review distribution options, 2) review a hard copy of the plan document, or 3) review the summary plan description for the plan. Be sure to check both the "Amendments" and "Distributions" sections of the plan document.

- Assuming a plan allows for in-service distributions, if the quality of advice and service that a plan participant receives from the plan is low, he or she would be a prime prospect for completing a rollover of an in-service distribution.

- Rollover accounts generally are subject to liberal in-service distribution rules as set forth in the plan document. Review the plan document for the in-service distribution provisions, and use the participant's plan account statement to determine if the participant has a rollover account. The account statement will also identify other money types.

- Distributions attributable to hardship are ineligible for rollover.

- Financial professionals with practices in areas holding a concentration of military personnel and their families should be aware of the new in-service distribution opportunity for individuals serving in the uniformed services.

Feedback for the review questions can be found at the end of the chapter.

1 With respect to employee salary deferrals in a 401(k) plan, which of the following lists accurately represents when employee salary deferrals may be distributed?

    A Attainment of age 59 ½, severance from employment, death, disability, plan termination and hardship

    B Severance from employment, death, disability, plan termination and hardship

    C Attainment of age 59 ½, death, disability, plan termination and hardship

    D Attainment of age 59 ½, severance from employment, death, plan termination and hardship

2 In which of the following situations would an employee be able to take a plan distribution while working?

    A 401(k) employee salary deferrals at age 55

    B Money purchase pension contributions at age 59 ½

    C Defined benefit plan employer contributions at age 60

    D 457(b) contributions for an unforeseeable emergency

3 What is the meaning of the "two-year bake rule" with respect to in-service distributions?

    A The employee must complete two years of service before being eligible to request an in-service distribution of employer profit sharing contributions.

    B If the employee's years of plan participation are fewer than five, he/she may only access profit sharing contributions on an in-service basis that have been in the plan for at least two years.

    C A plan must hold employee salary deferrals for a minimum of two years before a participant may access them.

    D A SEP plan may not distribute contributions that have not been in the IRA for two years.

4 What is the percentage amount of the early distribution penalty tax under IRC Sec. 72(t)(1)?

    A 6%

    B 10%

    C 15%

    D 50%

5 If a plan participant takes an in-service distribution of pre-tax assets, what could he/she do to avoid including the amount in his/her taxable income?

A In-service distributions are not subject to taxation.

B Directly transfer the amount to a taxable brokerage account.

C Complete a rollover to an IRA.

D It is impossible to avoid immediate taxation.

Chapter Review Questions Feedback

1 With respect to employee salary deferrals in a 401(k) plan, which of the following lists accurately represents when employee salary deferrals may be distributed?

    A Attainment of age 59 ½, severance from employment, death, disability, plan termination and hardship

    B Severance from employment, death, disability, plan termination and hardship

    C Attainment of age 59 ½, death, disability, plan termination and hardship

    D Attainment of age 59 ½, severance from employment, death, plan termination and hardship

    A *Correct, these are the sanctioned distribution triggering events for employee salary deferrals as specified in IRC Sec. 401(k)(2)(B)(i)).* Chapter 5 Page 124

    B *Incorrect, attainment of age 59 ½ could also be a distribution triggering event for employee salary deferrals.*

    C *Incorrect, severance from employment could also be a distribution triggering event for employee salary deferrals.*

    D *Incorrect, applicable Internal Revenue Code sections provide the general legal framework for retirement plan distributions, but not the specific triggering events for a particular plan.*

2 In which of the following situations would an employee be able to take a plan distribution while working?

    A 401(k) employee salary deferrals at age 55

    B Money purchase pension contributions at age 59 ½

    C Defined benefit plan employer contributions at age 60

    D 457(b) contributions for an unforeseeable emergency

    A *Incorrect, 401(k) employee salary deferrals may not be distributed prior to age 59 ½ while the participant is working.*

    B *Incorrect, money purchase pension plans may not distribute plan assets while the participant is working.*

    C *Incorrect, defined benefit plans may not distribute plan assets prior to age 62 while the participant is working.*

D *Correct, 457(b) plans may distribute assets while the participant is working if he/she experiences an unforeseeable emergency as defined in Treasury Regulation 1.457-6(c)(2).* Chapter 5 Page 126

3 What is the meaning of the "two-year bake rule" with respect to in-service distributions?

A The employee must complete two years of service before being eligible to request an in-service distribution of employer profit sharing contributions.

B If the employee's years of plan participation are fewer than five, he/she may only access profit sharing contributions on an in-service basis that have been in the plan for at least two years.

C A plan must hold employee salary deferrals for a minimum of two years before a participant may access them.

D A SEP plan may not distribute contributions that have not been in the IRA for two years.

A *Incorrect, if the employee's years of plan participation are fewer than five, he/she may only access profit sharing contributions on an in-service basis that have been in the plan for at least two years.*

B **Correct, pursuant to Revenue Ruling 68-24, if the employee's years of plan participation are fewer than five, the IRS believes that contributions must be held in the plan for two years before they can be considered eligible for in-service distribution.** Chapter 5 Page 134

C *Incorrect, employee salary deferrals may not be distributed on an in-service basis prior to the attainment of age 59 ½.*

D *Incorrect, IRA assets are distributable at any time for any reason.*

4 What is the percentage amount of the early distribution penalty tax under IRC Sec. 72(t)(1)?

A 6%
B 10%
C 15%
D 50%

A *Incorrect, 6% represents the IRS penalty tax applicable to excess IRA contributions.*

B **Correct, pursuant to IRC Sec. 72(t) the amount of penalty tax that applies to a distribution taken prior to attaining age 59 ½ is 10%.** Chapter 5 Page 137

C *Incorrect, 15% represents the IRS penalty tax applicable to a prohibited transaction.*

D *Incorrect, 50% represents the IRS penalty tax applicable for failure to take a required minimum distribution.*

5 If a plan participant takes an in-service distribution of pre-tax assets, what could he/she do to avoid including the amount in his/her taxable income?

  A In-service distributions are not subject to taxation.
  B Directly transfer the amount to a taxable brokerage account.
  C Complete a rollover to an IRA.
  D It is impossible to avoid immediate taxation.

A *Incorrect, in-service distributions of pre-tax amounts are includable in the recipient's taxable income in the year distributed.*

B *Incorrect, the in-service distribution will still be treated as a taxable distribution.*

C *Correct, the assets will retain their tax-deferred status if they are rolled over to an IRA or other eligible plan.* Chapter 5 Page 136

D *Incorrect, if the distribution recipient completes a rollover to an IRA or other eligible plan, taxation is deferred.*

CHAPTER 6

Roadblocks to Rollovers

Chapter Goal

Historically, record keepers have aggressively worked to attract company retirement plan business, while simultaneously standing by and passively watching large individual account balances leach away from their organizations in the form of rollovers as employees change jobs or retire. Rollover retention rates are low – only 25 percent of rolling participants choose their current provider.[1] Recently, however, many record keepers have realized that there are many actions they may take to increase the likelihood that their organizations will retain these often profitable accounts. For many financial professionals, this shift in asset retention strategy by record keepers has meant that winning rollover business has become more difficult, and that heightened knowledge and the application of best practices have become essential in order to be able to successfully compete in the rollover marketplace. This chapter will cover the many real and perceived impediments to the rollover process. Each of these "roadblocks" will be explained, followed by some suggested best practices for overcoming them.

Learning Objectives

✓ Recognize the four types of roadblocks to rollover success.

✓ Identify the three steps involved with managing the rollover process.

✓ Associate mitigation tactics with rollover roadblocks.

[1] The Asset Management Industry: Outcomes Are the New Alpha, McKinsey & Company, 2012

The Impact of Rollovers

Rollover transactions often represent the beginning of a new client relationship. Consequently, the client's experience with the rollover process can set the tone for the entire future relationship with the client. If the client's expectations are not met during the rollover process, not only will the client be less likely to invest other assets with a financial professional, the chances of the financial professional retaining the rollover assets are greatly diminished.

There are three primary reasons why rollover transactions engender such great anxiety among both financial professionals and clients. The first reason for heightened anxiety is that rollovers often involve large sums of pre-tax money. That means, if a rollover transaction is not handled properly, it will become taxable. When dealing with balances that are often valued in the millions, a rollover mistake can be extremely costly to the individual rolling over the assets (and to the financial professional, as well, if he or she is responsible for the error). The second reason for rollover anxiety is that retirement assets often literally represent a person's life's savings. Consequently, any losses to these assets have a direct impact on how the individual will be able to live in retirement. Therefore, losses involving these assets strike at the very heart of a person's sense of financial security.

Of course, the first and second reason for rollover anxiety would be merely academic if it weren't for the third reason for rollover anxiety, which is, there are many parts and many players involved in the rollover process, and much that can go wrong during a rollover transaction. When such high stakes are combined with a high risk for error, it's no wonder that rollovers are a cause of great concern for both clients and financial professionals.

This chapter will explore the most common potential problems that may arise during the rollover process. In addition to identifying these problems, referred to as "roadblocks," the chapter will also provide ways to avoid and limit these problems, which will ultimately lead to greater customer satisfaction and more rollover business for financial professionals and their organizations.

Types of Rollover Roadblocks and Strategies to Overcome

There are four general types of rollover roadblocks: regulatory, plan document, psychological, and administrative.

Regulatory Roadblocks

Regulatory roadblocks are created by Congress and the IRS, and are impossible to avoid if a retirement plan wishes to retain tax-favored status. These are the red-tape roadblocks that are inherent in saving in a tax-favored retirement plan. With regulatory roadblocks, the best one can do is to be aware of all requirements and to satisfy the requirements in the simplest way possible. Regulatory roadblocks can include the following.

Triggering Events

Participants in 401(k) plans, profit sharing plans, money purchase pension plans, target benefit plans, defined benefit plans, 403(b) plans, 457 plans, and employee stock ownership plans (ESOPs) must satisfy a distribution triggering event before the money in their accounts can be distributed. The specific triggering event rules are covered in greater detail in Chapter 4.

Eligible Rollover Distributions

Understanding the rules relating to rollovers and their portability among the different plan types is paramount in reducing roadblocks and setting expectations during the rollover process. Eligible rollovers and portability are discussed in greater detail in Chapter 7.

Spousal Signature Requirements

Some retirement plans require a spousal signature on the distribution request form. Sometimes these plans are known as "REA" plans. REA refers to the Retirement Equity Act of 1984 that created the spousal consent requirements, which were created to protect spousal rights in connection with retirement plan benefits. Many 401(k) plans are exempt from the REA spousal consent requirements; however, all defined benefit and money purchase plans are subject to the spousal consent requirements.

Mandatory 20 Percent Withholding On Indirect Rollovers

A distribution recipient will only receive 80 percent of the total value of a plan distribution if the distribution could have been directly rolled over to another plan, but was not. Federal tax law requires the distributing plan to withhold and remit the other 20 percent of the distribution to the IRS as pre-payment of federal income taxes. Some view the mandatory withholding as a penalty; it is not. It is merely a mechanism to pre-pay one's tax liability. Note that IRA distributions are not subject to the mandatory 20 percent withholding rate.

Plan Document Roadblocks

The employer sponsoring the plan can draft the plan in a manner that limits the forms of payment from the plan, and the form of payment can affect whether a distributed amount is eligible for rollover or not. For example, a defined benefit plan could mandate the only form of payment to a participant is an annuity over the life of the participant. A participant generally cannot roll over amounts to an IRA or other eligible retirement plan unless the plan they are participating in provides for a lump sum distribution.

Understanding the plan and its provisions are the key to dealing with many of the plan document roadblocks. A good practice is to obtain a copy of the plan document or, at minimum, the summary plan description. These documents can often be procured online from the employer's benefits web site. The documents will provide the information about plan payout options, which is crucial to helping the individual understand what his or her options are, and to navigate the options and choices available in the plan.

For example, in-service distributions are a commonly misunderstood provision. Plans may permit in-service distributions of some or all money types, and knowing what a given plan allows can often help advisers to help their clients gain greater access to their retirement assets through a rollover long before normal retirement age. A scenario illustrating this sort of situation follows.

EXAMPLE:

The Plan Does Not Allow for In-Service Distributions (or Does It?)

A financial professional was working with a new client who was a 57-year-old, human resources director for a medium-sized company. The client had $410,000 in the company 401(k) plan, and she was dissatisfied with the investment products and choices. Normal retirement age was 62, and the plan did not appear to contain an in-service distribution option. Consequently, the client assumed she could not take a distribution until she retired.

Upon reviewing her statement, the advisor noticed that a little over $300,000 of the $410,000 plan balance was in a rollover account, which the client had rolled into the plan from a prior employer six years earlier. A closer review of the plan documents revealed the plan did permit in-service distributions of rollover account money. This is a common provision that allows participants to take distributions of rollover amounts at any time. The financial professional was able to help the client take over $300,000 out of the 401(k) plan and roll the amount over to an IRA.

Psychological Roadblocks

Psychological roadblocks are a bit more complicated than regulatory roadblocks because they are often created by a client's own antagonistic attitudes toward the rollover process. These roadblocks may be the result of bad past experiences, misperceptions about the rollover process, or unfamiliarity with tax rules. Providing client reassurance and education, as necessary, can be crucial to overcoming psychological roadblocks.

Some psychological roadblocks are conscious and easily identifiable, and others are subconscious and may be difficult for the person experiencing them to put into words. However, in either case, a psychological roadblock is often a powerful impediment to a person pursuing a rollover strategy.

Dealing with the psychological roadblocks is a process of managing expectations. As was mentioned earlier, it is important to ask clients about past rollover experiences to attempt to determine what they know and don't know about rules relating to retirement plans and rollovers. The following issues are representative of some of the most common psychological roadblocks.

"The Rollover Process Is Too Complex"

Faced with seemingly overwhelming paperwork and other hurdles, many participants adopt an avoidance strategy to rollovers because they feel they are too complex. Essentially, the client is overwhelmed by the perception that the process is inordinately complex. Not surprisingly, the pile of poorly written regulatory notices that individuals often receive when they become eligible to receive distributions from their employers typically serve to reinforce this perception. Often the client feels overwhelmed by technical information, and feels he or she has no where to turn for help.

One strategy for dealing with this type of roadblock starts with outlining the rollover process in general terms so that the client is not overwhelmed with details. Clearly illustrating the process and the parties involved with the rollover will help to demystify the rollover experience for the client and help to minimize the client's sense that rolling over retirement plan assets is an overwhelming task. The financial professional should keep this explanation as concise as possible as an overly elaborate explanation will simply reinforce the client's sense that there is too much work involved in rolling over assets.

401(k) Direct Rollover	401(k) Indirect Rollover
Plan ⟶ IRA	Plan IRA ⤷ Participant ⤴
Distribution goes directly to plan	Distribution goes to participant
No federal withholding	Federal withholding applies
No taxation	Taxed on amounts not rolled over
No 60-day time limit	Rollover must occur within 60 days

Following a high-level description of the rollover process, next the advisor should explain his or her role in the process. For example, the financial professional should inform the client how he or she will be requesting rollover paperwork (usually on the phone or online), and that he or she will be available to assist the client in completing the forms. The financial professional should also inform the client that he or she will be forwarding the paperwork to the appropriate parties on behalf of the client. The financial professional can also assure the participant that he or she will track the process to ensure its successful completion.

Another strategy that should be employed at the first sign that the client is wavering in his or her commitment to rolling over assets is to show him or her what it may cost over the long-run to not roll over a distribution. This can often be accomplished with some simple illustrations in a brochure that deals with the subject, or, better still, by performing a computer projection that shows the anticipated financial benefit of rolling the assets over.

EXAMPLE:

401(k) Plan Participant Assumptions

Participant Date of Birth	02/21/1963
First Year of Plan Participation	1986
Distribution Amount	$100,000.00
Tax Filing Status	Married Filing Joint
Taxable Income Pre-retirement	$120,000.00
Retirement Age	67
Anticipated Rate of Return Prior to Retirement	10.000%
Tax Rate Prior to Retirement	25.00%
Tax Rate During Retirement	15.00%
Payout Years	30
Anticipated Rate of Return During Payout	7.000%

Projected Annual Income Options:

Tax Treatment	Projected Annual Income (After-Taxes)
No Rollover/Ordinary Income	$22,313.57
Rollover to Traditional IRA	$62,759.59

"These Plan Assets Cannot Be Rolled Over"

It is very common for clients to be unaware of rollover options and distribution choices that are available to them. For example, many plan participants are unaware if their plan allows for in-service distributions, or if their defined benefit plan has a lump sum distribution option. This roadblock is one of the easiest to resolve because it is usually based on a misunderstanding of the facts. A review of the plan documentation will settle the matter. Plan documentation can include

- the summary plan description,
- the plan document, and/or
- printouts from the employer's benefits web site.

Financial professionals can help clients obtain plan documentation from their employers and assist with the review process. Plan participants have the right under the Employee Retirement Income Security Act of 1974 (ERISA) to request and receive a copy of the plan document from the sponsoring employer (ERISA Sec. 104(b)(4)).

Moreover, financial professionals can help to facilitate a better understanding of which assets are eligible for rollover and which ones are not by providing clients with access to IRS Publication 590 (which contains a good explanation of qualified plan/IRA rollover rules and requirements), and IRS Publication 571 (which contains a good explanation of 403(b)-related rollover rules and requirements). Both publications are accessible free of charge on the IRS' web site www.irs.gov.

"A Retirement Plan Distribution Is a Windfall"

Some recipients of eligible rollover distributions see the assets as "found money," and want to use them for major purchases. Even though this is often an extremely expensive way to finance large purchases, once a person has earmarked the assets for a different purpose other than for rollover, it can be difficult to convince him or her that it would be better to find a different way to finance those purchases.

Of course the biggest downfall of keeping an otherwise eligible rollover distribution is the immediate tax liability. Perhaps by reminding the client that he or she will need to include the distribution in taxable income for the year, must immediately pay 20 percent for federal income tax withholding, and may be subject to a 10 percent early distribution penalty tax if he or she is under age 59½, will be enough to convince the client that a rollover is the better option if saving for retirement is the goal.

Administrative Roadblocks

Administrative roadblocks are logistical problems related to the provider, product or employer that have the potential for making the rollover process harder than it has to be. Although some problems, such as processing issues, are out of the hands of the participant and financial professional, and may require the provider to make major capital expenditures to fix, many administrative roadblocks can be mitigated by financial professionals becoming more aware of the specific rollover processing so that potential problems can be avoided before they occur.

Administrative roadblocks are generally related to getting the correct information, receiving the proper paperwork, and processing the paperwork. These roadblocks can be the most troublesome (and least predictable) to navigate. To start, the financial professional should alert the client at the onset of a rollover transaction that sometimes unforeseen circumstances occur during the rollover process. The financial professional should continue by assuring the client that he or she will be monitoring the process and will work with the client to overcome any unforeseen obstacles that may come up as quickly as possible. Some common administrative roadblocks include the following.

"The Distribution Paperwork Is Hard to Obtain"

Many vendors use a "hide-and-seek" strategy with respect to forms in order to retain dollars. They make it difficult to find and use rollover paperwork, thereby discouraging the rollover.

If this is the case, the financial professional and client should contact the employer or the service provider together to inquire about the process and the form requirements. In some cases, the forms are available online. Unfortunately, many times the only distribution forms available online are those that only permit rollovers to the current vendor. If the participant wants to roll over assets to another vendor, he or she must contact a customer service representative who often has been trained to encourage the client to leave the funds with the current provider. To avoid losing the rollover in such cases, it is important for the financial professional to be on this call with the participant. At the call's onset, clearly state that the financial professional is present, and that the client has decided to roll over the money to another IRA. Obtain an estimated time of arrival for the forms as well as the name, employee number, call-back number, and e-mail address of the client service representative. This information may be useful if the forms do not arrive when promised.

"The Rollover Process Is Unduly Burdensome"

Some organizations that hold assets attempt to retain the potential rollover in such an aggressive manner that the participant feels that he or she must "run the gauntlet," before a rollover is permitted. For example, the current provider may provide initial rollover paperwork promptly, but the paperwork may only allow for a direct rollover into an IRA with the current provider. In order to roll over the distributed assets to a different vendor, the individual may be required to speak with a service representative of the current provider. The service representative could potentially be another "hurdle" that the distribution recipient must leap before being able to move his or her assets somewhere else. Here again, the financial professional can help set realistic expectations for the client, and also help them overcome stubborn service representatives of the current provider.

"I'm Not Eligible for a Distribution"

In this scenario the individual is told he or she is not eligible for a distribution (when, in fact, he or she is). It is not uncommon for vendors or the employer to misstate or misunderstand when a participant is eligible to take a distribution. Often, in-service distribution options are misunderstood and not accurately communicated to individuals. A review of the plan documentation will set the record straight as to whether or not a participant is eligible for a distribution.

"I'll Have to Pay Extra Fees"

Some participants may incur surrender charges if they move their plan dollars within certain timeframes. These back-end charges are often not well disclosed, nor understood by participants. Unfortunately, many people don't learn the details of these penalties, and come to believe that if they ever move their money, they will have to pay a penalty.

Misunderstanding of Income Tax Withholding Rules and Early Distribution Penalties

There is a great deal of client confusion surrounding the mandatory withholding rules that apply to certain eligible rollover distributions. Many participants confuse the 20 percent mandatory income tax withholding on eligible rollover amounts that are not directly rolled over with the early distribution penalty. Some people think the 20 percent mandatory income tax withholding covers the early distribution penalty (it does not, withholding is merely a prepayment of anticipated income taxes on the amount distributed) or they think that they have to pay a 20 percent penalty whenever they take a distribution.

Signature Guarantees

Many vendors require a signature guarantee if the account exceeds a certain size or the check is to be mailed to an address other than the participant's. The signature guarantee is typically obtained from a financial institution such as a bank. It becomes one more step in the distribution process.

Lost Paperwork

Sometimes distribution paperwork mysteriously "disappears" shortly after its arrival at the employer or the investment provider. Often there is little or no tracking, and the client is told he or she must resend the paperwork.

It is generally prudent for financial professionals to make copies of rollover forms for clients as well as to obtain signatures on two completed sets of forms. This precaution is for situations where one of the parties in the process misplaces a copy of the forms. This practice adds very little administrative burden if it is done at the beginning of the rollover process, but it can save a great deal of time and frustration if something happens to the first set of forms.

Once rollover forms are ready for submission, they should be sent using a method that can be tracked. Obtaining signature guarantees often slows the rollover process. Some financial professionals meet with the client and drive them to the financial institution to obtain the signatures and expedite the process.

Belief There Will Be a Loss of Other Benefits

Individuals are sometimes told, erroneously, that if a distribution is taken from an employer-sponsored plan, the individual will lose some other benefit (health coverage, life insurance, vacation pay, etc). These statements are often designed to scare participants, particularly retirees, and if the statements are known to be untrue by those who make the claims, they are also fraudulent representations. However, in less egregious cases, the false statements may simply come about as a result of poor training for plan representatives.

Stating That Rollover Distributions Are Not Available

Under this situation the individual is told the plan does not permit a rollover to an IRA (or other retirement plan) and the amounts must be paid directly to the individual and be subject to the mandatory 20 percent withholding.

Contacting the Current Vendor

The process of navigating the phone system and communicating with an often uncooperative client service representative can be a demoralizing experience for most clients. Again, the management of expectations is important at this stage of the process. Offering to get on the phone with the client in order to protect his or her interests will go a long way to assuring the client that the financial professional is on his side and will make sure the process stays on track.

If a Vendor Refuses to Cooperate

If the vendor refuses to process a rollover request, more assertive strategies may have to be employed. The first step in the escalation process is contacting the general client service area and asking to speak with a supervisor or manager. This should be done with the client in a three-way call. If the account in question is in an insurance product, consider contacting the state insurance commission to enlist their help with the recalcitrant carrier. Another option is to insist on speaking to the legal department of the current provider. The fiduciary approach is a strategy that has proven to be effective in certain situations. If the employer has approved the distribution, the vendor should make the payout pursuant to the employer's instructions. The employer maintaining the plan is a fiduciary and the plan administrator. Service parties are required to follow the instructions of the plan administrator. If a service provider does not follow the plan administrator's instructions, the service provider runs the risk of becoming a plan fiduciary. A discussion with the legal counsel of the vendor regarding the liabilities associated with fiduciary status can be effective in speeding up the distribution process.

How to Address Rollover Roadblocks in General

The most important aspect of dealing with rollover roadblocks, regardless of the type, is to manage the client's overall expectations regarding the rollover process. Managing expectations is a three-step process that begins with talking with the client to understand what his or her expectations or preconceived notions may be regarding the rollover process. This requires asking probing questions. Possible questions could be these.

Step 1: Identify Expectations and Preconceived Notions

- Have you rolled over money in the past?
- What was the process like?
- How long did it take?

Often the participant may not have a direct experience with an IRA rollover but may have preconceived notions regarding the process because of comments made by family, friends or co-workers. These should also be explored with a few more questions.

- What have you heard about the rollover experience?
- Are you aware of any co-worker's or friend's rollover experiences?

Step 2: Monitor and Communicate

Once the client's expectations and preconceptions are understood, they can be managed. In managing a clients' expectations, financial professionals should commit to do the following.

- Monitor the progress of the transaction and keep the client informed about the progress. Notify him or her immediately regarding any unexpected obstacles. The process may take some time even under ideal conditions, but if unplanned problems arise, the client needs to know that his or her financial professional will do what it takes to resolve them as quickly as possible.

- Do as much as possible to ensure the process does not become overly burdensome to the client.

- Do everything in your power to ensure that the money is safely moved.

The financial professional must use the plan and keep the client informed about the transaction's status. Since clients may have different preferred methods of communication (e.g., e-mail, phone, in person), it is wise to determine their preferred method of communication at the beginning of the transaction. Some financial professionals use a weekly status e-mail for outstanding rollover clients. This e-mail communication lets the client know what has occurred during the week and what the next steps are. Of course, for some clients, such a communication might get lost in the flurry of other e-mails they receive, so it pays to find out clients' feelings on these types of communications in advance.

In order to ensure the rollover process proceeds smoothly, financial professional need a formal tracking mechanism.

Step 3: Track the process

1 A Plan for Tracking the Rollover Process

This plan will provide for follow up at critical steps in the process, and provide communication regarding the status of the rollover to the client. The plan should be reviewed before the rollover process begins as this is the core of managing expectations.

2 A Tracking Mechanism

The tracking doesn't have to be an elaborate process. It does need to quickly help the financial professional know where things are in the rollover process at any given time.

With a process like this in place, the financial professional is well positioned to identify problems and address them, while managing the client's expectations. If a roadblock occurs, the client is told about it in a timely manner, and the financial professional adjusts the strategy to overcome the obstacle. Once the hurdle is passed, the financial professional reminds the client that he or she is looking out for them, and reassures the client that he or she will keep the process moving.

Defined Benefit Plans and Distribution Options

Another common impediment to rollovers relates specifically to defined benefit plans. Many participants believe that they must take annuitized payments from their defined benefit plans, which, of course, would be ineligible for rollover. However, many defined benefit plans have a lump sum distribution option of which participants are often unaware.

Scenario: A Defined Benefit Plan Provides a Surprise Rollover

A financial professional in St. Paul, Minnesota had a new client. The client was 56 years old, single, and a life-long employee of a phone company, with annual income of approximately $40,000. The client had approximately $18,000 in an IRA with a local credit union and wanted help in investing it. Initially, the client told the financial professional that he had no other assets other than a small home. The financial professional asked him about his phone company employment. The client was a participant in a large collectively bargained defined benefit plan. The plan had a lump sum distribution option. The client was surprised to hear of the lump sum option. After some research and analysis the client elected to take the lump sum distribution from the defined benefit plan. The defined benefit plan rollover was almost $1.1 million.

- Dealing with rollover roadblocks is always easier if the financial professional has taken the time to build a relationship with the client before the rollover transaction. Often when a client's first experience with a financial professional is a rollover transaction, which turns out to be nothing but a string of problems, the relationship may be irreparably harmed and the client may even decide to cancel the rollover transaction.

- Consequently, it is very important to have a process in place to reduce the likelihood of problems. A rollover process must involve managing client expectations through timely and clear communication, and include a clearly defined mechanism for tracking the process as well as for escalating problems when necessary.

- Remember, an efficient rollover process can be a sales tool that can help a financial professional differentiate himself or herself from other financial professionals who only talk "product" not "process."

- The following table summarizes potential roadblocks to rollovers and suggests management strategies.

Client Roadblock	Management Strategy
Spousal signatures	Know when spousal signatures are necessary and communicate that to the client at the beginning of the process.
Signature guarantees	Take the client to the financial organization for signatures to expedite this process.
The client does not think he or she is eligible for a rollover.	Request a copy of the plan statement and summary plan description to verify distribution options, including in-service distributions.

Client Roadblock	Management Strategy
Client expects the rollover process will be quick and easy.	Discuss with the client the overall process so he or she understands how many steps and players are involved. Highlight his or her required actions and emphasize that you (the financial professional) will handle every other aspect that does not require his or her involvement. Be ready to provide technical and moral support when the client may have to talk to a hostile customer service representative.
The rollover process is too much trouble for me to even want to attempt it.	Break the rollover process down into easily digestible steps. Be prepared to show the client the financial benefits of rolling assets over versus doing nothing. Offer to handle the paperwork and tracking processes.
The client fails to follow through on paperwork requests.	Follow up with the client on a regular basis, and offer to sit down with the client to assist with the paperwork process, if necessary.
The financial professional will do all the work.	Be sure to be upfront about what the client must do, but assure the client that you (the financial professional) will do everything else possible to facilitate the rollover.
The client is upset with the amount of time and trouble surrounding the transaction.	Manage expectations early on. It may take a while, but emphasize that "we will get through it." The best way to avoid this situation is to clearly discuss the process with the client before starting the transaction, and to give him or her advance warning that there may be certain parts of the transaction that may not be within your control.
The client is unable to find forms, or determine where forms are to be sent.	Perform an online search for plan documents and forms. Forms may be available under the current vendor's web site or former employer's web site. If this does not work, contact the human resources area of the former employer. Be on the call with the client.

Client Roadblock	Management Strategy
Lost and delayed forms.	Get copies of all forms. Have two sets of signed forms. Problems with lost forms can be greatly alleviated by making copies or having the client fill out and sign two sets of forms. Also, sending documents overnight not only cuts down on transit time, but can allow for the tracing of lost documents, making it more likely that they will be recovered.
The client has disputes with the plan administrator about plan distribution provisions, including rollover availability in general, ability to directly roll over assets, withholding requirements, and other issues.	Some issues are a matter of law and cannot be over-ridden by a plan document. This includes issues relating to mandatory withholding and availability of direct rollovers. Be familiar with these statutory and regulatory issues. For other issues that are plan specific, be sure to have a copy of the plan document, or at least the summary plan description, and flag the sections in question. Although one would think that a plan administrator would know what is available under a plan, this is not always the case, so it pays to do research. This is an area where one's willingness to look after a client's interests can be beneficial in strengthening the financial professional/client relationship. Develop a dispute resolution strategy. For example, Step 1: Obtain a copy of the plan document for review. Plan participants have the right to request and receive a copy of the actual plan document from the employer (ERISA Sec. 104(b)(4)). Step 2: Follow the plan's claim's procedure. Step 3: Discuss areas of dispute with the plan administrator. Step 4: If no resolution is apparent, it may be necessary to escalate the issue by involving the Department of Labor (ERISA 502(a)). For more information on claims procedures, see the Department of Labor publication, *Filing a Claim for Your Retirement Benefits* at www.dol.gov/ebsa or call toll free at 1.866.444.EBSA (3272), or e-mail www.askebsa.dol.gov
The client must satisfy some unusual administrative requirements.	Occasionally, a form will include unusual signature requirements, such as an employer signature for a simplified employee pension (SEP) plan distribution. Depending on the flexibility of the plan administrator, it may be possible to have such a bogus requirement waived. Otherwise, comply.

Client Roadblock	Management Strategy
The client must interact with the current vendor's client service representatives in order to get rollover information.	The financial professional and client should contact the client service representative together to make the request, in order to make sure the client service representative understands that the rollover decision has already been made after careful consideration.
The 20 percent federal income tax withholding was misapplied to an eligible rollover distribution that was directly rolled over.	Go back to the provider and have the provider correct and rollover the remaining 20 percent.
The rollover request is lost.	Sometimes there is no formal tracking process in place. In such cases, a financial professional must develop his or her own process. Nothing can damage a relationship as much as the client thinking that a financial professional is not handling important paperwork with care.
The client is dealing with an uncooperative vendor or employer.	Follow the plan's claim's procedures as outlined in the Summary Plan Description. If ordinary efforts at diplomacy fail, an escalation process is necessary. Generally, the first escalation measure is to talk to the person who manages the client service representatives. If this does not result in satisfactory action, the next step is generally to escalate the matter to the organization's in-house legal counsel. This is often very effective because the legal counsel generally will see the risk involved with failing to expedite the process, and will make the necessary calls to get the process moving again. However, in cases where even this effort fails, advisors may need to help their clients file a complaint with the insurance commissioner for a group annuity product, or the Department of Labor if the plan has failed to follow the requirements of ERISA.. For more information on claims procedures, see the Department of Labor publication, Filing a Claim for Your Retirement Benefits at www.dol.gov/ebsa or call toll free at 1.866.444.EBSA (3272), or e-mail www.askebsa.dol.gov

Feedback for the review questions can be found at the end of the chapter.

1 Which of the following lists represents common categories of roadblocks to rollovers?

    A Over spending, longevity, inflation and market
    B Flat dollar, pro rata, integrated and new comparability
    C Regulatory, plan document, psychological and administrative
    D Social Security insolvency, low savings rate and rising healthcare costs

2 What is the most important aspect of dealing with roadblocks to rollovers regardless of type?

    A Manage the plan participant's expectations
    B Maintain copies of rollover forms
    C Obtain signature guarantees
    D Request a copy of the plan participant's account statement

3 In a situation where the plan participant is dealing with an uncooperative client service representative regarding a rollover request submitted to a plan service provider, in what order would you execute the following steps to remedy the situation in the most efficient way possible?

    A Escalate the issue with the service provider's upper management, notify the service provider's legal counsel, file a complaint with the Department of Labor
    B Notify the service provider's legal counsel, escalate the issue with the service provider's upper management, file a complaint with the Department of Labor
    C File a complaint with the Department of Labor, escalate the issue with the service provider's upper management, notify the service provider's legal counsel
    D The order of the steps does not matter.

4 Which of the following is *NOT* one of the steps in the managing the rollover process?

    A Identify expectations and preconceived notions
    B Monitor and Communicate
    C Submit a rollover request form to the IRS
    D Track the process

5 Which of the following would be a plan document roadblock that would preclude a rollover?

    A 20% mandatory withholding
    B The complexity of the rollover process
    C Signature guarantees
    D Plan only offers an annuity

1 Which of the following lists represents common categories of roadblocks to rollovers?

    A Over spending, longevity, inflation and market
    B Flat dollar, pro rata, integrated and new comparability
    C Regulatory, plan document, psychological and administrative
    D Social Security insolvency, low savings rate and rising healthcare costs

A *Incorrect, these are types of risks to retirement income.*

B *Incorrect, these are types of contribution allocation methods.*

C *Correct, based on the types of common roadblocks to rollovers, they can be classified under these four general categories.* Chapter 6 Page 148

D *Incorrect, these are types of Baby Boomer financial pressures.*

2 What is the most important aspect of dealing with roadblocks to rollovers regardless of type?

    A Manage the plan participant's expectations
    B Maintain copies of rollover forms
    C Obtain signature guarantees
    D Request a copy of the plan participant's account statement

A *Correct, a plan participant's frustration level with rollover roadblocks can be greatly reduced if he/she has realistic expectations about the rollover process.* Chapter 6 Page 156

B *Incorrect, this is a tactic that can be used to facilitate a rollover if a plan administrator loses the original paperwork.*

C *Incorrect, this is a requirement that could be considered a type of roadblock that the plan administrator may put up to delay the rollover process.*

D *Incorrect, this is a tactic that may be helpful in assessing the plan participant's potential rollover situation.*

3 In a situation where the plan participant is dealing with an uncooperative client service representative regarding a rollover request submitted to a plan service provider, in what order would you execute the following steps to remedy the situation in the most efficient way possible?

    A Escalate the issue with the service provider's upper management, notify the service provider's legal counsel, file a complaint with the Department of Labor
    B Notify the service provider's legal counsel, escalate the issue with the service provider's upper management, file a complaint with the Department of Labor
    C File a complaint with the Department of Labor, escalate the issue with the service provider's upper management, notify the service provider's legal counsel

D The order of the steps does not matter.

A *Correct, this represents the proper chain of communication based on levels of authority.*
Chapter 6 Page 156

B *Incorrect, it would be in efficient to contact the service provider's legal counsel before attempting to resolve the issue with the service provider's upper management.*

C *Incorrect, the Department of Labor recommends a plan participant first follow the plan's claim filing procedure, and file a complaint with its office only if the plan has failed to follow ERISA legal requirements.*

D *Incorrect, option A is the most efficient process and follows Department of Labor recommendations.*

4 Which of the following is *NOT* one of the steps in the managing the rollover process?

    A Identify expectations and preconceived notions
    B Monitor and Communicate
    C Submit a rollover request form to the IRS
    D Track the process

A *Incorrect, the first step in managing the rollover process is to identify the investor's expectations and preconceived notions with respect to rollovers.*

B *Incorrect, the second step in managing the rollover process is to monitor progress and communicate the progress to the investor.*

C *Correct, there is no requirement for the IRS to receive a copy of the rollover request form.*
Chapter 6 Page 155

D *Incorrect, tracking the rollover process is the third step in managing the rollover process.*

5 Which of the following would be a plan document roadblock that would preclude a rollover?

    A 20% mandatory withholding
    B The complexity of the rollover process
    C Signature guarantees
    D Plan only offers an annuity

A *Incorrect, this represents a regulatory roadblock as it is mandated by the IRS; however, withholding does not preclude a rollover.*

B *Incorrect, this represents a psychological roadblock; however, the level of complexity does not preclude a rollover.*

C *Incorrect, this represents an administrative roadblock; however, signature guarantees, once obtained, do not preclude a rollover.*

D *Correct, annuitized payments are not eligible for rollover.* Chapter 6 Page 149

CHAPTER 7

"Rollable" and "Nonrollable" Dollars

Chapter Goal

Two of the most common problems associated with rollover transactions are the failure to understand what types of plan assets are eligible for rollover, and which plans are considered "eligible retirement plans" for rollover purposes. If a participant rolls over ineligible dollars, or rolls eligible dollars to an ineligible plan, he or she may face taxation and penalties. Moreover, a rollover failure will likely have a negative impact on a person's long-term ability to save adequately for retirement.

Upon completion of this chapter the reader will understand which retirement plan dollars are eligible to be rolled over and which are not, as well as the types of plans that are considered eligible retirement plans for rollover purposes.

Learning Objectives

✓ Distinguish the four types of individuals who are eligible to complete a rollover.

✓ Recognize the four key differences between direct and an indirect rollovers to and from qualified retirement plans.

✓ Identify the seven major categories of plans that are eligible retirement plans for rollover purposes.

✓ Differentiate between eligible and ineligible rollover amounts.

✓ Apply the requirements for completing a nonspouse beneficiary rollover.

"Rollable" Plans

Law changes that took effect in 2002 greatly expanded the types of plans that are eligible for rollover. As a result, rollable plans include the following (IRC Sec. 402(c)(8)(B), 403(b)(8)(A), 457(e)(16)(A)).

"401(a) plans," which include 401(k), profit sharing, money purchase pension, "Keogh" or "HR 10" (an obsolete term that refers to profit sharing or defined benefit plans established for sole proprietors or partners), defined benefit, target benefit, employee stock ownership, and stock bonus plans

Traditional IRAs

SIMPLE IRAs (after two years of participation)

Simplified Employee Pension (SEP) IRAs

403(a) plans (i.e., qualified annuity plans where all plan assets are invested in annuity contracts)

403(b) tax-sheltered annuities and custodial accounts

457(b) plans maintained by state and local governmental entities

Rollovers from Retirement Plans to Roth IRAs

The Pension Protection Act of 2006 (PPA-06) allows a participant who receives a distribution after December 31, 2007, from an eligible retirement plan to directly roll over all or a portion of the amount to a Roth IRA. The portion of the distribution which has not been taxed will be included in the participant's income for the applicable year.

For this purpose an eligible retirement plan is a tax-qualified retirement plan under IRC Sec. 401(a) (e.g., a 401(k), profit sharing, defined benefit plan, etc.), a tax-sheltered annuity (IRC Sec. 403(b)) plan), or a governmental 457(b) plan. The present rules that apply to rollovers from a traditional IRA to a Roth IRA (i.e., conversion rules) apply. For example, a rollover from a 401(k) plan to a Roth IRA is includible in gross income (except to the extent it represents a return of after-tax contributions), and the 10 percent early distribution penalty tax does not apply. Prior to 2010, an individual with adjusted gross income of $100,000 or more could not roll over amounts from a tax-qualified retirement plan directly into a Roth IRA.

IRS Notice 2008-30 provides additional guidance on retirement plan-to-Roth IRA conversions.

Who May Complete a Rollover?

Prior to 2007, only a plan participant, IRA owner, or his or her spouse beneficiary had the right to complete a rollover (IRC Secs. 402(c)(1), 402(c)(9), 408(d)(3)). Beginning with distributions in 2007, the Pension Protection Act of 2006 (PPA-06) includes non-spouse beneficiaries in the list of those eligible to complete rollovers as well.

It is important to be aware of the changes to the definition of spouse pursuant to a Supreme Court ruling, and as further clarified in IRS and Department of Labor (DOL) pronouncements. The definition of spouse includes same-sex individuals, as well as opposite-sex individuals, who are legally married under state law. The Supreme Court ruled in *United States v. Windsor* that Section 3 of the Defense of Marriage Act (DOMA) was unconstitutional. As a result, the federal government must recognize same-sex married couples who were married in states that permit such marriages. The court's decision did not affect Section 2 of DOMA, which continues to allow individual states to refuse to recognize the validity of same-sex marriages entered into in other states. However, the IRS announced in Revenue Ruling 2013-17, and the DOL followed suit in Technical Release No. 2013-04, that same-sex couples who were legally married in jurisdictions that recognize same-sex marriages (i.e., either in U.S. states, U.S. territories or other countries) will be treated as married for federal tax and ERISA law purposes, regardless of the couple's current state of residence. This means, for example, if a same-sex couple is married in Minnesota (a state that recognizes same-sex marriage) and subsequently moves to Texas (a state that does not recognize same-sex marriage), then the couple will still be considered married for federal tax and ERISA purposes, including for employee benefits and contributing to an IRA, as well as for filing status, claiming personal and dependency exemptions, taking the standard deduction and claiming the earned income tax credit or child tax credit. Qualified retirement plans were required to comply with these rules as of September 16, 2013. The IRS and DOL have promised to issue additional guidance on plan amendments and any necessary corrective measures plan sponsors may need to take.

Designated Nonspouse Beneficiary Rollovers

As a result of PPA-06, starting January 1, 2007, a nonspouse beneficiary, who receives distributions from an eligible retirement plan may roll over the benefits to an inherited Traditional IRA. Prior to 2007, only spouse beneficiaries had the ability to roll over the benefits to a Traditional IRA. Subsequent distributions from the beneficiary IRAs are made based on the IRA beneficiary rules. These rule changes provide the financial professional with a great reason to meet with clients and beneficiaries to review and devise beneficiary distribution strategies.

On January 10, 2007, the Treasury Department and the IRS issued Notice 2007-7 to provide guidance on several rules contained in the PPA-06 that relate to distributions from IRAs and qualified retirement plans. The guidance addresses many questions on PPA-06 distribution provisions, including the new rules for rollovers from qualified plans to IRAs for nonspouse beneficiaries. Section V of Notice 2007-7 specifically addresses nonspouse beneficiary rollovers, and is reproduced in the following paragraphs. Please refer to Chapter 10 for more details on the nonspouse beneficiary rollover option. The February 13, 2007 issue of the IRS' online newsletter, Employee Plan News, offers further clarification of Notice 2007-7.

Note: The Workers, Retirees and Employees Recovery Act of 2008 made a direct rollover by a nonspouse beneficiary a required plan provision.

Excerpt from IRS Notice 2007-7

V. SECTION 829 OF PPA '06

Under § 402(c)(11) of the Code, which was added by § 829 of PPA '06, if a direct trustee-to-trustee transfer of any portion of a distribution from an eligible retirement plan is made to an individual retirement plan described in § 408(a) or (b) (an "IRA") that is established for the purpose of receiving the distribution on behalf of a designated beneficiary who is a nonspouse beneficiary, the transfer is treated as a direct rollover of an eligible rollover distribution for purposes of § 402(c). The IRA of the nonspouse beneficiary is treated as an inherited IRA with in the meaning of § 408(d)(3)(C). Section 402(c)(11) applies to distributions made after December 31, 2006.

Q-11. Can a qualified plan described in § 401(a) offer a direct rollover of a distribution to a nonspouse beneficiary?

A-11. Yes. Under § 402(c)(11), a qualified plan described in § 401(a) can offer a direct rollover of a distribution to a nonspouse beneficiary who is a designated beneficiary within the meaning of § 401(a)(9)(E), provided that the distributed amount satisfies all the requirements to be an eligible rollover distribution other than the requirement that the distribution be made to the participant or the participant's spouse. (See § 1.401(a)(9)-4 for rules regarding designated beneficiaries.) The direct rollover must be made to an IRA established on behalf of the designated beneficiary that will be treated as an inherited IRA pursuant to the provisions of § 402(c)(11). If a nonspouse beneficiary elects a direct rollover, the amount directly rolled over is not includible in gross income in the year of the distribution. See § 1.401(a)(31)-1, Q&A-3 and-4, for procedures for making a direct rollover.

Q-12. Can other types of plans offer a direct rollover of a distribution to a non spouse beneficiary?

A-12. Yes. Section 402(c)(11) also applies to annuity plans described in § 403(a) or (b) and to eligible governmental plans under § 457(b).

Q-13. How must the IRA be established and titled?

A-13. The IRA must be established in a manner that identifies it as an IRA with respect to a deceased individual and also identifies the deceased individual and the beneficiary, for example, "Tom Smith as beneficiary of John Smith."

Q-14. Is a plan required to offer a direct rollover of a distribution to a nonspouse beneficiary pursuant to § 402(c)(11)? (Obsolete: See note on previous page)

A-14. No. A plan is not required to offer a direct rollover of a distribution to a nonspouse beneficiary. If a plan does offer direct rollovers to nonspouse beneficiaries of some, but not all, participants, such rollovers must be offered on a nondiscriminatory basis because the opportunity to make a direct rollover is a benefit, right, or feature that is subject to § 401(a)(4). In the case of distributions from a terminated defined contribution plan pursuant to 29 C.F.R. § 2550.404a-3(d)(1)(ii), the plan will be considered to offer direct rollovers pursuant to § 402(c)(11) with respect to such distributions without regard to plan terms.

Q-15. For what purposes is the direct rollover of a distribution by a nonspouse beneficiary treated as a rollover of an eligible rollover distribution?

A-15. Section 402(c)(11) provides that a direct rollover of a distribution by a nonspouse beneficiary is a rollover of an eligible rollover distribution only for purposes of § 402(c). Accordingly, the distribution is not subject to the direct rollover requirements of § 401(a)(31), the notice requirements of § 402(f), or the mandatory withholding requirements of § 3405(c). If an amount distributed from a plan is received by a nonspouse beneficiary, the distribution is not eligible for rollover.

Q-16. If the named beneficiary of a decedent is a trust, is a plan permitted to make a direct rollover to an IRA established with the trust as beneficiary?

A-16. Yes. A plan may make a direct rollover to an IRA on behalf of a trust where the trust is the named beneficiary of a decedent, provided the beneficiaries of the trust meet the requirements to be designated beneficiaries within the meaning of § 401(a)(9)(E). The IRA must be established in accordance with the rules in Q&A-13 of this notice, with the trust identified as the beneficiary. In such a case, the beneficiaries of the trust are treated as having been designated as beneficiaries of the decedent for purposes of determining the distribution period under § 401(a)(9), if the trust meets the requirements set forth in § 1.401(a)(9)-4, Q&A-5, with respect to the IRA.

Q-17. How is the required minimum distribution (an amount not eligible for rollover) determined with respect to a nonspouse beneficiary if the employee dies before his or her required beginning date within the meaning of § 401(a)(9)(C)?

A-17. (a) General rule. If the employee dies before his or her required beginning date, the required minimum distributions for purposes of determining the amount eligible for rollover with respect to a nonspouse beneficiary are determined under either the 5-year rule described in § 401(a)(9)(B)(ii) or the life expectancy rule described in § 401(a)(9)(B)(iii). See Q&A-4 of § 1.401(a)(9)-3 to determine which rule applies to a particular designated beneficiary. Under either rule, no amount is a required minimum distribution for the year in which the employee dies. The rule in Q&A-7(b) of § 1.402(c)-2 (relating to distributions before an employee has attained age 70½) does not apply to nonspouse beneficiaries.

(b) Five-year rule. Under the 5-year rule described in § 401(a)(9)(B)(ii), no amount is required to be distributed until the fifth calendar year following the year of the employee's death. In that year, the entire amount to which the beneficiary is entitled under the plan must be distributed. Thus, if the 5-year rule applies with respect to a nonspouse beneficiary who is a designated beneficiary within the meaning of § 401(a)(9)(E), for the first 4 years after the year the employee dies, no amount payable to the beneficiary is ineligible for direct rollover as a required minimum distribution. Accordingly, the beneficiary is permitted to directly roll over the beneficiary's entire benefit until the end of the fourth year (but, as described in Q&A-19 of this notice, the 5- year rule must also apply to the IRA to which the rollover contribution is made). On or after January 1 of the fifth year following the year in which the employee died, no amount payable to the beneficiary is eligible for rollover.

(c) Life expectancy rule. (1) General rule. If the life expectancy rule described in § 401(a)(9)(B)(iii) applies, in the year following the year of death and each sub sequent year, there is a required minimum distribution. See Q&A-5(c)(1) of § 1.401(a)(9)-5 to determine the applicable distribution period for the nonspouse beneficiary. The amount not eligible for rollover includes all undistributed required minimum distributions for the year in which the direct rollover occurs and any prior year (even if the excise tax under § 4974 has been paid with respect to the failure in the prior years). See the last sentence of § 1.402(c)-2, Q&A-7(a). (2) Special rule. If, under paragraph (b) or (c) of Q&A-4 of § 1.401(a)(9)-3, the 5-year rule applies, the nonspouse designated beneficiary may determine the required minimum distribution under the plan using the life expectancy rule in the case of a distribution made prior to the end of the year following the year of death. However, in order to use this rule, the required minimum distributions under the IRA to which the direct rollover is made must be determined under the life expectancy rule using the same designated beneficiary.

Q-18. How is the required minimum distribution with respect to a nonspouse beneficiary determined if the employee dies on or after his or her required beginning date?

A-18. If an employee dies on or after his or her required beginning date, within the meaning of § 401(a)(9)(C), for the year of the employee's death, the required minimum distribution not eligible for rollover is the same as the amount that would have applied if the employee were still alive and elected the direct rollover. For the year after the year of the employee's death and subsequent years, see Q&A-5 of § 1.401(a)(9)-5 to determine the applicable distribution period to use in calculating the required minimum distribution. As in the case of death before the employee's required beginning date, the amount not eligible for rollover includes all undistributed required minimum distributions for the year in which the direct rollover occurs and any prior year, including years before the employee's death.

Q-19. After a direct rollover by a nonspouse designated beneficiary, how is the required minimum distribution determined with respect to the IRA to which the rollover contribution is made?

A-19. Under § 402(c)(11), an IRA established to receive a direct rollover on behalf of a nonspouse designated beneficiary is treated as an inherited IRA with in the meaning of § 408(d)(3)(C). The required minimum distribution requirements set forth in § 401(a)(9)(B) and the regulations there under apply to the inherited IRA. The rules for determining the required minimum distributions under the plan with respect to the nonspouse beneficiary also apply under the IRA. Thus, if the employee dies before his or her required beginning date and the 5-year rule in § 401(a)(9)(B)(ii) applied to the nonspouse designated beneficiary under the plan making the direct rollover, the 5-year rule applies for purposes of determining required minimum distributions under the IRA. If the life expectancy rule applied to the nonspouse designated beneficiary under the plan, the required minimum distribution under the IRA must be determined using the same applicable distribution period as would have been used under the plan if the direct rollover had not occurred. Similarly, if the employee dies on or after his or her required beginning date, the required minimum distribution under the IRA for any year after the year of death must be determined using the same applicable distribution period as would have been used under the plan if the direct rollover had not occurred.

"Nonrollable" Distributions

Some types of plan distributions, despite coming from rollable plan types, are not eligible for rollover. The tax code specifies certain types of assets or distributions that are not eligible for rollover (IRC Sec. 402(c)(4), Treas. Reg. 1.402(c)-2, Q&A 2 and Q&A 3). These nonrollable dollars include:

- required minimum distributions (with the exception of 2009 RMDs),
- substantially equal periodic payments,
- hardship distributions,
- loans that are deemed distributed,
- corrective distributions of excess contributions,
- dividends on employer securities,

- the cost of life insurance, and
- nonqualified deferred compensation plan distributions.

RMDs

RMDs are distributions that generally must be taken from a retirement plan when a plan participant turns age 70½. With qualified plans, it is possible for participants to delay taking RMDs past age 70½ if they are not considered an owner (i.e., owning five percent or less of the business), and they are still employed. IRA-based plans have no similar type of exception.

Generally, an RMD is not eligible for rollover (IRC Sec. 402(c)(4)(B)). If a qualified plan distribution recipient is subject to an RMD, and wants to complete a rollover of his or her balance, it is the responsibility of the plan trustee to make sure that the RMD is distributed to the participant before rolling over the remaining plan assets to another eligible retirement plan (Treas. Reg. 1.402(c)-1, Q&A 8). With respect to an IRA, the IRA owner is responsible for satisfying the RMD prior to completing a rollover (Treas. Reg. 1.408-8, Q&A 4).

Substantially Equal Periodic Payments

Substantially equal periodic payments are regular annual payments that are made for the life (or life expectancy) of the employee or the joint lives (or joint life expectancies) of the employee and his or her designated beneficiary (IRC Sec. 72(t)(2)(A)(iv)), or for a specified period of 10 years or more. If a series of substantially equal periodic payments is established, a distribution that represents one of the payments in that series is not eligible for rollover (Treas. Reg. 1.402(c)-2, Q&A 3). Substantially equal periodic payments are generally coded as a code 2 on the Form 1099-R.

Hardship distributions

Hardship distributions from a qualified plan are not eligible for rollover. This is a logical restriction given that the rules stipulate that the distribution recipient may only take out what is required to satisfy his or her hardship, and that he or she has exhausted all other means of satisfying the hardship (Treas. Reg. 1.401(k)-1(d)(3)) IRC Sec. 402(c)(4)(C)).

Loans Deemed Distributed

Loans from a qualified plan that are deemed distributed are not eligible for rollover (Treas. Reg. 1.402(c)-2, Q&A 4). Loans that are deemed distributed are coded with a code L on IRS Form 1099-R. A loan default should not be confused with a loan offset, which occurs when a participant's accrued benefit is reduced, or "offset," to repay the loan. A loan offset is an actual distribution; and is generally eligible for rollover. A loan offset will generally be coded as a 1 or a 7 on Form 1099-R, not as an L.

Corrective Distributions of Excess Contributions

There are several types of qualified plan corrective distributions of excess amounts that may not be rolled over (Treas. Reg. 1.402(c)-2, Q&A 4(a),(b), and (c)):

- Annual additions excess contributions,
- Excess salary deferrals,
- Excess contributions as a result of failing the actual deferral percentage test, and
- Excess aggregate contributions as a result of failing the actual contribution percentage test.

Corrective distributions from a qualified plan generally are coded with a code 8, P, D or E on Form 1099-R.

Excess contributions removed from an IRA will generally be coded with either an 8 or a P on Form 1099-R if they are not corrected. Because these distributions were not valid contributions in the first place, they are not eligible for roll over.

Dividends on Employer Securities

Dividends paid on employer securities held in an employee stock ownership plan (ESOP) are not eligible for rollover (Treas. Reg. 1.402(c)-2, Q&A 4(e)).

Cost of Current Life Insurance

The cost of current life insurance (net premium costs, also known as "PS 58" costs) is not eligible for rollover (Treas. Reg. 1.402(c)-2, Q&A 4(f)). When a distribution occurs, these costs are coded as a code 9 on IRS Form 1099-R.

Distributions From Nonqualified Deferred Compensation Plans

While distributions from governmental 457(b) plans are eligible for rollover (IRC Sec. 402(c)(8)(B)), distributions from other types of nonqualified deferred compensation plans are not.

Rollovers of After-Tax Amounts

At one time, after-tax amounts that were held in qualified plans were not eligible for rollover. As a result of the Economic Growth and Tax Relief Reconciliation Act of 2001 (EGTRRA), it is now possible for plan participants to rollover after-tax amounts between qualified plans through a direct rollover (as long as the receiving plan separately accounts for the after-tax assets), or through a rollover to a traditional IRA.

IRA owners may not roll over after-tax contributions from an IRA to a qualified plan, 403(b), or 457(b) plan. A special provision in the tax law allows an IRA containing after-tax assets to treat any rollover into a qualified plan as if it were coming first from the pre-tax assets.

Starting in 2007, the Pension Protection Act of 2006 clarified that after-tax amounts can be rolled from a qualified plan into a 403(b) contract as long as such trust separately accounts for the after-tax assets.

Direct and Indirect Rollovers Involving Qualified Plans

Since rollovers to and from qualified retirement plans are treated differently than rollovers to and from IRA-based plans, this text will examine these two types of rollovers separately.

Prior to 2002, a "qualified" plan for rollover purposes included plans described in IRC Sec. 401(a), for example, defined contribution plans, such as 401(k), profit sharing or money purchase pension plans, and defined benefit plans. However, as a result of changes in the laws governing rollovers to and from employer-sponsored retirement plans, other types of plans, such as 403(b) and governmental 457(b) plans, are now (as of 2002) treated as if they were qualified retirement plans for rollover purposes. Therefore, our treatment of qualified retirement plan rollovers includes 403(b) and governmental 457(b) plans, unless otherwise noted. Qualified plan rollovers fall into two categories: direct and indirect.

Direct Rollover

A direct rollover, as the name implies, is accomplished when plan assets move directly between plan trustees. At no point does the distribution recipient take constructive receipt of the assets. With a direct rollover, there is no time restraint for moving the assets from one trustee to another (as there is with an indirect rollover), although, obviously, customer service concerns dictate that the transaction take place in a timely fashion. Although a direct rollover is reportable to the IRS on Form 1099-R, federal withholding does not apply, and the direct rollover is nontaxable (Treas. Reg. 1.401(a)(31)-1, Q&A 3).

Indirect Rollover

With an indirect rollover, the distribution recipient takes actual or constructive receipt of the assets, and may hold the assets for up to 60 days before rolling them over to an eligible retirement plan. If assets are not rolled over within 60 days, they generally become ineligible for rollover, and are treated as taxable income. An indirect rollover is reportable to the IRS on Form 1099-R, and federal withholding rules apply. For federal withholding purposes, the distributing plan must withhold 20 percent of an eligible rollover distribution that is not directly rolled over, and remit the withheld amount to the IRS (Treas. Reg. 31.3405(c)-1).

Rollovers and Transfers Involving IRAs

When assets move between qualified retirement plans and IRAs, they may move as direct or indirect rollovers. However, when retirement assets move between IRAs, the transaction is referred to as either a rollover or a transfer.

IRA-To-IRA Rollover

For practical purposes, an IRA-to-IRA rollover looks very much like an indirect rollover involving a qualified plan. That is, the distribution

- is paid to the distribution recipient so that he or she has actual or constructive receipt of the assets,
- must be rolled over within 60 days in order to avoid taxation, and
- is reportable to the IRS.

There are several notable differences, however.

- An IRA owner is only allowed one distribution per IRA per 12-month period for rollover purposes.
- The same assets distributed from the IRA must be rolled over to the receiving IRA.
- IRA distributions are not subject to the mandatory 20 percent withholding rules of qualified plan indirect rollovers.

IRA-To-IRA Transfer

An IRA-to-IRA transfer, on the other hand, looks much like a direct rollover to or from a qualified retirement plan. However, unlike a direct rollover involving a qualified plan, an IRA-to-IRA transfer is not a reportable event. With an IRA-to-IRA transfer, it is possible for a distribution recipient to receive a transfer check and deliver it to the receiving institution as long as the transfer check is made payable to the receiving IRA and not the distribution recipient.

Roth and SIMPLE IRA Transfer/Rollover Limitations

Roth IRAs, savings incentive match plan for employees (SIMPLE) IRAs, and Roth 401(k) or Roth 403(b) contributions have transfer and rollover limitations.

Roth IRAs

Roth IRA owners may only roll over or transfer their Roth IRAs to other Roth IRAs (IRC Sec. 408A(e)).

Roth IRAs may receive rollovers from other IRAs (e.g., traditional IRAs, simplified employee pension (SEP) IRAs, and SIMPLE IRAs (after satisfying the two-year SIMPLE IRA participation period). Rollovers to Roth IRAs are known as "conversions," and require the IRA owner to include in income any taxable amounts converted.

Beginning in 2008, participants may roll over their qualified plans, 403(b) plans, and/or governmental 457(b) plans directly to a Roth IRA if they satisfy the rules for conversions. For example, a rollover from a tax-qualified retirement plan into a Roth IRA is includible in gross income (except to the extent it represents a return of after-tax contributions), and the 10 percent early distribution penalty tax does not apply. Prior to 2010, an individual with modified adjusted gross income of $100,000 or more could not roll over (i.e., convert) amounts from a qualified retirement plan directly into a Roth IRA.

Qualified Roth Contributions

For 2006 and later years, employers may include a qualified Roth contribution program in their 401(k) or 403(b) plans. Qualified Roth contributions may only be moved to another qualified Roth contribution program held by the participant, or to his or her Roth IRA (Treas. Reg. 1.401(k)-1(f)(3)(ii)).

SIMPLE IRAs

SIMPLE IRAs are unique with respect to rollovers from other plans because they may only receive rollovers and transfers from other SIMPLE IRAs. Furthermore, it is not possible to move SIMPLE IRA assets into another type of plan for the first two years after the SIMPLE IRA is established. This appears to be true even in cases where a SIMPLE IRA holder dies. However, once the two-year waiting period is up, assets can be moved from a SIMPLE IRA to another type of eligible plan.

IRS Rollover Chart

The IRS has put together the following rollover chart in an effort to help illustrate which retirement plan assets can move where, and when.

ROLLOVER CHART

6/7/2011

Roll From ↓ / Roll To →		Roth IRA	IRA (traditional)	SIMPLE IRA	SEP-IRA	457(b) (government)	Qualified Plan [1] (pre-tax)	403(b) (pre-tax)	Designated Roth Account (401(k), 403(b) or 457(b)[2])
	Roth IRA	YES	NO	NO	NO	NO	NO	NO	NO
	IRA (traditional)	YES[3]	YES	NO	YES	YES[4]	YES	YES	NO
	SIMPLE IRA	YES,[3] after two years	YES, after two years	YES	YES, after two years	YES,[4] after two years	YES, after two years	YES, after two years	NO
	SEP-IRA	YES[3]	YES	NO	YES	YES[4]	YES	YES	NO
	457(b) (government)	YES[3]	YES	NO	YES	YES	YES	YES	YES,[3,5] after 12/31/10
	Qualified Plan[1] (pre-tax)	YES[3]	YES	NO	YES	YES[4]	YES	YES	YES,[3,5] after 9/27/10
	403(b) (pre-tax)	YES[3]	YES	NO	YES	YES[4]	YES	YES	YES,[3,5] after 9/27/10
	Designated Roth Account (401(k), 403(b) or 457(b)[2])	YES	NO	NO	NO	NO	NO	NO	Yes, if a direct trustee to trustee transfer

[1] Qualified Plans include, for example, Profit-Sharing, 401(k), Money Purchase, and Defined Benefit plans.
[2] Governmental 457(b) plans, after December 31, 2010. [3] Must include in income. [4] Must have separate accounts.
[5] Must be an in-plan rollover

Practice Management Application

- Alert clients that distributions taken for reason of hardship are not eligible for rollover.

- Remind clients that required minimum distributions (RMDs) are not eligible for rollover. However, if a client takes more than his or her RMD for the year, that overage would be eligible for rollover.

- Other distributed amounts that are not eligible for rollover include the following:

  - Substantially equal periodic payments,
  - Hardship distributions,
  - Loans that are deemed distributed,
  - Corrective distributions of excess contributions,
  - Dividends on employer securities,
  - The cost of life insurance, and
  - Nonqualified deferred compensation plan distributions.

Chapter Review Questions

Feedback for the review questions can be found at the end of the chapter.

1   John Smith died leaving his 401(k) plan to his son, Tom, as primary beneficiary. Tom rolls over the balance to an inherited IRA. How must Tom title the inherited IRA?

    A Tom Smith
    B John Smith as beneficiary of Tom Smith
    C Tom Smith as Beneficiary of John Smith
    D Tom Smith and John Smith

2   Which of the following plans *WOULD NOT* be eligible for rollover?

    A Employee Stock Ownership (ESOP)
    B 457(f)
    C 403(b)
    D 401(k)

3   How would a plan participant complete an indirect rollover in order to avoid a taxable distribution?

    A Waive withholding and redeposit the entire distribution immediately
    B Redeposit the amount received within 30 days
    C Make up the amount withheld for federal taxes out-of-pocket and redeposit the total amount distributed within 60 days
    D Redeposit the total amount distributed within 90 days

4   Which of the following lists contain amounts that would be *INELIGIBLE* for rollover?

    A Hardship distributions, required minimum distributions, and substantially equal periodic payments
    B Distributions to nonspouse beneficiaries of qualified plans, distributions of employer stock with NUA, distributions of 401(k) after-tax contributions
    C All of the above
    D None of the above

5   Under which of the following scenarios would it be possible for the beneficiary to complete a rollover?

    A Mary, who is the daughter of an IRA owner, and beneficiary of his traditional IRA
    B Erin, who is the sister of a Roth IRA owner, and beneficiary of her Roth IRA

C John, the nephew of a profit sharing plan participant, and beneficiary of her plan account balance

D All of the above

Chapter Review Questions Feedback

1 John Smith died leaving his 401(k) plan to his son, Tom, as primary beneficiary. Tom rolls over the balance to an inherited IRA. How must Tom title the inherited IRA?

A Tom Smith

B John Smith as beneficiary of Tom Smith

C Tom Smith as Beneficiary of John Smith

D Tom Smith and John Smith

A *Incorrect, this would represent the titling used on IRAs that Tom owns outright that are not inherited.*

B *Incorrect, because Tom Smith is the beneficiary of John Smith.*

C *Correct, pursuant to IRS Notice 2007-7, IRAs inherited by nonspouse beneficiaries must be titled with the beneficiary's name first, followed by the phrase, "beneficiary of" and the original IRA owner's name.* Chapter 7 Page 168

D *Incorrect, an IRA may only be titled in the name of one owner.*

2 Which of the following plans *WOULD NOT* be eligible for rollover?

A Employee Stock Ownership (ESOP)

B 457(f)

C 403(b)

D 401(k)

A *Incorrect, an ESOP is an eligible plan for rollover purposes under IRC Sec. 402(c)(8)(iii).*

B *Correct, an 457(f) is not considered an eligible plan for rollover purposes under IRC Sec. 402(c)(8)(v).* Chapter 7 Page 175

C *Incorrect, a 403(b) is an eligible plan for rollover purposes under IRC Sec. 402(c)(8)(vi).*

D *Incorrect, a 401(k) plan is an eligible plan for rollover purposes under IRC Sec. 402(c)(8)(iii).*

3 How would a plan participant complete an indirect rollover in order to avoid a taxable distribution?

A Waive withholding and redeposit the entire distribution immediately

B Redeposit the amount received within 30 days

C Make up the amount withheld for federal taxes out-of-pocket and redeposit the total amount distributed within 60 days

D Redeposit the total amount distributed within 90 days

A *Incorrect, recipients of an eligible rollover distribution that is not directly rolled over cannot waive federal withholding.*

B *Incorrect, recipients of an eligible rollover distribution will only receive 80 percent of the distribution because the plan administrator must withhold 20 percent for federal income tax with holding purposes; if the recipient does not make up the withheld amount when completing the rollover, 20 percent of the full amount distributed will be deemed taxable.*

C *Correct, in order to avoid taxation, the withheld amount and the amount actually received must be rolled over within 60 days of receipt.* Chapter 7 Page 175

D *Incorrect, an indirect rollover must be completed within 60 days of receipt of the funds in order to avoid taxation.*

4 Which of the following lists contain amounts that would be *INELIGIBLE* for rollover?

A Hardship distributions, required minimum distributions, and substantially equal periodic payments

B Distributions to nonspouse beneficiaries of qualified plans, distributions of employer stock with NUA, distributions of 401(k) after-tax contributions

C All of the above

D None of the above

A *Correct, pursuant to IRC Sec. 402(c)(4), these items do not represent eligible rollover distributions.* Chapter 7 Page 173

B *Incorrect, these amounts are eligible for rollover pursuant to IRC. Sec. 402(c).*

C *Incorrect, list B contains amounts that are eligible for rollover*

D *Incorrect, list A contains amounts that are ineligible for rollover.*

5 Under which of the following scenarios would it be possible for the beneficiary to complete a rollover?

A Mary, who is the daughter of an IRA owner, and beneficiary of his traditional IRA

B Erin, who is the sister of a Roth IRA owner, and beneficiary of her Roth IRA

C John, the nephew of a profit sharing plan participant, and beneficiary of her plan account balance

D All of the above

A *Incorrect, an IRA is not one of the types of retirement plans that can offer a nonspouse beneficiary the option to complete a rollover.*

B *Incorrect, only an eligible individual can complete a rollover.*

C ***Correct, plans qualified under IRC Sec. 401(a) must offer nonspouse beneficiaries the option of completing a rollover.*** Chapter 7 Page 169

D *Incorrect, the nonspouse beneficiary of a traditional or Roth IRA may not complete a rollover.*

CHAPTER 8

Assessing the Advantages and Disadvantages of a Rollover Strategy

Chapter Goal

Helping clients to complete retirement plan rollovers can be a great way for financial professionals to build their practices. It is estimated that the rollover market annually will exceed $450 billion by 2017[1]. The opportunity is substantial considering, on average, only 45 percent of all eligible rollover distributions are fully rolled over.[2]

Financial professionals who attempt to take away business from competitors often find the process can be laborious, and sometimes fruitless. However, assisting potential clients with retirement plan distributions greatly improves a financial professional's chance of winning new business. In part, this is because an investor who is relatively satisfied with his or her current investment provider is generally reluctant to move his or her savings, even if another organization is offering a slightly better return. This reluctance to move investment dollars is sometimes referred to as "investment inertia."

Investment inertia basically means that once investment dollars are "at rest" they tend to stay "at rest." However, a retirement plan distribution changes this financial paradigm by putting retirement plan dollars "in motion," which makes the rollover event an ideal situation for take-away business. Furthermore, customers who are about to receive a rollover distribution often have a desire for guidance regarding their impending distributions—something that many financial organizations are reluctant to give. Perhaps this is why nearly *75 percent of high-value rollover distributions are moved to new providers!*[3] Satisfying a client's advice requirement associated with a rollover distribution can often translate into a long-term client relationship.

Learning Objectives

✓ Identify the three typical rollover targets.

✓ Distinguish between requirements for direct and indirect rollovers.

[1] Cerulli Report, 2012 [2] Employee Benefits Research Institute, Notes, November 2013, Vol. 34, Number 22
[3] Spectrem Group Survey, 2010

✓ Appy the rules related to automatic rollovers of small plan balances (i.e., "cash-outs").

✓ Identify the six leading situations where a rollover to an IRA may not be in the client's best interest.

✓ Recognize the key elements of a rollover notice.

Rollover Targets

There are three main types of rollover targets: job changers, current plan participants who are eligible for in-service distributions, and retirees. Although spouse beneficiaries (and some nonspouse beneficiaries beginning in 2007) may also be rollover targets, this rollover topic will be covered in Chapter 10, under beneficiary issues.

Job Changers

Job changers are often overlooked as a source of rollover business; however, there are significantly more people that change jobs every year than there are people who retire. A job change can be a rollover opportunity that could trigger the need for advice—and an opportunity to establish a long-term investing relationship.

Between the ages of 18 and 46, on average, an individual will hold an average of 11.3 jobs.[4] Furthermore, the average job-changer's rollover is estimated to be $20,781, so, on average, job-changer rollovers are certainly worth pursuing from an asset acquisition standpoint.[5]

Job-Changers' Need for Advice

Some job changers have a job change thrust upon them, such as in the case of a layoff or termination. In most cases, however, job changers change jobs of their own free will. Although both types of job changers often have needs for financial advice relating to rollover distributions, there are some very different dynamics between these two types of job changers. For one thing, people who have just been laid-off are probably more concerned about getting a new job than they are about rolling over their retirement assets. Understanding this can help a financial professional market to these individuals.

For example, rather than the advisor pushing his or her ability to help these individuals with their rollovers, financial professionals may want to develop a "job seekers" brochure, which contains a number of helpful tips on how to find a job in the area, as well as a brief description of the rollover services that the adviser can provide, including the ability to help clients find ways to take penalty-free distributions from their rollover distributions. For financial professionals who take this approach, it is important to make sure that the brochure contains high quality job seeking information, because

[4] Bureau of Labor Statistics, July 2012 [5] Employee Benefits Research Institute, Notes, November, 2013

this brochure serves as an opportunity for the financial professional to build credibility with clients. If clients find the job search information useful, they are more likely to trust the financial professional's expertise in the area of rollovers, as well.

Financial professionals who want to be more ambitious may want to consider offering a job hunting seminar, which includes a segment on rollovers. One type of seminar that would have a great deal of appeal to anyone who is looking for a job, voluntarily or not, would be a free seminar on how to write a great resume. If you are not a resume expert, you might want to pair with a professional resume writer to provide a joint presentation.

These ideas for marketing to job-changers are just a few of the many activities that might attract job-changers to seek out financial professionals regarding possible rollovers. In the case of a large lay-off, an advisor could also consider mailing to any known existing clients that work at the company, emphasizing the financial profession-al's willingness to assist them with their rollover needs. Financial professionals could contact the human resources department of the company involved to offer a brief pres-entation on rollovers to the employees that are being laid off, or get the company's approval to leave behind informational flyers in the company lunch room or other appropriate location. Also, for those financial professionals who want to be super proactive, it doesn't hurt to develop relationships with directors of local human resources departments, and offer to work with any employees who are leaving employ-ment.

Current Plan Participants Eligible for In-service Distributions

Although job-changers are often a difficult market to identify, individuals who are eligi-ble for in-service distributions are often even more difficult to identify because, although certain plan types may allow for in-service distributions, they are not required to do so. Chapter 5 of this text covers the types of plans that may offer in-service dis-tributions and the conditions under which they may be taken. The information in Chapter 5 can serve as a rule of thumb when targeting this market. For example, if a client is under age 59½, he or she generally will only be eligible for an in-service distri-bution of profit sharing or rollover dollars (if applicable), since employee salary defer-rals generally cannot be distributed prior to age 59½ (IRC Sec. 401(k)(2)(B)). Conversely, individuals who are age 59½ or older may be able to take in-service distri-butions because they have reached the normal retirement age under the plan.

Keep in mind that these are only rules of thumb, and that it is necessary to check the provisions of the individual's retirement plan in order to know for sure whether in-serv-ice distributions are allowed. Because of the plan specific nature of these provisions, it is not unusual to experience a lot of hit and miss adventures when reviewing plan documents for in-service distribution provisions.

Retirees

New retiree rollovers are the most coveted of all the rollover targets because they are generally the largest. The average plan balance of a 401(k) participant in his or her 60s with 20-plus years of service is approximately $160,000 to $209,000.[6] However, waiting to target an individual in his or her 60s in order to win his or her rollover business is often not as fruitful as one might think. Why? Because at that late stage in the financial planning game, the soon-to-be retiree is more likely to roll over assets with a financial professional with which he or she has an existing financial relationship (rather than with a complete stranger). Therefore, although financial professionals should not neglect marketing rollover services to clients age 60 and older, it is important to keep in mind that the relationships built with younger pre-retirees may prove to be the best source for acquiring future rollover assets. Financial professionals who start retirement discussions early with their clients, and who provide assistance to them in managing their portfolios during the wealth accumulation years, will likely be the surviving financial professionals in retirement who will help their clients transform their retirement savings into retirement income.

The Rollover Notice

Internal Revenue Code Section (IRC Sec.) 402(f) requires a plan administrator of a plan qualified under IRC Sec. 401(a), 403(a), 403(b), or 457(b) to provide a written notice to any recipient of an eligible rollover distribution. This notice is sometimes referred to as the "402(f) notice," because the rules for how it must be written and the information it must contain are found in IRC Sec. 402(f).

Although the 402(f) notice is required to be written in a manner that is readily understandable by the typical distribution recipient, it can be a source of confusion for clients because it often covers a great deal of information—much of which is not very interesting to the average person. Because this notice can be rather dry and long, it presents an opportunity for the financial advisor to offer "free assistance" to distribution recipients.

The timing for delivery of the 402(f) notice cannot be less than 30 days prior to a distribution (however, this minimum time period may be waived by the recipient), nor greater than 180 days (90 days prior to 2007) before the distribution is made (Treas. Reg. 1.402(f)-1, Q&A 2). The Pension Protection Act of 2006 (PPA-06) extended the 90-day period to 180 days. PPA-06 also directs the Secretary of the Treasury to modify the applicable regulations to reflect the extension of the notice period to 180 days, and to provide that the description of a participant's right, if any, to defer receipt of a distribution shall also describe the consequences of failing to defer such receipt.

Even if a client who is about to receive an eligible rollover distribution does not ask for assistance in understanding the 402(f) notice, a financial professional should always ask to see a copy of this notice because it may contain essential information that the client should be made aware of before starting the rollover process. For example, the notice may discuss after-tax dollars, the tax treatment of stocks, or payments made over a long period of time.

[6] Employee Benefits Research Institute, Issue Brief No. 380, December, 2012

Pursuant to IRC Sec. 402(f), the written explanation must describe the

- Direct rollover rules,

- Mandatory income tax withholding rules for distributions not directly rolled over,

- Tax treatment of distributions not rolled over, and

- Circumstances under which distributions may be subject to different restrictions and tax consequences after being rolled over.

Advantages and Disadvantages of Rollovers

Once the types of assets and payout options available to the client are determined, and a rollover is one of them, financial professionals may want to ask some additional questions to determine whether a rollover really is in the client's best interest. The following list includes some scenarios where a rollover of qualified plan assets may not be the best option for a client.

Distribution in Connection With a Qualified Domestic Relations Order

If an individual is under age 59½, and is awarded a portion of his or her spouse's retirement plan account balance pursuant to a qualified domestic relations order (QDRO) as a result of legal separation or divorce, it may not be in the client's best interest to roll over the assets if he or she anticipates needing them before turning age 59½. Why? Distributions from a qualified retirement plan pursuant to a QDRO are not subject to the early distribution penalty; a QDRO is an exception to the penalty (IRC Sec. 72(t)(2)(c)). However, if the assets are rolled to an IRA, they will become subject to the early distribution penalty, unless another exception applies.

Distribution Recipient Is Age 55 or Older, But Not Yet Age 59½

If a participant separates from service during the calendar year he or she turns age 55 or a later year, any plan distributions he or she takes are not subject to the 10 percent early distribution penalty tax (IRC Sec. 72(t)(2)(A)(v)). However, if the assets are rolled to an IRA, they will become subject to the early distribution penalty tax, unless another exception applies.

EXAMPLE

Jordan leaves employment in May and turns age 55 in July. Because she is turning age 55 in the year of separation, all distributions from her 401(k) plan made to her in July and thereafter will not be subject to the early distribution penalty tax.

Governmental 457(b) Plan Distributions Prior to Age 59½

Distributions from a governmental 457(b) plan are not subject to the early distribution penalty tax (IRC Sec. 4974(c) and IRC Sec. 72(t)(1)). However, if plan assets are rolled over to an IRA, they will become subject to the early distribution penalty if the IRA owner is under age 59½. Moreover, amounts rolled over to a governmental 457(b) plan from an IRA, qualified retirement plan, or 403(b) plan must be separately accounted for, and when distributed prior to attaining age 59½, will be subject to the early distribution penalty tax (IRC Sec. 72(t)(9)).

Spouse Beneficiary Under Age 59½

Upon the death of a plan participant or IRA owner, retirement plan and IRA distributions to a spouse beneficiary under age 59½ are not subject to the early distribution penalty tax (IRC Sec. 72(t)(2)(A)(ii)). However, if inherited plan assets are rolled over to the spouse's own IRA, they will become subject to the early distribution penalty tax if the spouse beneficiary is under age 59½.

Eligibility for Net Unrealized Appreciation (NUA) or Special Tax Treatments

If an individual's retirement plan account balance contains company stock, or he or she is eligible for special tax treatment, you should take the time to help your client determine whether it would make more sense to roll over the assets or use the special tax treatment. Chapter 12 deals with the issue of special tax treatment and NUA in more detail.

Defined Benefit Plan Lump Sum/Rollover vs. Annuity Option

The biggest consideration in whether to select a defined benefit plan annuity or a lump sum distribution and rollover, is whether a client feels confident that he or she will be able to outperform the promised benefit under the defined benefit plan in his or her own IRA. Several factors will go into this calculation, including how long the client expects to live, whether he or she is married, and how spousal benefits are handled under the plan.

Direct and Indirect Rollovers

Once it has been determined that a rollover is in a client's best interest, the next task is to determine whether to move the assets in a direct or indirect rollover.

Direct Rollover

In general, it is almost always in a client's best interest to move assets directly rather than indirectly, because direct rollovers are not subject to 20 percent mandatory federal income tax withholding. Also, there is much less risk that the rollover will be disqualified, because it is not subject to the 60-day rollover rule.

Generally, a direct rollover is requested from the plan administrator using either a direct rollover request form provided by the plan administrator, or one provided by the organization that will receive the rollover distribution. Before using the receiving organization's direct rollover request form, be sure to check that the retirement plan administrator will accept it, since some administrators require that participants use their forms only.

Once the forms are completed, copies should be made (in case the original copies do not make it to their intended destination), and the financial professional should plan to follow up at regular intervals to be sure that the transaction progresses.

Indirect Rollovers

Although it is generally in a client's best interest to move assets by means of a direct rollover, there are occasions when a client may have a need to hold assets outside a retirement plan for a period of time (not to exceed 60 days) prior to rolling them into an IRA. The distribution recipient will need to understand that the plan administrator will withhold 20 percent of the distribution for federal income tax purposes, and if he or she cannot make up that amount out of pocket along with the rest of the distribution at the point of roll over, any amount not rolled over within 60 days may become subject to an early distribution penalty tax, and will be considered taxable income.

Financial professionals can play an instrumental role in helping a client monitor the 60-day rollover period. If a client surpasses the 60-day rollover time limit, it may be possible for him or her to obtain a waiver of the time limit from the IRS.

The 60-day rollover requirement is waived automatically if all of the following apply.

1 The financial institution receives the funds on behalf of the distribution recipient before the end of the 60-day rollover period.

2 The distribution recipient followed all the procedures set by the financial institution for depositing the funds into an eligible retirement plan within the 60-day period (including giving instructions to deposit the funds into an eligible retirement plan).

3 The funds are not deposited into an eligible retirement plan within the 60-day rollover period solely because of an error on the part of the financial institution.

4 The funds are deposited into an eligible retirement plan within one year from the beginning of the 60-day rollover period.

5 It would have been a valid rollover if the financial institution had deposited the funds as instructed.

If the distribution recipient did not qualify for an automatic waiver, he or she can apply to the IRS for a waiver of the 60-day rollover requirement. To obtain a waiver, the distribution recipient must submit a request for a ruling from the IRS, pursuant to Revenue Procedure 2003-16. Furthermore, every request for extension of the 60-day rollover period must be accompanied by the appropriate user fee (See Revenue Procedures 2008-4 and 2008-8 for details.)

In determining whether to grant a waiver, the IRS will consider all relevant facts and circumstances, including the following:

- whether errors were made by the financial institution (other than those described under automatic waiver, above),
- whether the distribution recipient was unable to complete the rollover due to death, disability, hospitalization, incarceration, restrictions imposed by a foreign country or postal error,
- whether the distribution recipient used the amount distributed (i.e., he or she cashed the check), and
- how much time has passed since the date of distribution.

"Cash Outs" and Mandatory Rollovers

Pension benefit plans under Title I of the Employee Retirement Income Security Act of 1974 (ERISA) may contain a provision that allows certain accounts to be distributed without the consent of the plan participant. The provision that allows for these distributions is found under IRC Sec. 411(a)(11) and allows plan sponsors to distribute accrued benefits to certain separated participants without their consent as long as the participant's accrued benefit does not exceed a present value of $5,000. These forced payments are referred to as "cash outs." In 2001, the Economic Growth and Tax Relief Reconciliation Act (EGTRRA) was enacted. EGTRRA requires plans to automatically roll over to IRAs cash outs valued at more than $1,000 if the participant does not direct otherwise. EGTRRA also directed the Department of Labor (DOL) to issue regulations providing "safe harbors" under which a plan administrator's designation of an institution to receive the automatic rollover, and the initial investment choice for the rolled-over funds would be deemed to satisfy the employer's fiduciary responsibility. Although providing direct rollovers is only required for mandatory distributions of over $1,000, the safe harbor requirements that the DOL issued in 2004 (29 CFR Sec. 2550.404a-

2) also can be applied to direct rollovers of distributions of $1,000 or less. In 2005, the IRS released Notice 2005-5, which provided further clarification regarding the safe harbor provisions surrounding automatic rollovers of cash outs.

The safe harbor rules specify that for any mandatory distribution greater than $1,000, a "402(f)" distribution notice must be provided to inform the participant that the failure to elect to receive a mandatory distribution directly, or to provide the plan administrator with information as to where to directly roll over the mandatory distribution, will result in the mandatory distribution being directly rolled over to an IRA. The safe harbor rules also state that it is possible for an employer to establish IRAs to receive automatic rollovers for any participants who do not elect to receive the distribution directly or have the distribution rolled over to an eligible retirement plan of his or her choice. These safe harbor rules went into effect for cash outs made on or after March 28, 2005, and may represent a good ongoing source of revenue for financial professionals who pursue this opportunity.

Large employers may process many of these cash out distributions per year, and if a financial professional is able to develop a simple rollover process for these employers, he or she may find that automatic rollovers of cash outs can be a fairly consistent and easy source of new accounts that are often fairly low maintenance.

When setting up an IRA for a participant who does not respond to the 402(f) distribution notice in a timely fashion, an employer may use the participant's most recent mailing address on file. The trustee, custodian, or issuer of the IRA must provide a disclosure statement to the file address, and provide a standard IRA revocation period. This requirement is deemed satisfied even if the disclosure statement is returned as undeliverable by the U.S. Postal service.

Practice Management Application

- Customize client information based on the client's circumstances, whether a job changer, in-service distribution prospect, or a retiree.
- Review the 402(f) distribution notice with the client.
- Evaluate whether a rollover makes sense for a particular client. Sometimes a rollover may not be in his or her best interest.
- If a rollover is elected, review the rollover process, and manage client expectations.
- For indirect rollovers, carefully monitor the 60-day rollover time limit.
- Discuss mandatory rollovers of cash outs.

Chapter Review Questions

Feedback for the review questions can be found at the end of the chapter.

1 Why are in-service distribution rollover candidates difficult to identify?

    A In-service distribution options are plan specific.

    B The IRS must rule whether an individual is eligible for an in-service distribution.

    C Severance of employment for distribution purposes is based on the facts of circumstances of each case.

    D An employer is not required to inform its participants that the plan offers in-service distributions.

2 Why might a former spouse, who is awarded a portion of a retirement plan account balance through a qualified domestic relations order (QDRO), choose NOT to roll the assets to his/her own IRA?

    A The former spouse is not eligible to roll over amounts received through a QDRO.

    B If he/she is under age 59½, distributions from the IRA could be subject to an early withdrawal penalty.

    C Federal withholding at a rate of 20% would apply if the former spouse directly rolled the amount to an IRA.

    D Amounts withdrawn from the retirement plan are not taxable, but would be if the amount is rolled to an IRA.

3 Which of the following statements regarding a rollover notice is *FALSE*?

    A It is also known as the 402(f) notice.

    B It must be written in a readily understandable manner.

    C It is delivered not less than 30 days and not more that 180 days prior to the distribution.

    D It is provided to recipients of amounts that are ineligible for rollover.

4 Under what circumstance(s) may the IRS waive the 60-day rollover requirement?

    A Under no circumstances may the 60-day rollover requirement be waived.

    B Pursuant to the IRS' automatic waiver criteria only.

    C Pursuant to a letter ruling request for a waiver only.

    D B and C

5 When may a plan sponsor force a cash-out of a plan participant's account balance without his/her consent?

A If a participant has a severance of employment and his/her account balance is less than $5,000.

B Upon reaching age 59½ and his/her account balance is greater than $5,000.

C At any time

D A plan sponsor may never force a cash-out.

Chapter Review Questions Feedback

1 Why are in-service distribution rollover candidates difficult to identify?

    A In-service distribution options are plan specific.

    B The IRS must rule whether an individual is eligible for an in-service distribution.

    C Severance of employment for distribution purposes is based on the facts of circumstances of each case.

    D An employer is not required to inform its participants that the plan offers in-service distributions.

    A *Correct, not all qualified plan types may offer in-service distributions; and plans are not required to offer in-service distributions.* Chapter 8 Page 185

    B *Incorrect, the IRS provides general guidelines for in-service distributions, but eligibility to receive an in-service distribution is determined at the plan level.*

    C *Incorrect, because in-service distributions are taken while the participant is still working; severance of employment is not a consideration.*

    D *Incorrect, if a plan offers in-service distributions, the employer must disclose this information to plan participants in the Summary Plan Description for the plan.*

2 Why might a former spouse, who is awarded a portion of a retirement plan account balance through a qualified domestic relations order (QDRO), choose NOT to roll the assets to his/her own IRA?

    A The former spouse is not eligible to roll over amounts received through a QDRO.

    B If he/she is under age 59½, distributions from the IRA could be subject to an early withdrawal penalty.

    C Federal withholding at a rate of 20% would apply if the former spouse directly rolled the amount to an IRA.

    D Amounts withdrawn from the retirement plan are not taxable, but would be if the amount is rolled to an IRA.

    A *Incorrect, a former spouse is eligible to roll over amounts received through a QDRO.*

B *Correct, distributions from the retirement plan pursuant to a QDRO are not subject to an early withdrawal penalty, but if the former spouse rolls the retirement plan assets to his/her own IRA, and he/she is under age 59½, amounts withdrawn from the IRA could be subject to the early withdrawal penalty.* Chapter 8 Page 187

C *Incorrect, 20% federal withholding would only apply if the former spouse withdraws the retirement plan assets and does not complete a direct rollover.*

D *Incorrect, amounts withdrawn from the retirement plan would be includable in taxable income in the same manner as they would be if withdrawn from a rollover IRA.*

3 Which of the following statements regarding a rollover notice is *FALSE*?

   A It is also known as the 402(f) notice.
   B It must be written in a readily understandable manner.
   C It is delivered not less than 30 days and not more that 180 days prior to the distribution.
   D It is provided to recipients of amounts that are ineligible for rollover.

A *Incorrect, the rollover notice is referred to as the 402(f) notice because the rules that govern the document are found in IRC Sec. 402(f).*

B *Incorrect, IRC Sec. 402(f) requires the rollover notice to be written in a manner that can be understood by the average plan participant.*

C *Incorrect, the Pension Protection Act of 2006 changed the distribution timing to not less than 30 and not more than 180 days prior to the distribution.*

D *Correct, IRC Sec. 402(f) requires plan sponsors provide the rollover notice to recipients of eligible rollover distributions.* Chapter 8 Page 186

4 Under what circumstance(s) may the IRS waive the 60-day rollover requirement?

   A Under no circumstances may the 60-day rollover requirement be waived.
   B Pursuant to the IRS' automatic waiver criteria only.
   C Pursuant to a letter ruling request for a waiver only.
   D B and C

A *Incorrect, The 60-day rollover requirement may be waived under the IRS' automatic waiver criteria or pursuant to an IRS letter ruling request for a waiver.*

B *Incorrect, in addition to the automatic waiver criteria outlined by the IRS, an individual may request a waiver by submitting a letter ruling request to the IRS.*

C *Incorrect, in addition to a waiver granted pursuant to an IRS letter ruling request, an individual may qualify for an automatic waiver.*

D *Correct, the 60-day rollover requirement may be waived pursuant to the IRS' automatic waiver criteria or after receipt of a letter ruling from the IRS.* Chapter 8 Page 190

5 When may a plan sponsor force a cash-out of a plan participant's account balance without his/her consent?

   A If a participant has a severance of employment and his/her account balance is less than $5,000.
   B Upon reaching age 59½ and his/her account balance is greater than $5,000.
   C At any time
   D A plan sponsor may never force a cash-out.

   A *Correct, pursuant to IRC Sec. 411(a)(11), if a participant leaves employment with a plan balance of less than $5,000, the plan sponsor may distribute the assets without the participant's consent.* Chapter 8 Page 190

   B *Incorrect, if a plan participant's account balance is $5,000 or greater, he/she must consent to a distribution in writing prior to the later of 1) age 62 or 2) the plan's normal retirement age.*

   C *Incorrect, except for plan balances of less than $5,000, a participant's consent is required for any distribution that is immediately distributable.*

   D *Incorrect, pursuant to IRC Sec. 411(a)(11), if a participant leaves employment with a plan balance of less than $5,000, the plan sponsor may distribute the assets without the participant's consent.*

CHAPTER 9

Required Minimum Distributions— Choices and Rules

Chapter Goal

One of the great benefits of qualified retirement plans and IRAs is that they provide an opportunity for tax-deferred growth on contributions made. However, except in the case of a Roth IRA, current tax laws require that individuals who take advantage of these savings arrangements must start taking mandatory distributions from them as of the "required beginning date" (RBD). These "required minimum distributions" (RMDs) must be taken annually. Furthermore, if a taxpayer fails to take his or her RMD in a timely manner, he or she becomes subject to a 50 percent federal excise tax on the amount that should have been distributed, but was not. Many clients appreciate assistance with satisfying their RMDs in the form of reminders and planning assistance. Providing these services can help to build general client satisfaction.

Learning Objectives

✓ Identify the four major categories of retirement plans that are subject to RMDs.

✓ Determine the RBD for taking RMDs, and the deadline for taking subsequent annual RMDs.

✓ Calculate RMDs using the proper life expectancy table and account balance.

✓ Apply the rules of RMD aggregation to a given fact pattern.

Plans Subject to RMDs

The RMD rules apply to all qualified employer sponsored retirement plans under IRC Sec. 401(a), as well as to IRC Sec. 403(b) arrangements, eligible deferred compensation plans under IRC Sec. 457(b), and all IRAs, with the exception of Roth IRAs. Generally, the RMD rules apply in the same manner to the retirement arrangements previously listed, although there are a few exceptions. The following paragraphs will highlight these exceptions.

RMDs - General Definition

RMDs are the minimum amounts that must be taken each year starting when a retirement account owner reaches his or her RBD. The amount that must be taken out each year is calculated based on the prior year-end balance of the account for which the RMD is being calculated, divided by a life expectancy factor (Treas. Reg. 1.401(a)(9)-5, A-1,and Treas. Reg. 1.408-8, A-6). A person may take out more than the RMD amount, but not less, without facing penalty. Furthermore, RMDs are not eligible for rollover treatment.

The RBD

An IRA owner's RBD is April 1 following the year the individual turns age 70½. For example, if Sarah turns 70½ in 2013, she must take her first RMD by her RBD, which is April 1, 2014.

If a person's birthday falls after June 30, then he or she will turn age 70½ in the year following the year he or she turns age 70. If a person's birthday falls on or before June 30, then he or she will turn age 70½ in the same year that he or she turns age 70.

A retirement plan participant's RBD is also April 1 following the 70½ year, unless the plan document allows for a delayed RBD for working participants. If a delayed RBD applies, then the plan participant's RBD is the later of

- April 1 following the 70½ year, or
- April 1 following the year of retirement.

Owners (defined as those who own more than five percent of the business) cannot delay their RBDs, and must begin RMDs by April 1 following the 70½ year.

(Note that an RMD cannot be delayed from an IRA regardless of whether an individual works beyond age 70½.)

Second and Subsequent Years' RMD Deadline

December 31 of the year is the deadline for taking an RMD for the second and all subsequent years.

IRA RMD Reporting

An IRA custodian, trustee, or issuer is responsible for providing an IRA owner in distribution status with an RMD statement by January 31 of each year. This statement may be provided along with the Fair Market Value (FMV) statement that is also due by that date. In the statement, the financial institution reports the date due and amount of the RMD. Alternatively, the financial institution may simply include the due date and an offer to calculate the RMD for the individual. Form 5498, if sent by January 31, may be used to satisfy the RMD statement requirement. If Form 5498 is used, RMD information is reported in boxes 11, 12a and 12b. Additionally, when the IRA custodian, trustee, or issuer generates the annual IRS Form 5498 for each IRA, it indicates on the form that an RMD is due to the IRA owner for the following year in Box 11.

2013 Form 5498 Instructions for Recipients Regarding RMDs

Box 11. If the box is checked, you must take an RMD for 2014. An RMD may be required even if the box is not checked. If you do not take the RMD for 2014, you are subject to a 50% excise tax on the amount not distributed. See Pub. 590 for details.

Box 12a. Shows the date by which the RMD amount in box 12b must be distributed to avoid the 50 percent excise tax on the undistributed amount for 2014.

Box 12b. Shows the amount of the RMD for 2014. If box 11 is checked and there is no amount in this box, the trustee or issuer must provide you the amount or offer to calculate the amount in a separate statement by January 31, 2014.

It is the responsibility of the IRA owner to make sure he or she satisfies the RMD for the year when one is required. When an RMD is taken, the distributing organization will issue an IRS Form 1099-R to report the distribution to the IRS and to the recipient.

Important Note: Please see IRS Notice 2009-9 for special reporting instructions related to the waiver of 2009 RMDs.

Form 5498 (2014) — IRA Contribution Information

2828 ☐ VOID ☐ CORRECTED		Version A, Cycle 5 Dimensions: 7.3" x 5.5"; .5" head margin to top line

TRUSTEE'S or ISSUER'S name, street address, city or town, state or province, country, and ZIP or foreign postal code

1 IRA contributions (other than amounts in boxes 2-4, 8-10, 13a, and 14a) $

OMB No. 1545-0747

2014

Form **5498**

IRA Contribution Information

2 Rollover contributions $

3 Roth IRA conversion amount $

4 Recharacterized contributions $

Copy A

TRUSTEE'S or ISSUER'S federal identification no.

PARTICIPANT'S social security number

5 Fair market value of account $

6 Life insurance cost included in box 1 $

For Internal Revenue Service Center
File with Form 1096.

PARTICIPANT'S name

7 IRA ☐ SEP ☐ SIMPLE ☐ Roth IRA ☐
8 SEP contributions $

9 SIMPLE contributions $

For Privacy Act and Paperwork Reduction Act Notice, see the 2014 General Instructions for Certain Information Returns.

Street address (including apt. no.)

10 Roth IRA contributions $

11 Check if RMD for 2015 ☐

12a RMD date $

12b RMD amount $

City or town, state or province, country, and ZIP or foreign postal code

13a Postponed contribution $

13b Year

13c Code

14a Repayments $

14b Code

Account number (see instructions)

15a FMV of certain specified assets $

15b Code(s)

Form **5498**   Cat. No. 50010C   www.irs.gov/form5498   Department of the Treasury - Internal Revenue Service

Do Not Cut or Separate Forms on This Page — Do Not Cut or Separate Forms on This Page

Retirement Plan RMD Reporting

IRC Sec. 401(a)(9) makes plan administrators responsible for ensuring RMDs are properly distributed from qualified retirement plans (e.g., 401(k) plans). When an RMD is disbursed, the distributing plan will issue an IRS Form 1099-R to report the distribution to the IRS and to the recipient.

Form 1099-R (2014)

9898 ☐ VOID ☐ CORRECTED

PAYER'S name, street address, city or town, state or province, country, and ZIP or foreign postal code

1 Gross distribution $

2a Taxable amount $

OMB No. 1545-0119

2014

Form **1099-R**

Distributions From Pensions, Annuities, Retirement or Profit-Sharing Plans, IRAs, Insurance Contracts, etc.

2b Taxable amount not determined ☐   Total distribution ☐

Copy A

PAYER'S federal identification number

RECIPIENT'S identification number

3 Capital gain (included in box 2a) $

4 Federal income tax withheld $

For Internal Revenue Service Center
File with Form 1096.

RECIPIENT'S name

5 Employee contributions /Designated Roth contributions or insurance premiums $

6 Net unrealized appreciation in employer's securities $

For Privacy Act and Paperwork Reduction Act Notice, see the 2014 General Instructions for Certain Information Returns.

Street address (including apt. no.)

7 Distribution code(s)   IRA/ SEP/ SIMPLE ☐

8 Other $ %

City or town, state or province, country, and ZIP or foreign postal code

9a Your percentage of total distribution   %

9b Total employee contributions $

10 Amount allocable to IRR within 5 years $

11 1st year of desig. Roth contrib.

12 State tax withheld $

13 State/Payer's state no.

14 State distribution $

Account number (see instructions)

15 Local tax withheld $

16 Name of locality

17 Local distribution $

Form **1099-R**   Cat. No. 14436Q   www.irs.gov/form1099r   Department of the Treasury - Internal Revenue Service

Do Not Cut or Separate Forms on This Page — Do Not Cut or Separate Forms on This Page

403(b) Plan Pre-1987/Post-1986 Balances

The RMD rules apply to the portion of the 403(b) plan balance that has accrued after December 31, 1986 (i.e., attributable to contributions made and all earnings credited after that date). If the amounts have been separately accounted, the pre-1987 account balance (i.e., the "grandfathered" balance) is not subject to the RMD rules. Therefore, the RMD is calculated using only the post-1986 balance. This rule applies equally to 403(b) annuity contracts, custodial accounts, and retirement income accounts. If the 403(b) issuer or custodian did not keep records to separately account for the grandfathered balance, the entire account balance will be treated as subject to the RMD rules (Treas. Reg. 1.403(b)-3, Q&A 2).

Any amount distributed in a calendar year from a 403(b) plan in excess of the RMD for a calendar year will be treated as paid from the pre-1987 account balance, if any.

The pre-1987 account balance must begin to be distributed no later than age 75.

Formula for Calculating RMDs

Prior year-end account balance ÷ life expectancy = RMD

IRA Prior Year-End Account Balance

This is the IRA balance on December 31 of the year before the distribution year (e.g., use the December 31, 2013, IRA balance for a 2014 RMD). Adjust this IRA balance by adding to the IRA balance any

- outstanding rollovers taken within the last 60 days of a year and rolled over after the first of the following year;
- outstanding transfers taken in one year and completed in the following year; and
- conversions along with the net income attributable to the December 31 balance for the year in which the conversion occurred.

Retirement Plan Prior Year-End Account Balance

This is the retirement plan balance as of the last valuation date in the year before the distribution year. Adjust this amount by

- adding any contributions or forfeitures allocated to the account after the valuation date, but made during the valuation year;
- subtracting any distributions made in the valuation year that occurred after the valuation date.

Determining Life Expectancy Factors

The life expectancy an account owner (either an IRA owner or retirement plan participant) uses to calculate his or her RMD is based on one of two tables provided by the IRS for this purpose. These tables can be found in Treas. Reg. 1.401(a)(9)-9, or in IRS Publication 590 (www.irs.gov). Most retirement account owners will use the Uniform Lifetime Table to determine RMDs during their lifetimes. There is only one exception, which will be explained later.

The Uniform Lifetime Table provides a joint life expectancy figure that is equivalent to the hypothetical joint life expectancy of the retirement account owner and a second individual who is 10 years younger. As previously stated, most retirement account owners will use the Uniform Lifetime Table, even if they have no named beneficiary.

In the case of the Uniform Lifetime table, the life expectancy factor to use in the RMD calculation is found by finding the age that the retirement account owner will turn in the year of the calculation, and using the corresponding life expectancy factor, as shown in the following table. For example, by referring to IRS Publication 590, an IRA owner who is 73 would determine that his or her applicable life expectancy for RMD purposes is 24.7 years.

Table III (Uniform Lifetime)

For use by: Unmarried Owners, Married Owners Whose Spouses Are Not More Than 10 Years Younger, and Married Owners Whose Spouses Are Not the Sole Beneficiaries of their IRAs

Age	Distribution Period	Age	Distribution Period
70	27.4	93	9.6
71	26.5	94	9.1
72	25.6	95	8.6
73	24.7	96	8.1
74	23.8	97	7.6
75	22.9	98	7.1
76	22.0	99	6.7
77	21.2	100	6.3
78	20.3	101	5.9
79	19.5	102	5.5
80	18.7	103	5.2
81	17.9	104	4.9
82	17.1	105	4.5
83	16.3	106	4.2
84	15.5	107	3.9
85	14.8	108	3.7
86	14.1	109	3.4
87	13.4	110	3.1
88	12.7	111	2.9
89	12.0	112	2.6
90	11.4	113	2.4
91	10.8	114	2.1
92	10.2	115 and over	1.9

The exception to using the Uniform Lifetime Table applies if a retirement account owner has a spouse beneficiary who is more than 10 years younger than he or she. In this situation, the retirement account owner will use the Joint and Last Survivor Table. The result of using the actual joint life expectancy of the account owner and his or her spouse beneficiary who is more than 10 years younger is a smaller RMD for the individual.

When using the Joint and Last Survivor Table, the account owner finds his or her age on one axis and the age of the spouse beneficiary on the other axis, and follows the corresponding column and row to find the appropriate joint life expectancy, as shown in the following graphic. For example, a 73-year-old account owner with a 60-year-old spouse beneficiary would use the joint life expectancy of a 73 and 60-year-old, which is 26.8.

Table III (continued) (Joint Life and Last Survivor Expectancy)

For use by: Married Owners Whose Spouses Are More Than 10 Years Younger, and Are the Sole Beneficiaries of their IRAs

Age	60	61	62	63	64	65	66	67	68	69
60	30.9	30.4	30.0	29.6	29.2	28.8	28.5	28.2	27.9	27.6
61	30.4	29.9	29.5	29.0	28.6	28.3	27.9	27.6	27.3	27.0
62	30.0	29.5	29.0	28.5	28.1	27.7	27.3	27.0	26.7	26.4
63	29.6	29.0	28.5	28.1	27.6	27.2	26.8	26.4	26.1	25.7
64	29.2	28.6	28.1	27.6	27.1	26.7	26.3	25.9	25.5	25.2
65	28.8	28.3	27.7	27.2	26.7	26.2	25.8	25.4	25.0	24.6
66	28.5	27.9	27.3	26.8	26.3	25.8	25.3	24.9	24.5	24.1
67	28.2	27.6	27.0	26.4	25.9	25.4	24.9	24.4	24.0	23.6
68	27.9	27.3	26.7	26.1	25.5	25.0	24.5	24.0	23.5	23.1
69	27.6	27.0	26.4	25.7	25.2	24.6	24.1	23.6	23.1	22.6
70	27.4	26.7	26.1	25.4	24.8	24.3	23.7	23.2	22.7	22.2
71	27.2	26.5	25.8	25.2	24.5	23.9	23.4	22.8	22.3	21.8
72	27.0	26.3	25.6	24.9	24.3	23.7	23.1	22.5	22.0	21.4
73→	26.8	26.1	25.4	24.7	24.0	23.4	22.8	22.2	21.6	21.1
74	26.6	25.9	25.2	24.5	23.8	23.1	22.5	21.9	21.3	20.8
75	26.5	25.7	25.0	24.3	23.6	22.9	22.3	21.6	21.0	20.5

Account Owner With Multiple Beneficiaries

In general, if a retirement account owner has named multiple beneficiaries, he or she will use the Uniform Lifetime table, even if the oldest beneficiary is a spouse beneficiary who is more than 10 years younger than the account owner. However, in situations where the beneficial shares of the IRA or retirement plan account are being separately accounted, then separate RMDs could be calculated for each separate account, and the RMD with respect to the portion attributed to the more-than-10-years-younger spouse beneficiary could be calculated using the Joint and Last Survivor Table (Treas. Reg. 1.401(a)(9)-8, A-2). The Uniform Lifetime Table would apply when calculating the RMD portions attributable to the other named beneficiaries.

Death or Divorce of Spouse Beneficiary During a Distribution Year

If the spouse is the sole beneficiary of the retirement account, and he or she dies during a distribution year, the RMD is calculated as if the deceased spouse beneficiary remained the beneficiary for the entire distribution year. For RMD purposes, any change in beneficiary would not take effect until the year following the year of the spouse beneficiary's death.

If a retirement account owner divorces and changes the beneficiary designation in the same year, then the former spouse beneficiary will not be considered for RMD purposes for that and subsequent years. If a divorced retirement account owner does not change the beneficiary designation in the year of divorce, then a change in beneficiary is effective in the year following divorce.

If Client Misses the RMD Deadline

If a retirement account owner fails to take an RMD by the applicable deadline (i.e., by the RBD for the first RMD, or by December 31 for each subsequent years' RMD), he or she will have an "excess accumulation." The penalty on an excess accumulation is 50 percent of the amount that should have been taken but was not (IRC Sec. 4974).

In other words, if Tom was required to take an RMD equal to $40,000 by December 31, 2012, and he did not, then he will owe an excise tax of $20,000. Tom would compute and report the excess accumulation penalty tax by using IRS Form 5329, which he would submit with his income tax return.

Thankfully, if the failure to take the full RMD in a timely manner is due to a reasonable error, and the retirement account owner takes steps to remedy the situation by taking as a distribution what should have been distributed, the IRS may waive the excess accumulations penalty tax. To request a waiver of this penalty tax, the retirement account owner must file a Form 5329, and submit a letter requesting a waiver of the penalty. The letter should include an explanation as to why the RMD was not timely taken, and the steps that have been taken to remedy the failure.

RMD Aggregation

The IRA RMD rules allow IRA owners to independently calculate the RMDs that are due from each IRA they own, total the amounts, and take the aggregate RMD amount from whichever IRA they choose. This is known as RMD aggregation (Treas. Reg. 1.408-8, Q&A9). A person may also aggregate RMDs as a beneficiary from IRAs inherited from the same owner.

403(b) plan participants may aggregate their RMDs (Treas. Reg. 1.403(b)-6(e). Just as with IRAs, RMDs must be separately determined for each 403(b) contract of an employee, then such amounts may then be totaled and the total amount taken from any one or more of the individual 403(b) contracts. However, only amounts in 403(b) contracts that an individual holds as an employee may be aggregated. Amounts in 403(b) contracts that an individual holds as a beneficiary of the same decedent may be aggregated, but such amounts may not be aggregated with amounts held in 403(b) contracts that the individual holds as the employee or as the beneficiary of another decedent. Distributions from 403(b) contracts will not satisfy the minimum distribution requirements for IRAs, nor will distributions from IRAs satisfy the RMD requirements for 403(b) contracts or accounts.

Retirement plan participants are not allowed to aggregate their RMDs (Treas. Reg. 1.401(a)(9)-8, Q&A 1).

Developing an RMD Strategy

An individual with multiple IRAs and/or retirement plans may want to consider adopting an RMD strategy to simplifying the RMD process. Taking RMDs from multiple IRAs and/or retirement plans can be a huge source of confusion and frustration. As was stated previously, individuals face a substantial penalty if they take less than the required amounts.

One RMD strategy that can simplify the process is asset consolidation with an IRA. Consolidating assets into a "Super" IRA for RMD purposes may help the IRA owner or plan participant

- Streamline RMD paperwork,
- Lower the number of distributions that must be taken,
- Reduce the chance of errors and IRS scrutiny,
- Increase investment buying power and allow for more sophisticated investment strategies,
- Reduce fees,

- Help with beneficiary organization and consolidation,

- Increase the potential for more consistent service, and

- Simplify retirement income planning overall.

Keep in mind a consolidation strategy may not always be suitable. A financial professional, or tax or legal professional can help an IRA owner or plan participant determine whether IRA consolidation for RMD purposes is appropriate for the individual.

It is important to note that RMDs cannot be rolled over to an IRA or other eligible plan (i.e., qualified plan, 403(b) plan or governmental 457(b) plan). However, amounts other than RMDs are generally eligible for rollover.

Asset consolidation for RMD purposes can be accomplished by combining eligible rollover amounts into one IRA, which could be referred to as a "Super" IRA. For example, following a distribution triggering event, qualified plan, 403(b) and governmental 457(b) assets (except any RMDs) may be rolled over to an IRA.

The same Super IRA that holds retirement plan rollover contributions can be used to consolidate IRA assets (i.e., traditional, and SEP) as well. What's more, after participating in a SIMPLE plan for two years, a participant can transfer his or her SIMPLE IRA assets to the same Super IRA that holds the individual's SEP, traditional IRA, and rollover contributions.

Another RMD strategy is one that involves directly transferring distributions to qualified charities. Qualified charitable distributions (QCDs) from IRAs first became available as a result of the Pension Protection Act of 2006 (PPA) beginning for tax year 2006. Initially, the provision was effective only for 2006 and 2007 tax years. However, the Emergency Economic Stabilization Act of 2008 extended the QCD provision of PPA through 2009. Then in 2010, the Tax Relief, Unemployment Insurance Reauthorization and Job Creation Act of 2010 extended the QCD again through 2011. The third extension for QCDs came with the passage of the American Taxpayer Relief Act of 2012, which allows QCDs for 2012 and through 2013.

The QCD RMD strategy may apply for IRA owners and IRA beneficiaries age 70½ or older who take distributions from their

- Traditional IRAs;

- Roth IRAs;

- "Inactive" (i.e., not receiving employer contributions) simplified employee pension plan (SEP) IRAs; and/or

- Inactive savings incentive match plans for employees (SIMPLE) IRAs.

For 2012 QCDs, an eligible IRA owner or IRA beneficiary could treat a distribution up to $100,000 made to a qualified charity through January 31, 2013, as a 2012 QDC in either of the following circumstances:

• The contribution was a cash contribution to the charity on or before January 31, 2013, of all or a portion of an IRA distribution that was taken in December 2012.

• The contribution was paid directly from the IRA to the charity on or before January 31, 2013, provided the contribution otherwise would have been a 2012 QCD if it had been paid to the qualified charity in 2012.

Eligible IRA owners and beneficiaries should keep records to substantiate the timing of contributions and distributions regarding any 2012 QCD made in January 2013.

For 2013 QCDs, an eligible IRA owner or IRA beneficiary can treat any 2013 IRA distributions up to $100,000, other than those claimed as a 2012 QCD as described above, that are transferred directly to a qualified charity, as a 2013 QCD.

For QCD purposes, eligible charities include those in described in § 170(b)(1)(A) of the Internal Revenue Code (IRC), other than supporting organizations described in IRC § 509(a)(3) or donor advised funds that are described in IRC § 4966(d)(2). Consequently, donations to private foundations, donor advised funds, charitable remainder trusts, charitable gift annuities or pooled income funds do not qualify as QCDs.

Because eligible IRA owners and beneficiaries may exclude QCDs from their taxable income for the applicable tax year, QCDs are not additionally tax-deductible as charitable contributions under IRC § 170.

QCDs

— Are limited to $100,000 annually;

— May be used to satisfy an IRA owner's or beneficiary's required minimum distribution for the year;

— Are not subject to federal income tax withholding rules; and

— Are not taken into account in determining any deduction for charitable contributions.

IRS RMD FAQs

The IRS has updated FAQs for those facing required minimum distributions. Financial advisors assisting clients who may be facing their first required minimum distributions (RMDs) from IRAs or workplace retirement plans, have an updated resource they can consider sharing with clients to help them better understand these IRS-mandated withdrawals. The IRS has a series of frequently asked questions (FAQs) on its web site (irs.gov), under the title "Retirement Plans FAQs regarding Required Minimum Distributions," which it updated in February 2013.

Questions addressed include the following:

1. What are RMDs?
2. What types of retirement plans require minimum distributions?
3. When must I receive my RMD from my IRA?
4. How is the amount of the RMD calculated?
5. What are the RMD requirements for pre-1987 contributions to a 403(b) plan?
6. Can an account owner just take a RMD from one account instead of separately from each account?
7. Who calculates the amount of the RMD?
8. Can an account owner withdraw more than the RMD?
9. What happens if a person does not take a RMD by the required deadline?
10. Can the penalty for not taking the full RMD be waived?
11. Can a distribution in excess of the RMD for one year be applied to the RMD for a future year?
12. How are RMDs taxed?
13. Can RMD amounts be rolled over into another tax-deferred account?
14. Is an employer required to make plan contributions for an employee who has turned 70½ and is receiving required minimum distributions?

Practice Management Application

- Contact 70-year-old clients. Consider sending them a "70½" birthday card with a reminder that they may be required to start taking distributions from their retirement accounts.

- Coordinate a client's RMD review with a beneficiary audit of accounts.

- Suggest consolidating multiple IRAs into a Super IRA to simplify the RMD process.

- For IRA owners, check the client's IRS Form 5498 for the RMD amount.

- Be aware of the difference between RMDs for IRA owners and retirement plan participants.

- Be sure to pursue the waiver of the excess accumulation penalty if just cause exists.

Chapter Review Questions

Feedback for the review questions can be found at the end of the chapter.

1 The RMD rules apply to owners of the following retirement savings arrangements, *EXCEPT*:

    A IRC Sec. 401(a) plans
    B IRC Sec. 408A Roth IRAs
    C IRC Sec. 403(b) plans
    D IRC Sec. 408 IRA plans

2 IRA-owner Sally turned 70 on April 1, 2013. What is her required beginning date (RBD) for taking required minimum distributions (RMDs)?

    A April 1, 2013
    B December 31, 2013
    C April 1, 2014
    D April 15, 2014
    E After she retires from her job.

3 Based on the following information, what would be Ron's RMD?

    Age = 76
    Prior year-end account balance = $50,000
    Life expectancy factor = 22

    A $658
    B $1,672
    C $2,273
    D $5,000

4 Most individuals will use which of the following life expectancy tables to calculate their RMDs?

    A Uniform
    B Single
    C Joint
    D SSA Period Life

5 With respect to RMD aggregation, which of the following statements is *TRUE*?

    A Plan participants may aggregate their RMDs from multiple 401(k) plans.
    B SEP IRA owners are prohibited from aggregating their SEP IRAs for RMD purposes.

C RMD aggregation rules were eliminated in 2012.

D An IRA owner may total the RMD amounts due from each of his or her IRAs and distribute the total amount from one IRA.

Chapter Review Questions Feedback

1 The RMD rules apply to owners of the following retirement savings arrangements, *EXCEPT*:

    A IRC Sec. 401(a) plans

    B IRC Sec. 408A Roth IRAs

    C IRC Sec. 403(b) plans

    D IRC Sec. 408 IRA plans

    A *Incorrect, pursuant to IRC Sec. 401(a)(9), owners of 401(a) plan balances must begin RMDs by their required beginning dates.*

    B **Correct, pursuant to Treasury Regulation 1.408A-6, Roth IRA owners are not required to take distributions from their Roth IRAs while they are alive.** Chapter 9 Page 197

    C *Incorrect, pursuant to IRC Sec. 401(a)(9), owners of 403(b) plan balances must begin RMDs by their required beginning dates.*

    D *Incorrect, pursuant to IRC Sec. 401(a)(9) owners of individual retirement accounts and individual retirement annuities must begin RMDs by their required beginning dates.*

2 IRA-owner Sally turned 70 on April 1, 2013. What is her required beginning date (RBD) for taking required minimum distributions (RMDs)?

    A April 1, 2013

    B December 31, 2013

    C April 1, 2014

    D April 15, 2014

    E After she retires from her job.

    A *Incorrect, an IRA owner's RBD is April 1 of the year following the year he/she turns age 70½. In this case, Sally's RBD is April 1, 2014.*

    B *Incorrect, this date represents the end of Sally's 2013 tax year.*

    C **Correct, an IRA owner's RBD is April 1 of the year following the year he/she turns age 70½.** Chapter 9 Page 197

    D *Incorrect, this date represents Sally's 2013 tax filing deadline, without extensions.*

    E *Incorrect, an IRA owner's RBD is April 1 of the year following the year he/she turns age 70½. Some participants in qualified retirement plans may delay their RBD until after retirement.*

3 Based on the following information, what would be Ron's RMD?

> Age = 76
> Prior year-end account balance = $50,000
> Life expectancy factor = 22

  A $658
  B $1,672
  C $2,273
  D $5,000

A *Incorrect, the RMD is calculated by dividing the prior year-end account balance by the life expectancy factor; this figure represents the prior year-end account balance divided by Ron's age of 76.*

B *Incorrect, the RMD is calculated by dividing the prior year-end account balance by the life expectancy factor; this figure represents Ron's age multiplied by the life expectancy factor of 22.*

C **Correct, the RMD is calculated by dividing the prior year-end account balance by the life expectancy factor.** Chapter 9 Page 200

D *Incorrect, the RMD is calculated by dividing the prior year-end account balance by the life expectancy factor; this figure represents the prior year-end account balance divided by 10.*

4 Most individuals will use which of the following life expectancy tables to calculate their RMDs?

  A Uniform
  B Single
  C Joint
  D SSA Period Life

A **Correct, pursuant to 1.401(a)(9)-9, the Uniform table applies in all RMD situations except when the spouse beneficiary is more than 10 years younger than the account owner.** Chapter 9 Page 201

B *Incorrect, the Single life expectancy table would apply for beneficiaries.*

C *Incorrect, the joint life expectancy table only applies in situations where the spouse beneficiary is more than 10 years younger than the account owner.*

D *Incorrect, the Social Security Administration (SSA) Period Life Table is used to evaluate the actuarial soundness of annuities, promissory notes, loans and mortgages.*

5 With respect to RMD aggregation, which of the following statements is *TRUE*?

  A Plan participants may aggregate their RMDs from multiple 401(k) plans.
  B SEP IRA owners are prohibited from aggregating their SEP IRAs for RMD purposes.

C RMD aggregation rules were eliminated in 2012.

D An IRA owner may total the RMD amounts due from each of his or her IRAs and distribute the total amount from one IRA.

A *Incorrect, pursuant to Treas. Reg. 1.401(a)(9)-8, A1, retirement plan participants may not aggregate their RMDs.*

B *Incorrect, a SEP IRA is a traditional IRA which can be aggregated from RMD purposes.*

C *Incorrect, the RMD aggregation rules still apply.*

D **Correct, this is the definition of RMD aggregation.** Chapter 9 Page 204

CHAPTER 10

Beneficiary Options and Issues

Chapter Goal

Upon completion of this chapter the reader will be better able to assess, recommend, and implement retirement plan beneficiary planning strategies.

Learning Objectives

✓ Differentiate between the beneficiary distribution options when death occurs before the RBD and when it occurs on or after the RBD.

✓ Identify the term designated beneficiary.

✓ Recognize the result of executing a qualified beneficiary disclaimer.

✓ Apply standard distribution rules to create a stretch IRA.

Technical Overview

The rules that govern beneficiary distribution options are primarily found in IRC Sec. 401(a)(9)(B) and underlying Treasury regulations (Treas. Reg. 1.401(a)(9)). Plan document language may further restrict the available options, so it is always important to review the distribution section of the plan document for specific options.

Distribution options for beneficiaries depend upon when the IRA owner or retirement plan participant dies. Beneficiaries have different distribution options depending on whether the IRA owner or plan participant died on or after his or her "required beginning date (RBD)," or before. The options also differ somewhat for spouse beneficiaries vs. nonspouse beneficiaries.

As of September 16, 2013, the definition of "spouse" changed pursuant to a Supreme Court ruling with respect to the Defense of Marriage Act, and as clarified for federal tax and employee benefits purposes in IRS and Department of Labor (DOL) pronouncements. Consequently, the definition of spouse includes same-sex individuals, as well as opposite-sex individuals, who are legally married under state law, regardless of the couple's current state of residence.

The RBD

The IRS encourages individuals to save for retirement in IRAs and employer-sponsored retirement plans. To that end, the IRS generally discourages individuals from taking distributions from their retirement plans during their wealth accumulation years. However, under IRS mandate, individuals must begin distributions from their retirement plans following their RBD. Generally, a person's RBD, will be April 1 of the year following the year he or she turns age 70½ (IRC Sec. 401(a)(9)(C)).

Question	Answer
Are there any special rules that allow individuals to delay their RBD?	Certain retirement plan participants (but not IRA owners) may be able to delay their RBD until after they retire. If the plan document so states, participants who own five percent or less of the employer, who are still working past age 70½, may delay their RBD until April 1 of the year following the year they retire (IRC Sec. 401(a)(9)(C)).

Who Is the Designated Beneficiary?

A designated beneficiary is an individual who is listed as a beneficiary under the IRA or retirement plan, and whose life expectancy is considered for distribution calculation purposes. An individual may be designated as a beneficiary under the plan either by the terms of the plan or, if the plan so provides, by an affirmative election by the IRA owner or plan participant.

An IRA owner or plan participant's designated beneficiary for distribution purposes is determined based on the beneficiaries listed as of the date of death, and who remain beneficiaries as of September 30 of the year following the year of the IRA owner or plan participant's death (i.e., the beneficiary determination date) (Treas. Reg. 1.401(a)(9)-4).

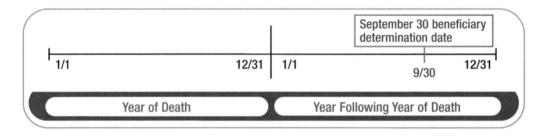

Question	Answer
What if a beneficiary takes a complete distribution of his or her share of retirement plan assets during the period from the date of death to the September 30th beneficiary determination date?	The individual is disregarded for purposes of determining the designated beneficiary.
What if a beneficiary disclaims his or her share of the retirement plan assets during the period from the date of death to the September 30th beneficiary determination date?	If the beneficiary executes a "qualified disclaimer" by the September 30th beneficiary determination date, then he or she is disregarded for purposes of determining the designated beneficiary.
What if the customer fails to follow through on paperwork requests?	Follow up with the client on a regular basis, and offer to sit down with the client to assist with the paperwork process, if necessary.

Question	Answer
What is a qualified disclaimer?	A qualified disclaimer is an irrevocable refusal by a beneficiary under the rules of IRC Sec. 2518(b) to accept an interest in property. See the section entitled "Beneficiary Disclaimers as Planning Tool" later in this text for further details.
What if a beneficiary dies during the period beginning on the IRA owner or plan participant's date of death and ending on the September 30th beneficiary determination date?	If a beneficiary dies during this period, the death has no effect on beneficiary determination. Therefore, despite the death, the deceased beneficiary will continue to be treated as the designated beneficiary as of the September 30th determination date for distribution purposes.
May a person other than an individual be a designated beneficiary?	No, only an individual may be a designated beneficiary for purposes of calculating distributions. A nonperson entity, such as an estate, may not be a designated beneficiary for calculation purposes. If a nonperson entity is listed as a beneficiary, the IRA owner or plan participant will be treated as having no designated beneficiary when determining amounts to distribute. However, see the following Q&A regarding trusts as beneficiaries.
Can a trust be a designated beneficiary?	If a "qualified trust" is named as beneficiary, the beneficiaries of the qualified trust may be designated beneficiaries for purposes of calculating distributions. A qualified trust is one that meets the requirements of Treas. Reg. 1.401(a)(9)-4, Q&A-5(b). See the section entitled "Qualified Trust as Beneficiary" for further details. While a nonqualified trust may be identified as a beneficiary, the underlying life expectancies of the beneficiaries of the trust may not be used for distribution calculation purposes.
Are there any special rules for a surviving spouse who is the sole beneficiary of the IRA or qualified plan?	If the spouse is the sole designated beneficiary of the IRA or qualified plan as of September 30th of the year following the year of death, and the designated spouse beneficiary dies before life expectancy payments have begun to him or her, then the designated beneficiary for distribution calculation purposes becomes the designated beneficiary of the (now deceased) spouse.

Distribution Options—Death Before the RBD

When the IRA owner or plan participant dies before reaching his or her required beginning date (RBD), unless the plan document is more restrictive, the beneficiary distribution options are

- the five-year rule,
- life expectancy payments,
- IRA transfer to own IRA (for a spouse beneficiary),
- rollover to own IRA or eligible plan (for a spouse beneficiary),
- rollover to a beneficiary IRA from an eligible plan (for a nonspouse beneficiary) (new for 2007 and later years), or
- lump sum payment.

Nonspouse Beneficiary Rollover Option

Effective in 2007 and for later years, the beneficiary rules are modified to allow nonspouse beneficiaries to directly roll over amounts from decedents' qualified plans into beneficiary IRAs. Subsequent distributions from the beneficiary IRAs are made based on the IRA beneficiary distribution rules. The IRS provided operational guidance for nonspouse beneficiary rollovers in Notice 2007-7. Effective January 1, 2010, plans must allow for nonspouse beneficiary rollovers as a result of the Worker, Retiree and Employer Recovery Act.

Key Points

- The rollover must be a direct rollover from a qualified retirement plan, 403(b) plan or governmental 457(b) plan. If a nonspouse beneficiary receives an amount from a plan, the distribution is not eligible for rollover.

- The IRA must be established in a manner that identifies it as an IRA with respect to a deceased individual, and also identifies the deceased individual and the beneficiary, for example, "Tom Smith as beneficiary of John Smith."

- If the named beneficiary of a deceased plan participant is a qualified trust, the plan administrator may make a direct rollover to an IRA established with the trust as beneficiary.

- Required minimum distributions (RMDs) are ineligible for rollover.

- If the plan participant dies before his or her RBD, and the five-year rule applies to the nonspouse beneficiary, for the first four years after the year the participant dies, no amounts payable to the beneficiary are considered RMDs. Accordingly, the nonspouse beneficiary is permitted to directly roll over his or her entire benefit until the end of the fourth year.

- Nonspouse beneficiaries may take advantage of a special rule when the five-year rule for distributions applies under the distributing plan. If the five-year rule applies, the nonspouse beneficiary, nevertheless, may determine RMDs under the plan using the life expectancy rule provided the direct rollover to a beneficiary IRA is made prior to the end of the year following the year of death. However, in order to use this rule, RMDs under the beneficiary IRA must be determined under the life expectancy rule using the same nonspouse beneficiary.

- If the plan participant dies before his or her RBD, and life expectancy payments apply, in the year following the year of death and each subsequent year, an RMD is due. All undistributed RMDs for the year in which the direct rollover occurs, and for any prior year, are ineligible for rollover.

- If the plan participant dies on or after his or her RBD, for the year of the participant's death, the RMD, which is not eligible for rollover, is the same as the amount that would have applied if the participant were still alive and had elected the direct rollover. For the year after the year of the participant's death and for subsequent years, RMDs are calculated using the longer of 1) the single life expectancy of the deceased plan participant, or 2) the single life expectancy of the nonspouse beneficiary.

- The rules for determining RMDs under the distributing plan with respect to the nonspouse beneficiary also must apply under the beneficiary IRA.

Special Considerations for Spouse Beneficiaries

When the IRA owner or plan participant dies before the RBD, a spouse beneficiary does not have to make a distribution decision until the earlier of December 31 of the year the deceased would have turned age 70½, or December 31 of year containing the fifth anniversary of the date of death.

If the spouse beneficiary chooses life expectancy payments, he or she may delay the onset of the payments until the end of the year the deceased would have turned age 70½.

The following table summarizes the distribution options available for beneficiaries of retirement plan assets when the owner dies before his or her RBD.

Death Before the RBD

Spouse as Sole Beneficiary	Nonspouse Beneficiary, or Spouse Is Not the Sole Beneficiary	No or Nonperson Beneficiary (e.g., an estate, nonqualified trust, charity, etc.)
1 **Five-Year Rule—** Assets are paid out by the end of the fifth year following the year of death	1 **Five-Year Rule—** Assets are paid out by the end of the fifth year following the year of death	1 **Five-Year Rule—** Assets are paid out by the end of the fifth year following the year of death
2 **Life Expectancy Payments** using the single life expectancy of the spouse beneficiary, determined in the year following the year of death, recalculated,[1] and beginning the later of 12/31 of the year following the year of death or 12/31 of the IRA owner's/plan participant's 70 ½ year.[3]	2 **Life Expectancy Payments** using the single life expectancy of the oldest beneficiary,[2] determined in the year following the year of death, nonrecalculated, and beginning 12/31 of the year following the year of the IRA owner's/plan participant's death.[4]	
3 **IRA Transfer—** A spouse may transfer the deceased's IRA to his/her own IRA.	3 **IRA Transfer—** A spouse may transfer his/her separate share of the deceased's IRA to his/her own IRA.	
4 **Rollover—** For an IRA or employer plan, a spouse may distribute and roll over the assets to his or her own IRA or eligible plan.	4 **Rollover—** For an IRA or employer plan, a spouse beneficiary may roll over his or her share to his or her own IRA or eligible plan. For an employer plan, a nonspouse beneficiary may roll over his or her share to a beneficiary IRA.	
5 **Lump sum**	5 **Lump sum**	
Regulatory Default: Single life expectancy payments.	*Regulatory Default:* Single life expectancy payments.	

1 Following the beneficiary's death, nonrecalculation of life expectancy applies.

2 If separate accounting applies, then each beneficiary's life expectancy may be used.

3 Following the beneficiary's death, nonrecalculation of life expectancy applies.

4 Ibid.

EXAMPLE: Five-Year Rule

Irma, age 56, died in 2014, leaving her IRA to her named beneficiary, Jack, her son. After considering his options, Jack elects to take the IRA assets under the five-year rule. Jack may take payments at any rate and in any amount, provided the entire IRA is depleted by December 31, 2019.

EXAMPLE: Life Expectancy Payments/Spouse Beneficiary

Nick died in 2014 at the age of 68, leaving his 64-year-old wife, Eileen, as the sole beneficiary of his retirement plan. Eileen could choose to take payments under the five-year rule, life expectancy payments, a lump sum distribution or rollover. Eileen elects life expectancy payments, but she will not begin taking the payments until December 31, 2016 (the year Nick would have turned 70½).

By the end of 2016, Eileen will determine her first beneficiary distribution by dividing the December 31, 2015, year-end balance of the retirement plan by her life expectancy (which is 20.2 for a 66-year-old). For each subsequent year, Eileen will recalculate her life expectancy by comparing her age to the single life expectancy table to determine a new life expectancy.

Sadly, Eileen dies in 2018 at the age of 68. Her year-of-death RMD is determined by dividing the December 31, 2017 year-end balance by her life expectancy of 18.6.

For 2019, the year following Eileen's death, the minimum payment is determined by dividing the December 31, 2018, year-end balance by Eileen's nonrecalculated life expectancy of 17.6, which is determined for each year that passes after the year of her death by subtracting one from her life expectancy that was set in the year of death.)

EXAMPLE: Nonspouse Beneficiary Rollover/Death Before the RBD

Scott, a single individual, named his brother, Jackson, as his beneficiary on his 401(k) plan. Unfortunately, Scott died at the young age of 47. Plan provisions require Jackson to distribute the assets according to the five-year rule for beneficiaries. Jackson's financial professional, however, informs Jackson about the new option to complete a nonspouse beneficiary rollover to a beneficiary IRA, and distribute the IRA assets using a life expectancy payment option. Jackson and his financial professional work with Scott's former employer to arrange for the direct rollover of the 401(k) balance to Jackson's beneficiary IRA before the end of the year following Scott's death.

Distribution Options—Death On or After the RBD

When the IRA owner or plan participant dies on or after reaching his or her RBD, unless the plan document is more restrictive, the beneficiary distribution options are

- life expectancy payments,
- IRA transfer to own IRA (for a spouse beneficiary),
- rollover to own IRA or eligible plan (for a spouse beneficiary),
- rollover to a beneficiary IRA from an eligible plan (for a nonspouse beneficiary) (for 2007 and later years), or
- lump sum payment.

The following table summarizes the distribution options available for beneficiaries of retirement plan assets when the owner dies on or after his or her RBD.

Death On or After the RBD

Spouse as Sole Beneficiary	Nonspouse Beneficiary, or Spouse Is Not the Sole Beneficiary	No or Nonperson Beneficiary (e.g., an estate, nonqualified trust, charity, etc.)
1 **Life Expectancy Payments,** beginning by 12/31 of the year following the year of death, using **the longer of** the single life expectancy of the spouse beneficiary, recalculated, or, IRA owner/plan participant determined in the year of death, nonrecalculated[1]	1 **Life Expectancy Payments,** beginning by 12/31 of the year following the year of death, using **the longer of** the single life expectancy of the oldest beneficiary[2], nonrecalculated, determined in year following the year of death, or IRA owner/plan participant, determined in the year of death, nonrecalculated[3]	**Life Expectancy Payments,** beginning by 12/31 of the year following the year of death, using the single life expectancy of the IRA owner/plan participant determined in the year of death, nonrecalculated
2 **IRA Transfer—** A spouse beneficiary may transfer the deceased's IRA to his/her own IRA.	2 **IRA Transfer—** A spouse may transfer his/her separate share of the deceased's IRA to his/her own IRA.	
3 **Rollover—** For an IRA or eligible plan, a spouse beneficiary may distribute and roll over the assets to his/her own IRA or eligible plan.	3 **Rollover—** For an IRA or eligible plan, a spouse beneficiary may distribute and roll over his/her share to his/her own IRA or eligible plan. For an eligible plan, a nonspouse beneficiary may roll over his or her share to a beneficiary IRA.	
4 **Lump sum payment.**	4 **Lump sum payment.**	

1 Following the death of the beneficiary, nonrecalculation of life expectancy applies

2 If separate accounting applies, then each beneficiary's life expectancy may be used independently.

3 Following the death of the beneficiary, nonrecalculation of life expectancy applies.

Recalculation Vs. Nonrecalculation of Life Expectancy

Recalculation or nonrecalculation of life expectancy are processes that become important for the beneficiary following the death of the IRA owner or plan participant because they affect the life expectancy figure that is used in distribution calculations. Regulations dictate when one or the other applies. Recalculation and nonrecalculation are each defined next. Before death, the life expectancy figure used to calculate an IRA owner's or plan participant's RMD is always recalculated.

Recalculation

When applying recalculation, life expectancy is re-determined each year by referring to the appropriate life expectancy table.

Nonrecalculation

With nonrecalculation, life expectancy is set in a particular year by referring to the appropriate life expectancy table, and the life expectancy factor is then reduced by one for all subsequent years.

Importance of Separate Accounts with Multiple Beneficiaries

Separate accounting of multiple beneficiary shares allows each beneficiary to determine his or her distribution independently. If separate accounts are not established, or are not properly maintained, beneficiary distributions must be determined based on the oldest beneficiary.

Separate accounts must be established no later than December 31 of the year following the year of the individual's death, and must reflect the separate interests of the beneficiaries of the IRA or plan account balance as of the IRA owner or plan participant's death. Separate accounting must also allocate all gains, losses, contributions and forfeitures on a reasonable and consistent basis to each beneficiary.

EXAMPLE:

Before her death on December 25, 2013, Camille completed a beneficiary designation form, naming multiple beneficiaries for her plan account balance. The plan set up separate accounts for each beneficiary by the end of 2014. (Note that separate accounts must be established by the end of the year following the year of death in order to allow the beneficiaries to use them for distribution purposes.) Because the beneficiary accounts were properly and timely established, they are treated as being in place as of Camille's death. Therefore, Camille's beneficiaries may determine their 2014 distributions based on the separate accounts.

Disclaiming Benefits as a Planning Tool

A beneficiary may disclaim a whole or partial interest in inherited property, and be treated as if he or she had never had rights to the property (IRC Sec. 2518(b)). By executing a "qualified disclaimer" of benefits, the disclaimant effectively relieves himself or herself of any tax consequences of receiving (and potentially gifting) the property that would have otherwise applied. Therefore, disclaimers are typically used as a tax planning tool. However, individuals may also choose to use a beneficiary disclaimer as a pseudo legacy planning tool, and disclaim their beneficial interests so that others may receive the assets. This usage is limited by the qualified disclaimer rules, which require that the disclaimant may not choose to whom the disclaimed assets will eventually pass.

What is a Qualified Disclaimer?

The disclaimer must be in writing.

The disclaimer must be given to the holder of the property's legal title (e.g., the IRA or plan administrator) not later than nine months after the later of 1) the death of the original owner (e.g., IRA owner or plan participant), or 2) the day on which such person attains age 21.

The disclaimant shall not have accepted the disclaimed interest or any of its benefits. The disclaimed interest shall pass—without direction on the part of the disclaimant— to any remaining beneficiaries.

A beneficiary of an IRA or retirement plan account balance that properly disclaims inherited assets during the period between the IRA owner's or plan participant's death and September 30 of the year following the year of death will not be considered a designated beneficiary (Treas. Reg. 1.401(a)(9)-4, Q&A-4).

Qualified Trust as Beneficiary

A qualified trust is one that meets the following requirements (Treas. Reg. 1.401(a)(9)-4, Q&A 5(b)).

1 The trust is valid under state law,

2 The trust is irrevocable (either during the IRA owner or plan participant's life or becomes so at his or her death),

3 The trust has identifiable beneficiaries, and

4 The trustee of the trust provides the IRA or plan administrator with a copy of the trust instrument (or qualifying trust documentation) by October 31 of the year following the year of the IRA owner or plan participant's death.

If a qualified trust is the beneficiary of an IRA or retirement plan, then the beneficiary distribution options as outlined in the previous tables apply to the beneficiaries of the qualified trust, with the following exceptions.

- A spouse beneficiary of a qualified trust does not have the ability to treat an IRA inherited through the trust as his or her own by transferring or redesignating the arrangement.

- When multiple beneficiaries are named within the qualified trust, separate accounting rules may not be applied. Consequently, for distribution purposes, the age of the oldest beneficiary must be used.

- The ability of a spouse beneficiary of a qualified trust to distribute and roll assets to his or her own IRA or retirement plan through the trust has only been authorized through IRS private letter rulings, which may only be relied upon by the individuals who requested the rulings. The ability to complete the rollover hinges upon the spouse's level of control of the trust.

- An employer plan may make a direct rollover to an IRA on behalf of a trust where the trust is the named beneficiary of a decedent, provided the beneficiaries of the trust meet the requirements to be designated beneficiaries. The IRA must be established as an inherited or beneficiary IRA with the trust named as the beneficiary. In such case, the beneficiaries of the trust are treated as designated beneficiaries of the decedent, provided the trust is a qualified trust as explained in previous paragraphs.

Tax Treatment of Distributions

Most retirement plan distributions will be taxed at the ordinary income tax rate applicable to the distribution recipient. There are exceptions, however. For more detail on the taxation of retirement plan distributions, refer to Chapter 11, Income Planning and Taxation Issues.

Stretch IRAs

Contrary to popular belief, a stretch IRA is not a unique type of IRA. Any regular IRA, saving incentive match plan for employees (SIMPLE) IRA or Roth IRA can be a stretch IRA. The stretching feature is achieved by applying standard distribution rules that allow beneficiaries to prolong payouts over an applicable life expectancy. According to Treasury regulations, following the death of an IRA owner or plan participant, typically, the beneficiary has the option to take life expectancy payments. Moreover, if the beneficiary has not exhausted the payments upon his or her death, a subsequent beneficiary may continue the payments over the course of the remaining schedule.

EXAMPLE:

Herb, age 75, has an IRA valued at $2 million. His wife, Judith, who is 20 years his junior, is his beneficiary. The couple has a special-needs child, Richard, who is 30 years old. Herb has been taking RMDs based on the joint life expectancy of Judith and himself. As a result of failing health, Herb passes away.

Rather than treat the IRA as her own, which would subject her to the early distribution penalty tax for any amounts taken before she reaches age 59½, Judith begins life expectancy payments as a beneficiary, and names Richard as the beneficiary of her inherited IRA. At age 58, Judith dies. Richard may continue distributions from the IRA over Judith's remaining life expectancy, nonrecalculated.

Beneficiary Distribution Options for Roth IRAs

A unique characteristic of the Roth IRA is that Roth IRA owners are not subject to the RMD rules. So, while the Roth IRA owner is alive, he or she need never distribute Roth IRA assets. This trait makes the Roth IRA a great tool for wealth accumulation for beneficiaries. Distribution options for Roth IRA beneficiaries follow those as outlined previously when death occurs before the RBD. As part of those options, following the death of the Roth IRA beneficiary, distributions may be continued over any remaining life expectancy, applying nonrecalculation.

- Conduct beneficiary audits for clients as a value-added service. Many IRA owners and retirement plan participants fail to keep their beneficiary designations up-to- date. As a result, beneficiary designations may no longer reflect the desires of the benefactor, and may conflict with other beneficiary documentation, which could lead to undesirable legal and tax issues.

The following court case underscores the importance of regular beneficiary audits with your clients. The case of *Gallagher v. Gallagher*, United States District Court, District of Massachusetts, February 26, 2013, provides an unfortunate reminder of how essential a beneficiary audit is to ensure your clients' wishes upon death are fulfilled. Although a detailed legal review of the case is beyond the scope of this material, the general situation in the case at hand is not that uncommon: A legally married, plan participant, who was separated from his spouse, named his son as primary beneficiary of his 401(k) plan account balance, without first obtaining spousal consent to do so. Upon the plan participant's death, both the estranged spouse and son claimed the 401(k) plan balance. The court noted that despite the participant's intention to leave his 401(k) plan account to his son, the participant was still legally married to his estranged wife. Therefore, she was still entitled to the benefit under law and the terms of the 401(k) plan. Clearly, a beneficiary audit with a financial advisor could have averted the unintentional result.

One of the simplest — yet most overlooked — estate planning tools is correctly designating beneficiaries on retirement plans, investment accounts and life insurance policies, and regularly reviewing these elections especially following changes in life's circumstances. Many investors mistakenly believe that an up-to-date will can ensure the desired disposition of their assets. Generally, however, a will does not override beneficiary designations on retirement plans and IRAs, annuity and life insurance policies, or brokerage accounts.

Beneficiary audits

- provide a reason to review beneficiary designations, options at time of death, and possible tax strategies;
- help clients and beneficiaries avoid estate and income tax problems;
- are a great way to prospect for new leads;
- can serve as a catalyst to discuss account consolidation; and

- help to ensure the client and beneficiary's planning strategies are compatible.
- Generally, a person's will will not override the beneficiary designations for annuity contracts, retirement plans and IRAs.
- Suggest an account consolidation strategy in order to provide continuity in the beneficiary planning process.
- Many individuals automatically default to listing their spouse as beneficiary for all assets. Suggest this may not be the most prudent approach from a taxation standpoint.
- Minimize the tax burden for beneficiaries by aligning higher tax rate beneficiaries with no or lower tax rate assets.
- Meet with beneficiaries pre-mortem to preview options and discuss strategies.
- Use a beneficiary audit form (see sample that follows).

Sample Beneficiary Audit Form

Client Name			Date	
Asset	**Service Provider**	**Held At**	**Asset Size**	**Beneficiary**
Will				
Trust				
Insurance Policy				
Qualified Retirement Plan				

Asset	Service Provider	Held At	Asset Size	Beneficiary
Nonqualified Deferred Compensation Plan				
Regular IRA				
Roth IRA				
SIMPLE IRA				
Annuity				
Other				

Chapter Review Questions

Feedback for the review questions can be found at the end of the chapter.

1 What is the significance of September 30th of the year following the year of the IRA owner's death?

    A It is the date by which all assets must be paid out of the IRA.
    B It is the IRA valuation date.
    C It is the beneficiary determination date.
    D It is the reporting deadline for the decedent's estate.

2 Which of the following would qualify as a designated beneficiary for distribution calculation purposes?

    A Any individual
    B Non-qualifying trust
    C Charity
    D The estate

3 If an IRA beneficiary properly executes a qualified disclaimer, what is the result?

    A The IRA is excluded from the value of the decedent's estate.
    B The beneficiary has no rights to the property.
    C When distributed from the IRA, the assets are nontaxable.
    D The beneficiary can decide who or what should receive the assets.

4 Which of the following statements regarding a nonspouse beneficiary is *TRUE*?

    A A nonspouse beneficiary of an IRA may roll over the inherited assets to his/her own IRA.
    B A nonspouse beneficiary of a 401(k) plan may roll over the inherited assets to his/her own IRA.
    C A nonspouse beneficiary of a Roth IRA may roll the inherited assets to his/her own Roth IRA.
    D A nonspouse beneficiary of a qualified plan may roll over the inherited assets to an inherited IRA.
    E All of the above.

5 What variable(s) determine the distribution options available to a beneficiary of a retirement plan or IRA.

    A When the death occurs
    B Spousal status
    C Plan document provisions
    D All of the above.

Chapter Review Questions Feedback

1 What is the significance of September 30th of the year following the year of the IRA owner's death?

    A It is the date by which all assets must be paid out of the IRA.
    B It is the IRA valuation date.
    C It is the beneficiary determination date.
    D It is the reporting deadline for the decedent's estate.

    A *Incorrect, distribution of the IRA assets following the IRA owner's death depends on many variables, including whether there are beneficiaries and distribution options based on plan agreement language.*

    B *Incorrect, the IRA valuation date in the year of death is either the date of death, or December 31.*

    C **Correct, the IRA owner's designated beneficiary is determined based on the individuals listed as of September 30 of the year following the year of death.** Chapter 10 Page 214

    D *Incorrect, the executor of the decedent's estate generally files IRS Form 706 within nine months after the date of death.*

2 Which of the following would qualify as a designated beneficiary for distribution calculation purposes?

    A Any individual
    B Non-qualifying trust
    C Charity
    D The estate

    A **Correct, only a person may be a designated beneficiary.** Chapter 10 Page 215

    B *IIncorrect, a nonperson entity, such as a non-qualifying trust, has no life expectancy; therefore, the retirement account is treated as having no designated beneficiary when determining minimum distributions.*

    C *Incorrect, a nonperson entity, such as charity, has no life expectancy; therefore, the retirement account is treated as having no designated beneficiary when determining minimum distributions.*

    D *Incorrect, a nonperson entity, such as an estate, has no life expectancy; therefore, the retirement account is treated as having no designated beneficiary when determining minimum distributions.*

3 If an IRA beneficiary properly executes a qualified disclaimer, what is the result?

    A The IRA is excluded from the value of the decedent's estate.
    B The beneficiary has no rights to the property.

C When distributed from the IRA, the assets are nontaxable.

D The beneficiary can decide who or what should receive the assets.

A *Incorrect, a person's gross estate includes the value of all property, including IRAs, in which he/she had an interest at the time of death.*

B **Correct, a qualified disclaimer is an irrevocable refusal to accept an interest in property.**
Chapter 10 Page 223

C *Incorrect, amounts withdrawn from an IRA are includible in the recipient's taxable income.*

D *Incorrect, as part of the qualified disclaimer, the disclaimed interest shall pass without direction on the part of the disclaimant to the remaining beneficiaries.*

4 Which of the following statements regarding a nonspouse beneficiary is *TRUE*?

A A nonspouse beneficiary of an IRA may roll over the inherited assets to his/her own IRA.

B A nonspouse beneficiary of a 401(k) plan may roll over the inherited assets to his/her own IRA.

C A nonspouse beneficiary of a Roth IRA may roll the inherited assets to his/her own Roth IRA.

D A nonspouse beneficiary of a qualified plan may roll over the inherited assets to an inherited IRA.

E All of the above.

A *Incorrect, a nonspouse beneficiary cannot roll amounts into or out of the inherited IRA. He/she could make a trustee-to-trustee transfer as long as the IRA into which amounts are being moved is set up and maintained in the name of the deceased IRA owner for the benefit of the nonspouse beneficiary.*

B *Incorrect, a nonspouse beneficiary may roll over the inherited assets to an inherited IRA.*

C *Incorrect, a nonspouse beneficiary cannot roll amounts into or out of the inherited Roth IRA. He/she could make a trustee-to-trustee transfer as long as the Roth IRA into which amounts are being moved is set up and maintained in the name of the deceased IRA owner for the benefit of the nonspouse beneficiary.*

D **Correct, nonspouse beneficiaries may directly roll over amounts from decedents' qualified plans a beneficiary or inherited IRA.** Chapter 10 Page 221

E *Incorrect, only item D. is accurate.*

5 What variable(s) determine the distribution options available to a beneficiary of a retirement plan or IRA.

A When the death occurs

B Spousal status

C Plan document provisions

D All of the above.

A *Incorrect, in addition to when the death occurs (i.e., whether on or after the required beginning date (RBD), or before), spousal status and the options outlined in the plan document affect the available options.*

B *Incorrect, in addition to spousal status, when the death occurs and the options outlined in the plan document affect the available options.*

C *Incorrect, in addition to the plan document provisions, when the death occurs and spousal status also affect the available options.*

D **Correct, when determining beneficiary distribution options, it is important to consider when the death occurred, whether the individual is a spouse or not, and what options are detailed in the plan document.** Chapter 10 Page 221

CHAPTER 11

Retirement Income and Taxation Issues

Chapter Goal

Upon completion of this chapter the reader will be better able to assess, recommend, and implement retirement income and taxation planning strategies.

Learning Objectives

✓ Associate the appropriate federal tax treatment with the type of retirement income.

✓ Select the appropriate IRS forms and procedures for purposes of reporting federal income, estate and gift taxes.

✓ Apply federal income tax withholding rules to retirement plan distributions.

✓ Differentiate the tax implications between Traditional IRAs and Roth IRAs.

✓ Distinguish key characteristics between fixed and variable annuity products.

Overview of Retirement Distributions and Their Taxation

Distributions from retirement plans and IRAs are generally fully taxable as ordinary income for tax purposes. However, there are a few exceptions, such as cases where a retirement plan or IRA contains a cost basis, or where a distribution from a qualified retirement plan is eligible for one of several special tax treatments. Therefore, in most cases, if a person takes a distribution in a year that he or she is in a high tax bracket, the individual will pay more taxes on the distribution than if he or she had taken the distribution in a year a lower tax bracket applied.

Planning retirement distributions in order to minimize income taxation and penalties is a basic component of good distribution planning. However, in order to properly accomplish this goal, one must understand which types of retirement assets are taxable, which are partially taxable, and which are not taxable at all. Further, in cases where a distribution is taxable, one must know whether it is taxable as ordinary income or if it is eligible for one of several special tax treatments available to certain distributions from qualified retirement plans.

Furthermore, in addition to most distributions being subject to income taxes, some distributions may also be subject to penalty taxes. Knowing when these penalties apply and how to avoid them is an important part of being able to help clients harvest their retirement wealth efficiently.

The following table summarizes the various types of retirement income and the taxability of each type.

Type of Income	Taxability
Liquidation of investment basis	Tax free
Roth IRA	Qualified distributions are tax free; other distributions may be taxable and subject to penalty depending on ordering rules
Social Security	Potentially taxable as ordinary income depending on income level
Qualified dividend income	Up to 20% tax rate
Long-term capital gains	Up to 20% tax rate
Pension income	Taxed as ordinary income, plus 10% penalty for early withdrawal
Traditional IRA and 401(k) distributions	Taxed as ordinary income, except for after-tax amounts, plus 10% penalty for early withdrawal

Taxation of Traditional IRA Distributions

Traditional IRA owners may take distributions from their IRAs at any time. Distributions from traditional IRAs are taxable as ordinary income to the recipient, except to the extent the distributions represent a return of nondeductible contributions. If an IRA owner made only deductible contributions to an IRA, when distributions are taken, the individual would treat the entire amount of the distribution as ordinary income on his or her income tax return. However, when an IRA owner makes nondeductible contributions to a traditional IRA, he or she creates a cost basis in the arrangement. The traditional IRA distribution rules require that a portion of each distribution be allocated between nondeductible (cost basis) contributions, and deductible contributions and earnings to determine the amount subject to taxation.

If the IRA owner has made nondeductible contributions to an IRA, he or she must file IRS Form 8606, Nondeductible IRA, with his or her income tax return. The IRA owner will also use Form 8606 for the year a distribution is taken. Publication 590, Individual Retirement Arrangements (IRAs), contains a worksheet that IRA owners may use to help calculate the taxable amount of their IRA distributions.

Formula for Determining Taxation of IRA Distributions

To determine the taxability of IRA distributions, IRA owners use the following formula (Notice 87-16 and Announcement 86-121).

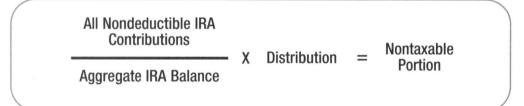

$$\frac{\text{All Nondeductible IRA Contributions}}{\text{Aggregate IRA Balance}} \times \text{Distribution} = \text{Nontaxable Portion}$$

The fraction's numerator is the total amount of the individual's nondeductible contributions to all traditional IRAs (reduced by amounts that were previously recovered), and the denominator is the aggregate value of all of the individual's traditional IRAs (determined as of the end of the calendar year and including current year distributions).

EXAMPLE:

Sam owns two traditional IRAs. He made all his deductible contributions to IRA #1, and all his nondeductible contributions to IRA #2. Sam takes a distribution from IRA #2 and (wrongly) assumes that he will not be taxed on the amount because it is a return of his nondeductible contributions. Sam's financial professional informs him of the IRA distribution rules that require him to apply the pro rata taxation formula to his distribution to determine the taxable and nontaxable portion.

Sam's nondeductible IRA contributions	$4,000
Sam's aggregate IRA balance	$20,000
Sam's distribution amount	$2,000

$$\frac{\$4,000}{\$20,000} \times 2,000 = \$400$$

After applying the formula, Sam and his financial professional determine that $1,600 of his $2,000 distribution is taxable as ordinary income and only $400 is nontaxable.

Taxation of Roth IRA Distributions

Roth IRA owners may take distributions from their Roth IRAs at any time. "Qualified distributions" (as defined later) from Roth IRAs are tax and penalty free (IRC Sec. 408A(d)(2)). The taxability of nonqualified Roth IRA distributions depends on the distribution ordering rules of Treas. Reg. 1.408A-6. Many Roth IRA owners are surprised to learn that many nonqualified Roth IRA distributions are also tax and penalty free.

Roth IRA Qualified Distribution

For a distribution from a Roth IRA to be considered qualified and, therefore, free from tax and penalty, it must satisfy the following two requirements. The Roth IRA owner must meet both requirements.

1 The distribution must occur after a five-year period that begins with the first year during which the Roth IRA owner makes a contribution or, if earlier, a conversion.

2 The distribution occurs after the Roth IRA owner experiences one of the following events:

- attainment of age 59½; or
- disability;

- first-time home purchase ($10,000 lifetime limit); or
- death.

Roth IRA Distribution Ordering Rules

When Roth IRA assets are distributed, the IRS views them as coming out in the following order.

1 Regular contributions

2 Conversions on a first-in-first-out basis, taxable portion first, followed by nontaxable portion

3 Repeat 2 for each conversion

4 Earnings

The following chart summarizes the tax and/or penalty consequences for a Roth IRA distribution based on the distribution ordering rules. The chart identifies qualified distributions and nonqualified distributions with or without a penalty exception under IRC Sec. 72(t).

Ordering Rules	Qualified Distribution	Nonqualified Distribution	
		Client Has a Penalty Exception	Client Does Not Have a Penalty Exception
1 Contributory Dollars	No tax; No penalty	No tax; No penalty	No tax; No penalty
2 Taxable Conversion Dollars (Client paid taxes at the time of the conversion)	No tax; No penalty	No tax; No penalty	No tax; Subject to penalty if within 5 years of the conversion*
3 Nontaxable Conversion Dollars	No tax; No penalty	No tax; No penalty	No tax; No penalty
4 Earnings	No tax; No penalty	Subject to tax; No penalty	Subject to tax; Subject to penalty

*Roth IRA conversions have their own "five-year clocks," based on the year of conversion. If a Roth IRA owner takes a distribution of conversion dollars within five years of the conversion, the Roth IRA holder could be subject to a penalty.

Taxation of Retirement Plan Distributions

Generally, distributions from retirement plans, such as 401(k) plans, are taxable as ordinary income when distributed. But when contributions to retirement plans are made on an after-tax basis, meaning, they are made with dollars that have already been taxed when they are contributed, they create a cost basis in the retirement plan, and will not be taxed when they are distributed.

Sources of cost basis within a qualified plan include the following.

1 After-tax contributions (including Roth contributions)
2 PS-58 costs (premiums paid for current insurance protection that are taxable to participants when they are paid)
3 Loan repayments after a default

Taxation

Most retirement plan distributions will be either fully taxable or partially taxable when distributed. Each of these two scenarios is discussed later in this section.

Changes Under PPA-06

As a result of the Pension Protection Act of 2006 (PPA-06), retired public safety employees may take tax-free distribution of up to $3,000 from qualified plans, 403(b) or 457 plans to purchase health or long-term care insurance (effective 2007).

Taxpayers age 70½ and older may make a "qualified charitable distribution" from an IRA and exclude up to $100,000 dollars of the amount from taxable income if it is paid directly to a charitable organization through 2013 as a result of the American Taxpayer Relief Act of 2012.

Fully Taxable Distributions

Generally, if a retirement plan participant takes a distribution that has no cost basis, he or she must include the entire amount of the distribution in ordinary income for the year the distribution is made. In this case, the higher a person's marginal tax rate in the year he or she takes a retirement distribution, the more the individual will pay in taxes as a result of the distribution.

Partially Taxable Distributions

If a retirement plan participant takes a distribution from a plan that contains a cost basis, he or she will not include the entire amount in income. The distribution recipient will have to apply a formula to determine what portion of the distribution is the return of cost basis and excludable from income. The formula the plan participant will use depends upon whether the distribution is a periodic or nonperiodic payment. Each is discussed next.

Periodic Payments

Periodic payments are amounts paid at regular intervals (such as weekly, monthly, or yearly) for a period of time greater than one year (such as for 15 years or for life). These payments are also known as annuity payments. To determine the taxability of a periodic payment, a plan participant may use the "Simplified Method" or the "General Rule." Please see IRS Publication 575 for more details.

Under the Simplified Method, a plan participant determines the amount of each payment that will be excluded from taxation by taking the total cost basis and dividing it by the anticipated number of annuity payments. The anticipated number of annuity payments is based upon life expectancy or the terms of the contract. IRS Publication 575, Pension and Annuity Income, contains a worksheet that participants may use to calculate the taxable portion of their periodic payments.

Qualified plan and 403(b) plan participants who began receiving periodic payments on or after November 19, 1996, must use the Simplified Method to determine taxability. Special rules applied to those participants who were required to begin distributions after July 1, 1986, and before November 19, 1996. Typically, they could use either the General Rule or Simplified Method. Prior to July 2, 1986, the General Rule applied in most cases.

For annuity payments that begin after 1986, the amount excluded from taxation may not exceed the actual cost basis in the plan. In cases where an annuitant dies before recovering the entire tax basis, the unrecovered basis at the death of the last annuitant may be recovered as a miscellaneous itemized deduction on the final return of the last annuitant to die and is not subject to the two percent of adjusted gross income limit.

EXAMPLE:

Joe has $10,000 of cost basis in his qualified retirement plan. He intends to take annuity payments each month for 15 years. The amount of each payment that will be excluded from taxation will be $10,000/180 = $55.56. If Joe is taking a life annuity, and lives longer than the 15 years that is anticipated, he will no longer be able to exclude $55.56 from taxation after 15 years has elapsed; rather, the entire amount of each payment will become taxable at that time.

For a life annuity, the number of months used to determine the amount of cost basis that can be excluded from each payment is determined by dividing the cost basis by the life expectancy of the annuitants. For term annuity payments, the cost basis is divided by the total number of payments that will be made under the contract.

Nonperiodic Payments

Nonperiodic payments include all distributions other than annuity-type payments and corrective distributions. The taxable amount of a nonperiodic distribution depends on whether it is made before the "annuity starting date," or on or after the annuity starting date. The annuity starting date is either the first day of the first period for which a plan participant receives an annuity payment under the contract or the date on which the obligation under the contract becomes fixed, whichever is later.

The amount of basis that may be excluded from income when a distribution is in the form of a nonperiodic payment rather than an annuity payment is determined before each distribution, and may vary from one distribution to the next depending on several factors including whether the nonperiodic payment is taken before or on or after the annuity starting date, in the case of distributions taken on or after the annuity starting date, whether the distribution reduces the amount of future annuity payouts, and if it does, how much cost basis has been distributed before the particular nonperiodic distribution is taken.

Nonperiodic Payments Taken On or After the Annuity Starting Date: There are four different scenarios possible when a nonperiodic payment is taken on or after the annuity starting date. The first case involves a distribution that does not reduce subsequent annuity payments, such as in the case of a cost-of-living increase that is not considered an annuity payment. This type of nonperiodic payment will be fully taxable in the year the participant receives it.

Nonperiodic Payments That Reduce Already Established Periodic Payments: It is also possible to receive a nonperiodic payment after the annuity starting date that will reduce annuity payments after they have already begun. In this second case, a portion of the nonperiodic payment may be excluded from income. The following equation is used to determine what portion of the nonperiodic payment will be excluded from income.

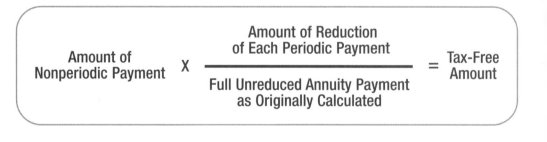

$$\text{Amount of Nonperiodic Payment} \times \frac{\text{Amount of Reduction of Each Periodic Payment}}{\text{Full Unreduced Annuity Payment as Originally Calculated}} = \text{Tax-Free Amount}$$

Nonperiodic Payment Made at Time Annuity Payments Start: If annuity payments have not yet commenced, the taxation of a nonperiodic payment taken immediately before they commence should be determined using the Simplified Method as described in the section on periodic payments.

Distribution In Full Discharge of Contract After Annuity Payments Have Started: The amount of the distribution that should be included in income due to a refund, surrender, redemption, or maturity of a contract, is the amount of the distribution that exceeds the remaining cost in the contract after accounting for all previous amounts that have been excluded from income.

Distributions Taken Before the Annuity Starting Date: For nonperiodic payments taken before the annuity starting date, it is very important that the amount that may be excluded from income be calculated at the time of each distribution, because the amount excluded from each payment is likely to vary with each distribution. The formula to calculate the amount that may be excluded from a particular distribution is as follows. Note that separately tracked, pre-1987 employee contributions may be recovered tax free, in most cases, without the need to apply the following formula.

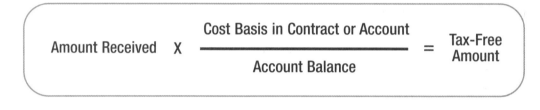

$$\text{Amount Received} \times \frac{\text{Cost Basis in Contract or Account}}{\text{Account Balance}} = \text{Tax-Free Amount}$$

Reporting

Payers who process distributions from IRAs, IRA-based employer plans, qualified retirement plans, 403(b) plans and governmental 457(b) plans report distributions to the IRS and the distribution recipient using IRS Form 1099-R, Distributions From Pensions, Annuities, Retirement or Profit-Sharing Plans, IRAs, Insurance Contracts, etc.

Payers use Form W-2, Wage and Tax Statement, to report distributions from non-qualified plans under IRC Sec. 409A, and nongovernmental 457(b) plans. However, payers of distributions to beneficiaries of these plans report the payments on Form 1099-R.

Recipients of retirement plan distributions generally report them on the applicable version of IRS Form 1040. For example, IRA distributions are reported on lines 15a and 15b of IRS Form 1040, U.S. Individual Tax Return, while retirement plan and annuity distributions are reported on lines 16a and 16b. Taxpayers may need to file additional reporting forms (e.g., Form 4972, Tax on Lump Sum Distributions, Form 8606, Nondeductible IRAs, etc.) along with their Forms 1040 when they take certain types of IRA or retirement plan distributions.

Income Tax

The following tables, reflect the 2014 federal income tax rates based on filing status pursuant to Revenue Procedure 2013-35.

Single

If taxable income is over...	But not over...	The tax is:
$0	$9,075	10% of the amount over $0
$9,075	$36,900	$907.50 plus 15% of the amount over $9,075
$36,900	$89,350	$5,081.25 plus 25% of the amount over $36,900
$89,350	$186,350	$18,193.75 plus 28% of the amount over $89,350
$186,350	$405,100	$45,353.75 plus 33% of the amount over $186,350
$405,100	$406,750	$117,541.25 plus 35% of the amount over $405,100
$406,750	no limit	$118,118.75 plus 39.6% of the amount over $406,750

Married Filing Jointly or Qualifying Widow(er)

If taxable income is over...	But not over...	The tax is:
$0	$18,150	10% of the amount over $0
$18,150	$73,800	$1,815 plus 15% of the amount over $18,150
$73,800	$148,850	$10,162.50 plus 25% of the amount over $73,800
$148,850	$226,850	$28,925 plus 28% of the amount over $148,850
$226,850	$405,100	$50,765 plus 33% of the amount over $226,850
$405,100	$457,600	$109,587.50 plus 35% of the amount over $405,100
$457,600	no limit	$127,962.50 plus 39.6% of the amount over $457,600

Married Filing Separately

If taxable income is over...	But not over...	The tax is:
$0	$9,075	10% of the amount over $0
$9,075	$36,900	$907.50 plus 15% of the amount over $9,075
$36,900	$74,425	$5,081.25 plus 25% of the amount over $36,900
$74,425	$113,425	$14,462.50 plus 28% of the amount over $74,425
$113,425	$202,550	$25,382.50 plus 33% of the amount over $113,425
$202,550	$228,800	$54,793.75 plus 35% of the amount over $202,550
$228,800	no limit	$63,981.25 plus 39.6% of the amount over $228,800

Head of Household

If taxable income is over...	But not over...	The tax is:
$0	$12,950	10% of the amount over $0
$12,950	$49,400	$1,295 plus 15% of the amount over $12,950
$49,400	$127,550	$6,762.50 plus 25% of the amount over $49,400
$127,550	$206,600	$26,300 plus 28% of the amount over $127,550
$206,600	$405,100	$48,434 plus 33% of the amount over $206,600
$405,100	$432,200	$113,939 plus 35% of the amount over $405,100
$432,200	no limit	$123,424 plus 39.6% of the amount over $432,200

Federal Income Tax Withholding on Distributions

Federal income tax withholding requirements with respect to a distribution depend upon whether the distribution is an eligible rollover distribution. For purposes of withholding, distributions from any IRA are not eligible rollover distributions.

Eligible Rollover Distribution From Retirement Plans

If an eligible rollover distribution is paid directly to an eligible retirement plan in a direct rollover, federal income tax withholding does not apply. However, if any part of an eligible rollover distribution is not directly rolled over to an eligible plan, the payer must withhold 20 percent of the portion that is paid to the recipient and includible in gross income. The distribution recipient cannot waive the 20 percent withholding. However, he or she may ask to have additional amounts withheld by completing Form W-4P, Withholding Certificate for Pension or Annuity Payments. The mandatory 20 percent withholding rules apply to qualified plans, 403(b) plans, and governmental 457(b) plans.

Employer securities and plan loan offset amounts that are part of an eligible rollover distribution must be included in the amount used to determine the mandatory 20 percent withholding. However, the actual amount to be withheld cannot be more than the sum of the cash and the fair market value of property (excluding employer securities and plan loan offset amounts). For example, if the only part of an eligible rollover distribution that is not a direct rollover is employer securities or a plan loan offset amount, the payer does withhold. However, any cash that is paid in the distribution must be used to satisfy the withholding on the employer securities or plan loan offset amount.

Any net unrealized appreciation (NUA) in qualifying employer securities distributed as part of a lump sum distribution that is excludable from gross income under the special tax rules for NUA is not included in the amount of any eligible rollover distribution that is subject to 20 percent withholding.

Payers are not required to withhold 20 percent of an eligible rollover distribution that, when aggregated with other eligible rollover distributions made to one person during the year, is less than $200.

For distributions that are not eligible for rollover, payers withhold depending on whether the distribution is a periodic or nonperiodic payment, as explained in the following paragraphs.

IRAs

The 20 percent mandatory withholding rule for eligible rollover distributions does not apply to distributions from any IRA, but withholding does apply to IRAs under the rules for periodic and nonperiodic payments.

For withholding purposes, payers must treat the entire amount of an IRA distribution as taxable (except for the distribution of excess contributions). Generally, Roth IRA distributions are not subject to withholding except on the earnings portion of excess contributions distributed under section 408(d)(4).

An IRA recharacterization is not subject to income tax withholding.

Periodic payments

For periodic payments, payers must withhold on the taxable portion of the distribution as though the periodic payments were wages, based on the recipient's Form W-4P. The recipient may request additional withholding on Form W-4P or waive withholding altogether. If a recipient does not submit a Form W-4P, payers must withhold by treating the recipient as married with three withholding allowances. (See Circular E, Employer's Tax Guide (Pub. 15), for wage withholding tables.)

Nonperiodic Payments

Payers must withhold 10 percent of the taxable part of a nonperiodic distribution. The recipient may request additional withholding on Form W-4P, or claim exemption from withholding.

Failure to Provide TIN

For periodic payments and nonperiodic distributions, if a distribution recipient fails to furnish his or her correct taxpayer identification number (TIN), or if the IRS notifies the payer before any distribution that the TIN furnished is incorrect, a recipient cannot claim exemption from withholding. For periodic payments, payers must withhold as if the recipient was single, and claiming no withholding allowances. For nonperiodic payments, the payer must withhold 10 percent. Note that backup withholding does not apply to IRA distributions.

Estate and Gift Taxes

Up to this point, this text has focused mainly on income tax issues related to IRA and retirement plan distributions. However, it is important to realize that estate and gift taxes may apply to retirement plan distributions in certain cases. For example, if a client takes a distribution from his or her IRA and gives it to someone, not only will that distribution be subject to income tax, it may also be subject to a federal gift tax. In addition, when a person dies, any money or property he or she owns may be subject to federal estate tax.

Fortunately, it is possible to make lifetime gifts up to a certain limit, and leave a certain amount to heirs, before these taxes are owed. We will discuss the basics of gift and estate taxes, as well as how much may be excluded from taxes in the following sections.

Estate Tax

Estate tax may apply to a decedent's taxable estate upon death. The taxable estate is the deceased person's gross estate less allowable deductions.

Gross Estate

The gross estate includes the value of all property in which the deceased had an interest at the time of death, including IRAs and retirement plans. The gross estate also includes the following:

- Life insurance proceeds payable to the deceased's estate or, if the policy was owned by the deceased, to the deceased's heirs

- The value of certain annuities payable to the estate or the deceased's heirs

- The value of certain property the deceased transferred within three years before death

- Trusts or other interests established by the deceased

Taxable Estate

The allowable deductions used in determining a person's taxable estate include, but are not limited to, the following. Refer to IRS Form 706, United States Estate (and Generation-Skipping Transfer) Tax Return, for complete deduction details.

- The marital deduction (generally, the value of the property that passes from the deceased's estate to his or her surviving spouse)

- Funeral expenses paid out of your estate

- Mortgages and debts owed at the time of death

- Charitable deductions

- Administration expenses of the estate

- Losses during estate administration.

Each person has a Unified Credit that he or she can use to offset gift and estate taxes. The following table shows the Unified Credit and Applicable Exclusion Amount for the calendar years in which a gift is made or a decedent dies after 2001.

After the net amount is computed, the value of lifetime taxable gifts (beginning with gifts made in 1977) is added to this number and the estate tax is computed. The estate tax is then reduced by the available Unified Credit. Presently, the amount of this credit reduces the computed tax so that only total taxable estates and lifetime gifts that exceed $5,340,000 in 2014, will potentially be subject to tax at a rate up to 40 percent. In its current form, the estate tax only affects the wealthiest two percent of all Americans.

	For Gift Tax Purposes		For Estate Tax Purposes	
Year	Unified Credit	Applicable Exclusion Amount	Unified Credit	Applicable Exclusion Amount
2002 and 2003	345,800	1,000,000	345,800	1,000,000
2004 and 2005	345,800	1,000,000	555,800	1,500,000
2006 thru 2008	345,800	1,000,000	780,800	2,000,000
2009	345,800	1,000,000	1,455,800	3,500,000
2010	330,800	1,000,000	Elect 2010 or 2011 Rules	
2011	1,730,800	5,000,000	1,730,800	5,000,000
2012	1,772,800	5,120,000	1,772,800	5,120,000
2013	2,045,800	5,250,000	2,045,800	5,250,000
2014	2,081,800	5,340,000	2,081,800	5,340,000

If estate taxes apply, the executor of the decedent's estate must file IRS Form 706. Generally, Form 706 is due nine months after the date of death. A six-month extension is available if the executor requests it prior to the due date, and the estate pays the estimated amount of tax before the due date.

Gift Tax

The gift tax applies to the transfer by gift of any property (IRC Sec. 2501, Chapter 12, Subtitle B). A person makes a gift if he or she gives property (including money), or the use of or income from property, without expecting to receive something of at least equal value in return. If a person sells something at less than its full value or if he or she makes an interest-free or reduced-interest loan, he or she may be making a gift.

The general rule is that any gift is a taxable gift. However, there are many exceptions to this rule. Generally, the following gifts are not taxable gifts.

- Gifts that are not more than the annual exclusion for the calendar year
- Tuition or medical expenses paid directly to a medical or educational institution for someone
- Gifts to a spouse
- Gifts to a political organization for its use
- Gifts to charities

Annual Exclusion

A separate annual exclusion applies to each person to whom a gifter makes a gift. The annual exclusion is $14,000 for 2014. Therefore, generally an individual can give up to the applicable dollar limit each to any number of people, and none of the gifts will be taxable. For example, each spouse in a married couple can separately give up to $14,000 to the same person in 2014 without making a taxable gift.

Gift Splitting for Married Couples

Married couples may also take advantage of gift splitting.

In 2014, gift splitting allows married couples to give up to $28,000 to a person without making a taxable gift. If a couple splits a gift, both the husband and wife must file a gift tax return to show that they agree to use gift splitting.

EXAMPLE:

Harold and his wife, Helen, agree to split the gifts that they made during 2014. Harold gives his nephew, George, $21,000, and Helen gives her niece, Gina, $18,000. Although each gift is more than the annual exclusion ($14,000), by gift splitting they can make these gifts without making a taxable gift.

Harold's gift to George is treated as one-half ($10,500) from Harold and one-half ($10,500) from Helen. Helen's gift to Gina is also treated as one-half ($9,000) from Helen and one-half ($9,000) from Harold. In each case, because one-half of the split gift is not more than the annual exclusion, it is not a taxable gift. However, each of them must file a gift tax return.

EXAMPLE 1

In 2014, Andy gives his niece a cash gift of $8,000. It is his only gift to her this year. The gift is not a taxable gift because it is not more than the $14,000 annual exclusion. Andy does not need to file Form 709.

EXAMPLE 2

Andy pays $15,000 of college tuition for Elizabeth directly to the college. Because the payment qualifies for the educational exclusion, the gift is not a taxable gift, and Andy does not need to file Form 709.

EXAMPLE 3

In 2014, Andy gives $25,000 to his 25-year-old son. The first $14,000 of his gift is not subject to the gift tax because of the annual exclusion. The remaining $11,000 is a taxable gift, but because Andy will use $11,000 of his Unified Credit, he will not have to pay gift tax. However, even though no gift tax is due, Andy still will have to file Form 709.

Applying the Unified Credit to Gift Tax

The Unified Credit is an amount that an individual can use to offset both estate tax and gift tax liabilities. The Unified Credit against taxable gifts is $2,081,800 for 2014. Any amount of the Unified Credit used to offset gift tax liabilities during life will reduce the amount available for future gift taxes, AND the amount available to offset estate tax liability at death.

When a gift tax is incurred, the taxpayer (donor) must use his or her Unified Credit to offset any gift tax owed (meaning the individual cannot pay the gift tax out of pocket).

Step 1: Determine which gifts are taxable.
Step 2: Figure the amount of gift tax on the total taxable gifts, using the IRS' graduated tax rate tables

For gifts made in 2014 the applicable exclusion amount is $5,340,000 with a top estate and gift tax rate of 40 percent.

The following table shows the Unified Credit and applicable exclusion amount for the calendar years in which a gift is made or a decedent dies after 2001.

Year	For Gift Tax Purposes		For Estate Tax Purposes	
	Unified Credit	Applicable Exclusion Amount	Unified Credit	Applicable Exclusion Amount
2002 and 2003	345,800	1,000,000	345,800	1,000,000
2004 and 2005	345,800	1,000,000	555,800	1,500,000
2006 thru 2008	345,800	1,000,000	780,800	2,000,000
2009	345,800	1,000,000	1,455,800	3,500,000
2010	330,800	1,000,000	NA	NA
2011	1,730,800	5,000,000	1,730,800	5,000,000
2012	1,772,800	5,120,000	1,772,800	5,120,000
2013	2,045,800	5,250,000	2,045,800	5,250,000
2014	2,081,800	5,340,000	2,081,800	5,340,000

Reporting

The Form 709, gift tax returns are filed annually. It is a separate return from a taxpayer's Form 1040.

Generally, a taxpayer subject to gift tax, or a split gifting must file Form 709 no earlier than January 1 of the year following the year of the gift, but not later than the tax return deadline (e.g., for a 2014 gift, no earlier than January 1, 2015 and no later than April 15, 2015.)

If the donor died during the year, the executor must file the donor's Form 709 not later than the earlier of

- the due date (with extensions) for filing the donor's estate tax return, or
- the tax filing deadline, including extensions granted for filing the donor's gift tax return.

Filing a Gift Tax Return

Generally, a person must file a gift tax return using Form 709 if any of the following apply.

- The person gave gifts to at least one person (other than his or her spouse) that are more than the annual exclusion for the year.
- A person and his or her spouse are splitting a gift.
- A person gave someone (other than his or her spouse) a gift of a future interest that he or she cannot actually possess, enjoy, or receive income from until some time in the future.
- A person gave his or her spouse an interest in property that will be ended by some future event.
- A person need not file a gift tax return to report gifts to (or for the use of) political organizations and gifts made by paying someone's tuition or medical expenses directly. A person is also not required to report on Form 709 deductible gifts made to charities as long as the entire interest in the property is gifted. A partial gift requires the filing of Form 709.

See Publication 950, Introduction to Estate and Gift Tax for more information. http://www.irs.gov/pub/irs-pdf/p950.pdf

Penalty Taxes

Generally, IRA owners or plan participants who receive plan distributions before reaching age 59½, will pay a 10 percent early distribution penalty on the amount taken, in addition to any taxes owed on the amount (IRC Sec. 72).

Early Distribution Penalty Exceptions

Fortunately, there are some exceptions to the early distribution penalty as outlined next (IRC Sec. 72(t)(2)).

- Death
- Disability
- IRS Levy on the plan
- Qualifying medical expenses
- Substantially equal periodic payments (qualified plan participants must have separated from service) for life or life expectancy
- Health insurance for certain unemployed individuals (IRA only)
- First-time home purchase expenses (IRA only, $10,000 lifetime limit)
- Higher education expenses of qualified individuals (IRA only)
- Separation from service in the year he or she attains age 55 or thereafter (qualified plan only)
- Employee Stock Ownership Plan (ESOP) dividends (qualified plan only)
- Qualified domestic relations order (QDRO) payments (qualified plan only)

If a participant separates from service during the calendar year he or she turns age 55 or thereafter, any plan distributions taken after the participant attains age 55 and separates from service are not subject to the 10 percent early distribution penalty tax. For example, Sarah leaves employment in May and turns age 55 in July. Because she is turning age 55 in the year of separation, all distributions made to her in July and thereafter will not be subject to penalty.

EXAMPLE

At age 35, Michael withdraws his entire plan balance of $100,000, without talking with his financial professional first (never a good idea!). When he files his income taxes for the year, Michael is shocked to learn that, by the time he pays an early distribution penalty on the distribution ($10,000), federal taxes at 25% ($25,000) and state and local taxes at 4% ($4,000), his $100,000 has shrunk to $61,000!

Changes Under PPA-06

As a result of the Pension Protection Act of 2006 (PPA-06), two new exceptions to the 10 percent early distribution penalty tax were created. The penalty is waived for

- qualifying reservists who have more than 179 days of active duty (effective for distributions after September 11, 2001); and
- public safety employees who separate from service after attaining age 50,

who are receiving distributions from governmental defined benefit plans (effective for distributions after August 17, 2006.

Lump Sum Distributions

Certain plan participants who receive "lump-sum" distributions, may be eligible for special tax treatments, such as capital gains or 10-year income averaging. Before discussing these special tax treatments, it is important to define the term lump-sum distribution.

A lump-sum distribution is the payment in one tax year of a plan participant's entire balance from all of the employer's qualified plans of one kind (e.g., pension, profit-sharing, or stock bonus plans).

The distribution must be taken on account of one of the following reasons.

- Because of the participant's death
- After the participant attains age 59½
- Because of the participant's separation of service from the employer (can not be used by self-employed individuals)
- Because the participant has become disabled (only applies to self-employed individuals)
- Made from a qualified pension, profit sharing or stock bonus plan

Distributions That Are Not Lump Sum Distributions

Distributions that fall into the following categories are not considered lump sum distributions for the purpose of eligibility for special tax treatment.

- Distributions that are partially rolled over to another plan or an IRA
- Any distribution if the plan participant elected to use either five- or 10-year income averaging at any time after 1986
- Distributions containing U.S. Retirement Plan Bonds
- Distributions made during the first five years a participant was in a plan, except in the case of the death of the participant
- Distributions that contains the current actuarial value of an annuity contract.
- Distributions to a 5% owner that are subject to penalties under

IRC Sec. 72(m)(5)(A)

- Distributions from an IRA

- Distributions from a tax-sheltered annuity

- Distributions including redemption proceeds of bonds rolled over tax free to a qualified pension plan from a qualified bond purchase plan

- A distribution from a qualified plan if the participant or his or her surviving spouse previously received an eligible rollover distribution from the same plan (or another plan of the employer that must be combined with that plan for the lump-sum distribution rules) and the previous distribution was rolled over tax free to another qualified plan or an IRA

- Distributions from a qualified plan that after 2001 has received a rollover from an IRA (other than a conduit IRA), a governmental 457 plan, or a tax-sheltered annuity

- Corrective distributions

- Distributions of lump-sum credits or payments from the Federal Civil Service Retirement System

Please see IRS Form 4972 for more details.

If an individual is eligible for special tax treatment on a lump sum distribution, it is important to realize that he or she has several options.

1 Report the part of the distribution from participation in the plan before 1974 as a capital gain, and the part from participation after 1973 as ordinary income.

2 Report the part of the distribution from participation before 1974 as a capital gain, and use the 10-year tax option on the part from participation after 1973.

3 If qualified, use the 10-year tax option to figure the tax on the total taxable amount.

4 Roll over the distribution.

5 Report the entire taxable amount as taxable income.

Income Averaging

A special tax option available only to plan participants (and their beneficiaries) born before January 2, 1936 who receive lump sum distributions, is the 10-year income averaging tax option. Under the 10-year income averaging option, taxpayers use a special formula to figure a separate tax on the ordinary income part of a lump-sum distribution. The plan participant pays the total tax for the year in which he or she receives the distribution. The amount due for the year of the distribution is calculated as if it had been received in equal amounts over a 10-year period.

The ordinary income part of the distribution is the amount shown in box 2a of Form 1099-R, minus the amount, if any, shown in box 3. Individuals can also treat the capital gains part of the distribution (box 3 of Form 1099-R) as ordinary income for the 10-year income averaging option if they do not choose capital gains treatment for that part.

Taxpayers complete Part III of Form 4972 to choose the 10-year tax option, and use the special tax rates shown in the instructions for Part III to figure the tax.

Capital Gains

Plan participants (or their beneficiaries) who receive lump-sum distributions from a qualified plan, where the respective plan participant was born before January 2, 1936, may be able to use capital gains tax treatment on the portion of the plan that accrued before 1974.

Capital gains tax treatment applies only to the taxable portion of a lump-sum distribution resulting from participation in the plan before 1974. The amount treated as capital gain is taxed at 20 percent. A taxpayer may elect this treatment only once for any plan participant, and only if the plan participant was born before January 2, 1936. The capital gains portion is reported on Form 1099-R, in box 3.

The taxpayer completes Form 4972 to elect the 20 percent capital gains tax treatment.

EXAMPLE

Arlo was born July 4, 1935. He spent his entire working career at The Big Fish Corporation (BFC). Arlo retired from BFC in 2006, and withdrew his entire qualified plan account balance. He received a total distribution of $175,000 ($25,000 of employee contributions plus $150,000 of employer contributions and earnings on all contributions).

The payer issued Arlo a Form 1099-R, showing the capital gain portion of the distribution (the part attributable to participation before 1974) as $10,000. Arlo elects 20% capital gain treatment for this part. Arlo enters $10,000 on Form 4972, Part II, line 6 and $2,000 ($10,000 x 20%) on Part II, line 7.

The ordinary income part of the distribution is $140,000 ($150,000 minus $10,000). Arlo elects to figure the tax on this part using the 10-year income averaging tax option. He enters $140,000 on Form 4972, Part III, line 8. Then he completes the rest of Form 4972 and includes the tax of $24,270 in the total on line 44 of his Form 1040.

Life Insurance

Some qualified plans permit participants to purchase life insurance with a portion of their individual accounts within the retirement plan. If life insurance is offered as an investment within a retirement plan, the following are some critical points to keep in mind. (Note that life insurance is not a permissible investment option for IRAs.)

Death benefits must be "incidental," meaning they must be secondary to other plan benefits.

For defined contribution plans, the amount of employer contributions and forfeitures that may be used to purchase whole or term life insurance benefits under a plan must be limited to 50 percent for whole life, and 25 percent for term policies. No percentage limit applies if the participant purchases life insurance with company contributions held in a profit sharing plan for two years or longer.

For a defined benefit plan, life insurance coverage is generally considered incidental if the amount of the insurance does not exceed 100 times the participant's projected monthly benefit.

If the plan uses deductible employer contributions to pay the insurance premiums, the participant will be taxed on the current insurance benefit. This taxable portion is referred to as the P.S. 58 cost.

Insurance premiums paid by self-employed individuals are not deductible.

A participant with a life insurance policy within a retirement plan, generally, may not roll over the policy (but he or she may swap out the policy for an equivalent amount of cash, and roll over the cash). Participants may exercise nonreportable "swap outs." In a life insurance swap out, the participant pays the plan an amount equal to the cash value of the policy in exchange for the policy itself. This transaction allows the participant to distribute the full value of his or her plan balance (including the cash value of the policy), and complete a rollover, while allowing the participant to retain the life insurance policy outside of the plan.

Anne has a life insurance contract in her 401(k) plan with a face value of $150,000, and a cash value of $25,000. She elects to swap out the policy and gives the administrator a check for $25,000. In return, the administrator reregisters the insurance policy in Anne's name (rather than in the plan's name), and distributes the contract to her. There is no taxable event and Anne may take a distribution (once she has a triggering event) and roll over the entire amount received.

Income in Respect of a Decedent

Traditional IRAs and retirement plans allow an individual to defer taxation on contributions, as well as any earnings on these contributions, until they are distributed. It is common that a decedent will have an undistributed, and therefore, untaxed portion remaining in his or her IRA or retirement plan at death. Whatever taxable amount is left in a decedent's account on the date of death is treated as "income in respect of a decedent" when it is distributed.

To determine what the "income in respect of a decedent" is for a distribution from a retirement account, one must determine the decedent's balance at the time of death, including unrealized appreciation and income accrued to date of death and subtract any basis (nondeductible contributions). Amounts distributed that are more than the decedent's entire IRA balance (includes taxable and nontaxable amounts) at the time of death are the income of the beneficiary. If the beneficiary of the retirement account is a surviving spouse who properly rolls over the amount to an account in his or her name, the distribution will not be currently taxable.

Effective in 2007, the beneficiary rules are modified to allow nonspouse beneficiaries to directly roll over amounts from decedents' qualified plans into beneficiary IRAs. Subsequent distributions from the beneficiary IRAs are made based on the IRA beneficiary distribution rules. Refer to Chapter 10, Beneficiary Options and Issues, for complete details.

Because "income in respect of a decedent" does not include basis, qualified Roth distributions are not considered income in respect of a decedent. However, if a Roth distribution is nonqualified, a portion of the distribution may be treated as income in respect of a decedent if it includes earnings.

Income in respect of a decedent must be included in the income of the recipient, whether that recipient is the decedent's estate, or a named beneficiary.

If a client has to include income in respect of a decedent in his or her gross income and an estate tax return was filed for the decedent, he or she may be able to claim a deduction for the estate tax paid on that income. For more information on the taxation of inherited IRAs, see Publication 559, Survivors, Executors, and Administrators.

Annuities

Annuities are popular, and sometimes controversial, investment vehicles for retirement planning. Historically, the annuity has been the primary tool used to provide retirement income to retirees. Modern annuity products have evolved to incorporate many additional features for investors and their beneficiaries. The following paragraphs will explore the original role of annuities, key annuity concepts, tax ramifications of annuities, and the evolving role annuities are playing in retirement income accumulation and income planning.

Original Role of the Annuity

The annuity product began quite simply. An individual purchased an annuity contract from an insurance carrier and received a stream of income over his or her lifetime. Initially, the products were simple and used to deliver lifetime income to the annuitant. Over the years these products have evolved to provide additional income options, for example, there are joint and survivor annuity products that provide income for the lives of the annuitant and a beneficiary.

Fixed and Variable Annuities

In an effort to understand annuities, it is important to grasp several key concepts that reside at the heart of annuities; become familiar with the various annuity-related questions that investors face; and realize the potential ramifications of annuity-related decisions.

An annuity is a contract between a consumer and an insurance company, under which the individual makes a lump-sum payment or series of payments to purchase the contract. In return, the insurer agrees to make periodic payments to the contract owner beginning immediately or at some future date. Annuities typically offer taxdeferred growth of earnings and may include a death benefit that will pay a named beneficiary a guaranteed minimum amount, such as the total purchase payments.

There are generally two types of annuities—fixed and variable. In a fixed annuity, the insurance company guarantees that you will earn a minimum rate of interest during the time that your account is growing. The insurance company also guarantees that the periodic payments will be a guaranteed amount per dollar in your account. These periodic payments may last for a definite period, such as 20 years, or an indefinite period, such as your lifetime or the lifetime of you and your spouse.

In a variable annuity, by contrast, an individual can choose to invest the purchase payments in a range of different investment options, typically mutual funds. The rate of return on the purchase payments, and the amount of the periodic payments that the individual will eventually receive, will vary depending on the performance of the investment options selected.

When determining the client's suitability for a variable annuity, the client should only consider buying a variable annuity if the insurance and annuity features meet the client's individual needs. Following that analysis, the client may want to consider the added benefits and options to the contract for an additional cost. Available features may include guaranteed minimum interest rates on the contract values or a wide variety of periodic payment options. The optional features are included in extra contract language called "riders."

Optional features will vary by insurance provider; it is important to review the prospectus for details. Other considerations may include the following,

- **Principal Guarantees**—Many contracts provide a principal guarantee option, which states that at the end of "X" years the value of the contract will not be less than the amount of the principal contribution.

- **Enhanced Death Benefit**—One type of enhanced death benefit feature provides the beneficiaries with a death benefit typically equal to the greater of the purchase payments or the highest contract anniversary value prior to death.

- **Lifetime Guaranteed Withdrawal Benefit**—This option allows the individual to withdraw a certain percentage of the contract's benefit base for life, regardless of the contract value. This option provides flexibility beyond the traditional annuitization options.

- **Guaranteed Partial Withdrawal Benefit**—This option allows a base withdrawal (for example, 5 percent of the contract benefit) to be taken each year for a specified time period (for example, 20 years). The guaranteed amount is available regardless of the contract value.

- **Guaranteed Minimum Income Benefit**—This option allows the participant to annuitize the contract based on the largest of several values. Typically, this is the larger of the contract value, the highest contract anniversary value or the value of the principal contributions increased by an annualized guaranteed rate.

Any guarantees in variable annuity contracts are subject to the claims paying ability of the issuing insurance company.

A variable annuity has different types of fees and charges that should be considered prior to investment. These may include a sales charge, mortality and expense risk charges, surrender charges, and administrative fees, as well as additional charges for optional features that may be elected.

Annuity Concepts

The concept of "annuitization" is important to understand. When a contract is, annuitized, it is in effect, converted into a promise to make a series of payments for the life of the annuitant (and perhaps their beneficiary), or for a defined period of time. The key to understanding annuitization is the focus on the contract being exchanged for a promise to pay benefits. The annuitant no longer owns a contract and will no longer receive statements reflecting the contract value. They will however receive a stream of payments that the annuitant cannot outlive.

Another concept similar to annuitization is that of periodic payments. Under a periodic payment situation the contract owner elects to receive payments from the annuity contract. The contract is not surrendered. This means the contract owner may only withdraw an amount no greater than the value of the contract. For example if an annuity contract is worth $40,000 the contract owner can withdraw up to $40,000 from the contract. Once the contract value is zero the contract is closed.

Conversely the contract owner could annuitize the contract in exchange for a promise of payments from the carrier. In the previous example the contract owner annuitizes the contract in exchange for a promise from the insurance carrier to pay the contract owner $4,800 per year for as long as the individual lives.

Tax Aspects of Annuities

The increase in the value of an annuity contract is generally not subject to Federal income tax until distributions occur from the contract. This tax deferred build-up within annuity contracts has been a key factor in the sale of annuity contracts. The tax deferred buildup within the annuity contract has no significance if the contract is held by an IRA or other qualified retirement vehicle. IRAs and other qualified retirement accounts are themselves subject to special Federal rules that also allow tax deferred build with the account until the amounts are distributed. Thus a key tax benefit of annuity contracts is moot when the contract is held in an IRA or similar retirement account.

Another unique aspect of an annuity contract is the tax implications of distributions from the contract. An annuity payment is usually part taxable and part not taxable. The taxable/non-taxable portion of an annuity payment is determined based on the exclusion ratio. This ratio is based upon the premiums paid into the annuity contracts (which generally have been taxed) divided by the expected return from the annuity payment. Because the buildup within the contract is tax deferred only the buildup, or increase in value, is taxable when distributed. Thus a portion of each annuity payment is taxable, and represents the distribution of the heretofore untaxed buildup with the contract and a non-taxable portion representing the previously taxed premiums made to the contract. Once the total amount of premiums paid into the contract are recovered through the exclusion ratio, all subsequent annuity payments are fully taxable.

If the annuity contract is held within an IRA or other qualified retirement vehicle the exclusion allowance is generally not applicable because the premiums paid to the contract are pretax dollars. Thus the amounts distributed, the pretax premiums and the increase in the value of the contract, have not yet been subject to Federal income tax so the entire portion of the payment is taxable to the recipient.

Evolving Role of Annuities

The evolution of annuity products has been driven by market demographics. Beginning with the passage of ERISA in 1974 billions of dollars in retirement savings have been set aside by the baby boomers. Baby boomer asset accumulation for retirement has had an enormous impact on the overall financial services industry. The insurance industry responded to this opportunity through the creation of new annuity products that focused on the accumulation of assets rather than distribution features. Many variable annuity products were deployed that allowed the consumer to select the investment vehicles within the annuity contract. These investment options are commonly known as sub-accounts and are similar to mutual funds in many respects.

Other features have been added to variable annuity contracts to enhance their overall competitiveness. Common features include guaranteed minimum accumulation benefits on the cash value within the contract, income benefit guarantees to provide downside market protection, enhanced death benefits, and life time withdrawal benefit guarantees even if the consumer does not annuitize the contract.

Obviously annuity contracts are complex products. Many consumers have purchased annuity contracts without understanding the ramifications of the products. Issues such as fees, surrender charges and the general understanding of how the products operate have surfaced to create confusion regarding the contract.

Perhaps the most common criticism of annuity contracts the fees and expenses. In many cases annuity contracts are significantly more expensive than mutual funds.

The question of fees and expenses should be viewed in the broader context of options and features and whether the client wants or needs the relatively expensive features or options within their contract. Ultimately the question of expenses is this: is the consumer getting what he/she is paying for, and does he/she understand and need what the individual is buying?

DOL Contemplates Merits of Lifetime Income Options in Retirement Plans

On February 2, 2010, the DOL, in conjunction with the IRS and Treasury Department, issued a formal request for comments from the financial community as well as the general public on how best to ensure that workers do not run out of money during retirement. In addition to examing the role of traditional annuities as a lifetime income option, the initiative seeks to explore "alternative income approaches" such as longevity insurance and managed advisory accounts. Testimony from the Department of Labor and Department of Treasury joint hearing and public comments are posted at the following web site: http://www.dol.gov/ebsa/regs/cmt-1210-AB33.html#2. Two formal hearings have also been held: one by the DOL and IRS in September 2010 and one by the HELP committee in February 2011. As a result of the hearings and public comments, Washington has responded with the following releases in support of lifetime income options in retirement plans.

White House report: "Supporting Retirement for American Families," 02/02/12 This is a report prepared by the Executive Office of the President, Council of Economic Advisers that discusses the importance of annuity products in managing the risk of outliving one's retirement assets.

Proposed regulations (REG-115809-11): Qualified longevity annuity contracts or QLACs. Deferred annuities that begin at a later age (e.g., 80 or 85) are known as longevity annuity contracts. These regulations would allow plan participants to exclude the value of QLACs from their account balances when calculating required minimum distributions.

Proposed regulations (REG-110980-10): Partial defined benefit plan annuity distributions. The primary impact of this proposed rule change would be to make it simpler and easier for a plan to offer an optional form of benefit that is a combination of a single-sum payment and an annuity.

Revenue Rule (Rev. Rul.) 2012-3: Qualified joint and survivor annuity (QJSA) and qualified preretirement survivor annuity (QPSA) rules for deferred annuities. Its purpose is to eliminate uncertainty about how 401(k) spousal protection rules apply when employees purchase deferred annuities from their plans. It describes how the QJSA and QPSA rules apply when a deferred annuity contract is purchased under a profit sharing plan in certain specified fact situations.

Rev. Rul. 2012-4: Rollover from defined contribution to defined benefit plan to obtain additional annuity. This revenue ruling provides guidance on how a participant who receives a lump-sum payment from his or her employer's defined contribution plan may be able to roll over some or all of the amount to the employer's defined benefit plan (if one exists) in order to receive an annuity from the defined benefit plan.

And still in the pre-rule stage, the Department of Labor (DOL) is exploring "annuity equivalent" participant benefit statements and annuity selection criteria guidance. As part of this initiative, the DOL will explore whether, and how, an individual benefit statement should and could present a participant's accrued benefits in a defined contribution plan (i.e., the individual's account balance) as a lifetime income stream of payments in addition to presenting the benefits as an account balance.

The Department of Labor (DOL) has posted a Lifetime Income Calculator on its web site (dol.gov) for use by participants in defined contribution (DC) retirement plans like 401(k) plans. The calculator allows such plan participants to project what their retirement plan account balances would look like as level monthly payments for their lifetime. The DOL's release of the calculator follows on the heals of the issuance of its recent notice in which it asks the public for comments on the best ways to illustrate a participant's DC plan account balance as a lifetime income stream.

The calculator uses an annuitization approach to estimate the monthly lifetime income payments that would be generated based on both the participant's current account balance and on the projected value of the account balance at retirement. For both balances, the calculator develops two, level lifetime payments: one for the life of the participant (with no benefits to any survivors) and the second for the joint lives of the participant and the spouse with a 50% survivor's benefit for the spouse's lifetime.

The DOL commented that "showing participants their retirement plan account balances as level monthly payments for their lifetime will help them assess their retirement readiness and plan for their retirement."

Medicare Surtaxes

Two additional taxes took effect 2013 and for later years on U.S. workers as a result of the Patient Protection and Affordable Care Act (PPACA). The taxes consist of two elements: 1) the additional Medicare hospital insurance (HI) tax on high wage earners; and 2) the unearned income Medicare contribution. Each is explained in a bit more detail in subsequent paragraphs.

Additional HI tax on high wage earners
The Federal Insurance Contributions Act (FICA) imposes tax on employers based on the amount of wages paid to an employee during the year. The tax imposed is composed of two parts: (1) the old age, survivors, and disability insurance (OASDI) tax equal to 6.2 percent of covered wages up to the taxable wage base ($117,000 in 2014); and (2) the HI tax amount equal to 1.45 percent of covered wages.

PPACA increases the employee portion of the HI tax by an additional tax of 0.9 percent on wages received in excess of the threshold amount. However, unlike the general 1.45 percent HI tax on wages, this additional tax is on the combined wages of the employee and the employee's spouse, in the case of a joint return. The threshold amount is $250,000 in the case of a joint return or surviving spouse, $125,000 in the case of a married individual filing a separate return, and $200,000 in any other case.

Unearned Income Medicare Contribution

Social Security benefits and certain Medicare benefits are financed primarily by payroll taxes on covered wages. FICA imposes tax on employers based on the amount of wages paid to an employee during the year. The tax imposed is composed of two parts: 1) the OASDI tax equal to 6.2 percent of covered wages up to the taxable wage base ($117,000 in 2014); and 2) the HI tax amount equal to 1.45 percent of covered wages. In addition to the tax on employers, each employee is subject to FICA taxes equal to the amount of tax imposed on the employer. The employee level tax generally must be withheld and remitted to the Federal government by the employer.

PPACA imposes, in the case of an individual, estate, or trust, an unearned income Medicare contribution tax beginning in 2013 and for later years. In the case of an individual, the tax is the 3.8 percent of the lesser of net investment income or the excess of modified adjusted gross income (MAGI) over the threshold amount. The threshold amount is $250,000 in the case of a joint return or surviving spouse, $125,000 in the case of a married individual filing a separate return, and $200,000 in any other case. MAGI is adjusted gross income increased by the amount excluded from income as foreign earned income.

Investment Income <u>includes</u> Income from:

- Interest

- Dividends

- Nonqualifed Annuities

- Royalties

- Rents

- Gain from the Sale/Disposition of certain property (Capital Gains)
- A trade or business that is considered a passive activity (under the passive loss rules) or is trading in financial instruments or commodities/related derivatives

But does not include:

- Qualified Retirement Plan Distributions

    - IRAs, 401(k)s, pensions, etc.

- Tax-exempt Income

    - Municipal bond interest

    - Excluded gain on the sale of a principal residence

    - Life insurance death benefits, etc.

- Self Employment income that is taken into account for SECA tax purposes

- Trade or business income other than income from a trade or business described in the final bullet on the left. However, income from the investment of working capital does not fall within this exception.

Steps that may prevent one from breaking through the MAGI income threshold merit consideration as a NIIT strategy — and tax-advantaged retirement plans are great vehicles to facilitate the moves. Pretax contributions to qualified retirement plans lower MAGI upfront, and the earnings they may generate while held in the plan grow tax-deferred. Any future distributions of pretax dollars from a plan would be taxable as ordinary income, and therefore would increase MAGI, but the distributions do not count under NII. 401(k) plans not only allow for pretax contributions, but, if designed properly, could also permit after-tax contributions (either designated Roth contributions or standard after-tax contributions). Although after-tax contributions are included in MAGI, they are not counted as NII. If they grow while held in the 401(k), any gain is tax-deferred and excluded from NII. When withdrawn, only the earnings on standard after-tax contributions are considered MAGI, not the principal. And, qualified distributions of designated Roth contributions (principal and earnings) are completely tax-free, meaning they are not included in NII or MAGI.

Nonqualified Deferred Compensation Plans

The first step in understanding nonqualified deferred compensation plans is to distinguish them from qualified retirement plans. Many of us are familiar with how qualified retirement plans work from a tax standpoint. With a qualified retirement plan, if the plans meet the requirements of Internal Revenue Code Section (IRC §) 401(a), the sponsoring corporation receives a tax deduction for the year contributions are made to the plan, and taxation of the assets and earnings to participants and beneficiaries is delayed until the assets are distributed.

In contrast, nonqualified deferred compensation plans are broadly defined as any elective or nonelective plan, agreement, method, or arrangement between an employer and an employee (or service recipient and service provider) to pay compensation some time in the future for services presently rendered. Employers may deduct compensation allocated to a nonqualified deferred compensation plan when the amount is includible in the employee's income; and taxation to the participant depends on whether the plan is "funded" or "unfunded" (defined later). Future payments are generally made in cash, but not always. The "nonqualified" moniker simply means they are plans that do not meet the requirements of a plan compliant with IRC §401(a) for federal tax-favored treatment (like a 401(k) plan is intended to be). Nonqualified deferred compensation plans are, instead, governed by IRC §409A. Note IRC § 457 covers nonqualified deferred compensation plans of state and local governmental entities and tax-exempt employers. "Ineligible" plans under IRC §457(f) are subject to the requirements of IRC §409A, whereas "eligible" plans under IRC §457(b) are not.

Why Have a Nonqualified Deferred Compensation Plan?
Besides offering qualified retirement plans, employers tend to offer nonqualified plans to attract, motivate, reward, and retain key, highly performing employees and executive talent. While qualified retirement plans are appealing, they are subject to restrictions (e.g., satisfying nondiscrimination requirements, limiting employer and employee contributions, and limiting the amount of compensation that may be considered for plan purposes), none of which apply in the nonqualified deferred compensation world. Nonqualified deferred compensation plans can provide a method of tax deferral above and beyond what can be provided through qualified retirement plans. A nonqualified

deferred compensation plan provides either tax deferral of the employee's compensation (salary and bonus) or deferral of the investment return, or both.

For employees, these plans can be used in conjunction with other forms of compensation, such as stock compensation plans to manage current taxation and to place more assets under tax deferred growth.

IRC §409A

The American Jobs Creation Act of 2004 added § 409A to the Internal Revenue Code. IRC § 409A provides new and comprehensive rules governing nonqualified deferred compensation arrangements. More specifically, IRC § 409A provides that, unless certain requirements are satisfied, all amounts deferred under a nonqualified deferred compensation plan for all taxable years are currently includible in gross income (to the extent not subject to a substantial risk of forfeiture and not previously included in gross income). IRC § 409A, generally, took effect with respect to amounts deferred in taxable years beginning after December 31, 2004.

The primary requirements of IRC Sec. 409A relate to 1) when salary deferral elections are made; 2) when compensation payments are made; and 3) how compensation payments are made.

First, employees who participate must make their elections to defer compensation, which are irrevocable, in the year *before* any services are performed to which the compensation relates (with some exceptions for new plan participants and performance-based compensation). For example, by December 31, 2014, employees would need to make deferral elections for compensation to be earned in 2015. Employees newly eligible to participate in a 409A plan can make their initial deferral elections within 30 days of becoming eligible. Note that the deferral election will apply only to compensation earned after the election. Employees who are subject to performance-based compensation (e.g., compensation tied to achieving established sales goals) can make their deferrals elections as late as six months before the end of the performance period. For purposes of the final regulations under IRC §409A, performance-based compensation is compensation to which a participant will be entitled upon satisfying organizational or individual performance goals for a performance period that is at least 12 months in duration.

Second, deferred compensation may only be paid on the occurrence of an event specified when the deferred compensation is created, and only if the event is on the approved list contained in the statute. Generally, there are only six statutorily sanctioned distribution events

- Separation from service;

- Disability;

- Death;

- A time or fixed schedule as specified under the plan;

- A change in ownership or effective control of the corporation; or

- The occurrence of an unforeseeable emergency.

Third, the acceleration of time or schedule of any payment under the plan is not allowed, except in limited cases as provided by the regulations. However, plans can permit a one time extension of the distribution period. In other words, if a participant initially chooses a distribution date in 2020, he or she cannot accelerate it to 2015, but, based on plan rules, he or she may be able to extend it to 2022.

A plan may dictate when the distribution is made, or the employee may be able to elect a distribution option such as January of 2020, five-year installment. Some plans permit a distribution selection each time the employee elects to defer compensation, and that distribution option could include an in-service distribution in order to cover a large expense such as college tuition while the employee is still working.

Common Categories of Nonqualified Deferred Compensation Plans

There are four basic categories of nonqualified deferred compensation plans: salary reduction arrangements, bonus deferral plans, Supplemental Executive Retirement Plans (SERPs) also known as "Top Hat" plans, and Excess Benefit Plans. A common question related to nonqualified deferred compensation plans is whether the "contributions" to the plan are made by the employer, the employee or both. That is qualified retirement plan thinking that does not fit in the nonqualified deferred compensation world. Regardless of the type of nonqualified arrangement—the amounts are considered *compensation to the employee.*

Salary Reduction Arrangements

Salary Reduction Arrangements simply defer the receipt of otherwise currently includible compensation by allowing the participant to defer receipt of a portion of his or her salary.

Bonus Deferral Plans

Bonus deferral plans resemble salary reduction arrangements, except they enable participants to defer receipt of bonuses.

SERPs or Top Hat Plans

Supplemental Executive Retirement Plans (SERPs) or Top-Hat plans are nonqualified deferred compensation plans maintained primarily for a select group of management or highly compensated employees.

Excess Benefit Plans

Excess benefit plans are nonqualified deferred compensation plans that provide benefits solely to employees whose benefits under the employer's qualified plan are limited by Internal Revenue Code §415. These plans are available to employees whose compensation exceeds the compensation limit for that year that may be considered for qualified retirement plans (i.e., $260,000 for 2014).

Important Concepts Associated with Nonqualified Deferred Compensation Plans

Funded vs. Unfunded Plans

Nonqualified deferred compensation plans are either funded or unfunded, though most are intended to be unfunded because of the tax advantages unfunded plans afford participants. Generally, a funded plan means less tax benefit.

A plan will be considered funded if the employer irrevocably places an amount for the benefit of the participant with a third party, and neither the employer nor any of its creditors has any current or contingent interest in that amount. A funded arrangement generally exists if the employer sets aside assets from the claims of the employer's creditors, for example in a trust or escrow account. A qualified retirement plan is the classic funded plan. A plan will generally be considered funded if the employer segregates assets so that they are identified or "ear marked" as a source to which participants can expect payment of their benefits. For nonqualified deferred compensation purposes, it is not relevant whether the assets have been identified as belonging to the employee. What is key is whether the employee has a beneficial interest in the assets. If the arrangement is funded, the benefit is likely taxable under IRC §§ 83 and 402(b), which relate to the taxation of property transferred to a person for performance of service. In other words, in exchange for having the security of a trust or escrow account, the employee loses the immediate tax benefit of deferring the receipt of additional taxable compensation.

A plan will be considered *unfunded* if the employer does not maintain a separate fund in connection with the plan or if it does maintain a fund in connection with the plan, it is subject to some current or contingent claim of the employer or its creditors. For example, in the case of a rabbi trust maintained in connection with a nonqualified plan, the participant must rely on the solvency of the employer, and in the event of the employer's bankruptcy or insolvency, the participant must have no rights to the assets of the rabbi trust or to the employer's general assets other than as a general unsecured creditor of the employer. An unfunded arrangement is one where the employee has only the employer's "mere promise to pay" the deferred compensation benefits in the future, and the promise is not secured in any way. The employer may simply keep track of the benefit in a bookkeeping account, or it may voluntarily choose to invest in annuities, securities, or insurance arrangements to help fulfill its promise to pay the employee. Similarly, the employer may transfer amounts to a trust that remains a part of the employer's general assets, subject to the claims of the employer's creditors if the employer becomes insolvent, in order to help it keep its promise to the employee. To obtain the benefit of income tax deferral, it is important that the amounts are not set aside from the employer's creditors for the exclusive benefit of the employee. If amounts are set aside from the employer's creditors for the exclusive benefit of the employee, the employee may have currently includible compensation.

Rabbi Trusts

An employer may establish a "rabbi trust" to provide a source of funds that can be used to satisfy the employer's obligations to participants under one or more nonqualified plans. The funds in the rabbi trust, however, remain subject to the claims of all of the employer's creditors, including the nonqualified plan participants, in the event of the employer's bankruptcy or insolvency. Participants in plans using rabbi trusts are taxed on contributions and any taxable earnings when the benefits are actually or constructively received.

Secular Trusts

A secular trust is an irrevocable trust that holds assets to be used for the exclusive purpose of paying nonqualified plan benefits. Typically, they are set up by the employer but treated for tax purposes (if properly structured) as established by the employee. Unlike the case with a rabbi trust, the assets of a secular trust are not subject to the claims of the employer's bankruptcy and insolvency creditors. Participants in plans using secular trusts are taxed on contributions and any taxable earnings as soon as they vest. It is important that a secular trust be structured so that the participating employees are treated as the grantors who have established the trust.

Taxation of Funded Plans

Generally amounts contributed to a funded nonqualified plan generally are includible in a participant's gross income at the time the participant becomes vested in the amounts. Deferred amounts in a funded arrangement are included in an employee's gross income under the Doctrine of Economic Benefit. Under the Economic Benefit Doctrine, if an individual receives any economic or financial benefit or property as compensation for services, the value of the benefit or property is currently includible in the individual's gross income. In this case, an employee would be required to include in current gross income, the value of assets that have been unconditionally and irrevocably transferred as compensation into a fund for the employee's sole benefit, if the employee has a nonforfeitable interest in the fund.

If property is transferred to a person as compensation for services, the employee will be taxed at the time of receipt of the property if the property is either transferable or not subject to a substantial risk of forfeiture (IRC §. 83). "Transferable" means a person has the ability to transfer his or her interest in the property to anyone other than the transferor from whom the property was received. However, property is not considered transferable if the transferee's rights in the property are subject to a substantial risk of forfeiture.

"Substantial risk of forfeiture" means the individual's right to receive the property is conditioned on the future performance of substantial services or on the nonperformance of services. In addition, a substantial risk of forfeiture exists if the right to the property is subject to a condition other than the performance of services and there is a substantial possibility that the property will be forfeited if the condition does not occur.

Taxation of Unfunded Plans

Generally, amounts contributed to an unfunded nonqualified plan generally are includible in a participant's gross income at the time the amounts are paid or made available to the participant. Deferred amounts in an unfunded arrangement are included in an employee's gross income under the Doctrine of Constructive Receipt. Under the constructive receipt doctrine, despite not taking actual possession of the income, the taxpayer is deemed to receive the income when it is credited to his account, set apart for him, or otherwise made available so that he may draw upon it at any time, or so that he could have drawn upon it during the taxable year if notice of intention to withdraw had been given. However, income is not constructively received if the taxpayer's control of its receipt is subject to substantial limitations or restrictions. See § 1.451-2(a) of the regulations.

Establishing constructive receipt requires a determination that the taxpayer had control of the receipt of the deferred amounts and that such control was not subject to substantial limitations or restrictions. It is important to scrutinize all plan provisions relating to each type of distribution or access option. It also is imperative to consider how the plan has been operated regardless of the existence of provisions relating to types of distributions or other access options. Devices such as credit cards, debit cards, and check books may be used to grant employees unfettered control of the receipt of the deferred amounts. Similarly, permitting employees to borrow against their deferred amounts achieves the same result. In many cases, the doctrine of constructive receipt operates to defeat the deferral objectives of employees possessing such control.

Deduction for Employer

For tax deduction purposes, employers may deduct amounts contributed to a nonqualified deferred compensation plan as *compensation* when the amount is includible in the employee's income [IRC §§ 83(h) and 404(a)(5)]. Interest or earnings credited to amounts deferred under nonqualified deferred compensation plans represent additional deferred compensation deductible under IRC § 404(a)(5).

Employment Taxes

Businesses must apply the appropriate payroll taxes to amounts contributed to non-qualified deferred compensation plans, including the following taxes:
- Federal Insurance Contributions Act (FICA) tax,
- Federal Unemployment Tax Act (FUTA) tax or
- Self-Employed Contributions Act (SECA) Tax.

The timing of when there is a payment of wages for FICA and FUTA tax purposes is not affected by whether an arrangement is funded or unfunded.

FICA

Nonqualified deferred compensation amounts are taken into account for FICA tax purposes at the later of when
- The services are performed or
- There is no substantial risk of forfeiture with respect to the employee's right to receive the deferred amounts in a later calendar year.

Thus, amounts are subject to FICA taxes at the time of deferral, unless the employee is required to perform substantial future services in order for the employee to have a legal right to the future payment. If the employee is required to perform future services in order to have a vested right to the future payment, the deferred amount (plus earnings up to the date of vesting) is subject to FICA taxes when all the required services have been performed. FICA taxes apply up to the annual wage base for Social Security taxes and without limitations for Medicare taxes.

FUTA
Nonqualified deferred compensation amounts are taken into account for FUTA purposes at the later of when
- Services are performed or
- There is no substantial risk of forfeiture with respect to the employee's right to receive the deferred amounts up to the FUTA wage base (determined by each state, but at least $7,000).

SECA
For non-employees, such as directors, SECA taxes apply up to the amount of the Social Security taxable wage base. Unlike FICA and FUTA taxes, SECA applies when income taxes apply.

Income Tax Withholding
Employers are required to withhold income taxes from nonqualified deferred compensation at the time employees actually or constructively receive the amounts.

Interest Credited to Amounts Deferred
In general, Treasury regulations at § 31.3121(v)(2)-1(a)(2)(iii) operate to exclude from wages any interest or earnings credited to amounts deferred under a nonqualified deferred compensation plan. However, this exclusion is limited to an amount that reflects a reasonable rate of return. In the context of an account balance plan, a reasonable rate of return is a rate that does not exceed either the rate of return on a predetermined actual investment or a reasonable rate of interest. In the context of a plan that is not an account balance plan, the rule only applies to an amount determined using reasonable actuarial assumptions. Thus, if a nonqualified deferred compensation plan credits amounts deferred with excessive interest, or pays benefits based on unreasonable actuarial assumptions, additional amounts are taken into account when the excessive or unreasonable amounts are credited to the participant's account. If the employer does not take the excess amount into account, then the excess amount plus earnings on that amount are FICA taxable upon payment.

Nonqualified Deferred Compensation Plan Linked to 401(k) Plan
Be aware that a nonqualified deferred compensation plan that references the employer's 401(k) plan may contain a provision that could cause disqualification of the 401(k) plan. IRC § 401(k)(4)(A) and Treas. Reg. § 1.401(k)-1(e)(6) provide that a 401(k) plan may not condition any other benefit (including participation in a nonqualified deferred compensation plan) upon the employee's participation or nonparticipation in the 401(k) plan. Watch

for things like a nonqualified deferred compensation plan provision that limits the total amount that can be deferred between the two plans or a NQDC provision that states that participation is limited to employees who elect not to participate in the § 401(k) plan.

Reporting and Withholding

IRS Notice 2008-115 contains the reporting and withholding requirements for nonqualified deferred compensation plans. An employer or payer will report all deferrals for the year under a nonqualified deferred compensation plan on a Form W-2 (Wage and Tax Statement) or a Form 1099-MISC (Miscellaneous Income) as taxable income. The Instructions to IRS Form W-2 and 1099-MISC provide further guidance and contain example charts for reporting.

Compensation Programs Involving Stock

Stock ownership at work can come in many forms and an employee may be participating in more than one type of program. Each kind of plan provides employees with some special consideration in price or terms. The five leading types of stock ownership arrangements are 1) stock options, 2) restricted stock and restricted stock units, 3) stock appreciation rights, 4) phantom stock and 5) employee stock purchase plans.

Overview of Stock Options

Stock options give employees the right to buy a certain number of their employing company's shares at a fixed price for a certain period of time, usually 10 years. Employee stock-option programs are typically authorized by a company's board of directors (and, historically, have been approved by the shareholders) and give the company discretion to award options to employees equal to a certain percentage of the company's shares outstanding. Employee stock options typically cannot be transferred, and consequently have no market value.

Key Stock Option Terms

Exercise: The purchase of stock pursuant to an option. Once an option is vested, the employee can then "exercise" it (i.e., purchase from the company the allotted number of shares at the strike price (see below), and then either hold the stock or sell it on the open market.

Option term: The length of time the employee can hold the option to buy before it expires.

Exercise price: The price at which the stock can be purchased. This is also called the "strike price" or "grant price." In most plans, the exercise price is the fair market value of the stock at the time the grant is made.

Spread: The difference between the exercise price and the market value of the stock at the time of exercise. This is the employee's gain in the value of the shares.

Under Water: When the option's strike price exceeds the market price of the stock, the option is technically worthless, or "under water."

In the Money: When the market price of the stock exceeds the strike price of the vested option, the option has value, or is "in the money."

Vesting: The requirement that must be met in order to have the right to exercise the option, which is usually the continuation of service for a specific period of time or the meeting of a performance goal. Options usually begin vesting after one year and vest fully after four years. If an employee leaves the company before his or her options vest, they are canceled.

Types of Stock Options
The Internal Revenue Code (IRC) recognizes two basic types of options: 1) "statutory" or "qualified" options; and 2) "nonqualified" options. Qualified options are considered as such because they receive favorable tax treatment if they meet the IRS' strict qualifications under IRC §§ 421-424. One requirement is that they be granted in a written plan document that is approved by the company's shareholders. Generally, the value of these options is not taxed to the employee nor deducted by the employer. Qualified options include Incentive Stock Options (ISOs) and Employee Stock Purchase Plans (ESPPs).

ISOs
ISOs are distinguishable by the following characteristics:
- They must designate the number of shares to be subject to the options;
- They must specify the classes of employees eligible to participate;
- The option price can be no less than the market value of the stock at the time of the grant;
- They must be exercised within 10 years from the time of grant;
- The market value of the stock for any incentive stock options exercisable in any year is limited to $100,000 for any individual for favorable tax treatment (options exceeding this limit are treated as nonqualifying); and
- Restrictions apply to individuals owning more that 10 percent of the outstanding stock.

ESPPs
ESPPs are distinguishable by the following characteristics:
- They must generally cover all full-time employees with at least two years of service (or all except highly compensated employees);
- They must exclude any employee who owns (or would own after exercising the options) five percent or more of the company's stock.
- The option price must be at least 85 percent of the fair market value of the stock either when the option is granted or when it is exercised, whichever is less;
- The options must be exercised within a limited time (no more than five years); and
- The plan must not allow any employee to accrue rights to purchase more than $25,000 in stock in any year.

Nonqualified options have no special tax criteria to meet, but they are taxable to the employee as wage income when their value can be established (which, the IRS says, is when they are no longer at risk of forfeiture and can be freely transferred). They are deductible by the employer when the employee includes them in income (IRC § 83).

Summary of Qualified vs. Nonqualified Stock Options

Characteristic	Qualified	Nonqualified
Type	ISOs or ESPPs	May be granted in unlimited amounts
Tax Treatment	• Tax is imposed to employee when the stock is sold • If the employee holds the stock for one year from purchase and two years from the granting of the option, the difference between the market price of the stock when the option was exercised and the price for which it was sold is taxed as long-term capital gain; and the employer is not allowed a deduction for these options. • If the option price was less than 100% of the fair market value of the stock when it was granted, the difference between the exercise price and the market price (the discount) is taxed as ordinary income. • If the employee does not hold the stock for the required time, the employee is taxed at ordinary income tax rates; and the employer is allowed a deduction. • The value of incentive stock options is included in minimum taxable income for the alternative minimum tax in the year of exercise • Excluded from FICA and FUTA taxes	• Taxed when exercised and all restrictions on selling the stock have expired • Tax is based on the difference

Impact of IRC §409A on Stock Options

IRC §409A applies to deferred compensation plans, and includes stock appreciation rights if the exercise price is less than the fair market value of the underlying stock on the date the stock appreciation rights are granted. IRC §409A generally provides that amounts deferred under a nonqualified deferred compensation plan for all taxable years are currently includible in gross income to the extent not subject to substantial risk of forfeiture and not previously included in gross income, unless certain requirements are met. Thus, stock options, subject to IRC §409A, are included in income when they vest rather than when they are exercised.

Stock Arrangement	Tax Impact
Restricted Stock and Restricted Stock Units	Employees choose whether to be taxed when restrictions lapse or when the right is first granted (see detail below)
Restricted and Control Securities	Taxed as income when restrictions on ability to sell satisfied
Phantom Stock	Taxed as ordinary income when employee exercises the right to the benefit
Stock Appreciation Rights	Taxed as ordinary income when employee exercises the right to the benefit

Restricted Stock and Restricted Stock Units

With restricted stock, employees are given shares or the right to purchase shares (maybe at a reduced price), but they cannot take possession of the shares until the employee meets certain requirements (or, the restrictions are lifted). Restrictions can include working for a set number of years, or meeting specified performance goals. The restrictions can phase out or cease immediately. While the employee holds the restricted stock, it may or may not provide dividends or voting rights. With restricted stock *units*, employees do not actually receive shares until the restrictions lapse.

There is some flexibility regarding taxation. Employees can choose whether to be taxed when the restrictions lapse or when the right is first granted. If taxation occurs when the restrictions lapse, employees will pay ordinary income tax on the difference between the current price and anything they may have paid for the shares.

Taxation upon grant may occur only if the individual files an IRC "§83(b) election" (relating to the transfer of property in connection with the performance of service). In that case, they pay tax on the difference (if any) between the current price and the purchase price at ordinary income tax rates, and then pay capital gains tax when they actually sell the shares. Thus, the value of property with respect to which this election is made is included in gross income as of the time of transfer, even though such property is not yet vested at the time of transfer (Revenue Procedure 2012-29). An 83(b) election carries some risk. If the employee makes the election and pays tax, but the restrictions never lapse, the employee does not get a refund of the taxes paid, nor does the employee get the shares. Recipients of restricted stock units are not allowed to make 83(b) elections.

The employer gets a tax deduction only for amounts on which employees must pay income taxes, regardless of whether the employee makes an 83(b) election.

Restricted stock is not subject to the deferred compensation plan rules under IRC §409A, but RSUs are.

Restricted and Control Securities

Not to be confused with restricted stock are restricted and control securities. The restriction, in this case, is based on security laws, not based on company plan rules. Generally, a stock is a restricted security if it is not registered with the Securities Exchange Commission (SEC) or it is acquired from an issuer or affiliate in a private sale. Investors typically receive restricted securities through private placement offerings, Regulation D offerings, employee stock benefit plans, as compensation for professional services, or in exchange for providing "seed money" or start-up capital to the company.

Control securities are those held by an affiliate of the issuing company. An affiliate is a person, such as an executive officer, a director or large shareholder, in a relationship of control with the issuer. Control means the power to direct the management and policies of the company in question, whether through the ownership of voting securities, by contract, or otherwise. An investor that buys securities from a controlling person or affiliate has acquired restricted securities, even if they were not restricted in the affiliate's hands.

Investors that acquire restricted securities or hold control securities must find an exemption from the SEC's registration requirements in order to be able to sell them in a public marketplace. SEC Rule 144 provides a safe harbor means for public resale of restricted and control securities if a number of conditions are met.

Rule 144 has five conditions:

1) satisfaction of a holding period;
2) availability of adequate, current, public information about the issuing company;
3) satisfaction of trading volume limits;
4) adherence to routine trading transactions; and
5) fulfillment of SEC filing requirements.

Phantom Stock Arrangements

Phantom stock arrangements involve the crediting of shares of stock to a service provider's account without ever issuing the actual shares to the employee. Despite their name, phantom stock plans are nonqualified deferred compensation arrangements, not stock arrangements. Typically, upon termination of employment, the individual is entitled to receive the cash value of the number of phantom shares that have been credited to the individual's account.

Phantom stock is considered nonqualified deferred compensation for purposes of wages if the employee has a legally binding right in a calendar year to the cash value of a certain number of shares that is to be paid in a later calendar year. Treasury Reg. § 31.3121(v)(2)-1(b)(4)(ii), and -1(b)(5) Ex. 8. provide a special timing rule for phantom stock that is nonqualified deferred compensation. If phantom stock is nonqualified deferred compensation within the meaning of IRC § 3121(v)(2), then, under the special timing rule, the value of the phantom stock is wages at the time credited to the employee's account. The amount of FICA wages is the fair market value of the phantom stock when credited to the employee's account. If the phantom stock is nonqualified deferred compensation, and the value of the phantom stock was included in FICA wages when credited to the employee's account, then any appreciation in the value of the stock is not FICA wages when the executive cashes-out the phantom stock. When the executive cashes out, any appreciation is gross income to the employee subject to federal income tax withholding.

Phantom stock is another promise-to-pay arrangement to pay a bonus or award in the form of the equivalent of either the value of company shares or the increase in that value over a period of time. For instance, a company could promise a new employee that it would pay her a bonus every five years equal to the increase in the equity value of the firm times some percentage of total payroll at that point. Or it could promise to pay her an amount equal to the value of a fixed number of shares set at the time the promise is made. Other equity or allocation formulas could be used as well. The taxation of the bonus would be much like any other cash bonus: Taxed as ordinary income at the time it is received. Phantom stock plans are not tax-qualified, so they are not subject to the same rules as Employee Stock Ownership Plans (ESOPs) and 401(k) plans, provided they do not cover a broad group of employees. If they do, they could be subject to ERISA rules. Unlike SARs, phantom stock may reflect dividends and stock splits. Phantom stock payments are usually made at a fixed, predetermined date.

Stock Appreciation Rights

Stock appreciation rights are another method of compensating employees or independent contractors. In this arrangement, an employer agrees to pay an employee an amount equal to the appreciation or gain on the company's stock over a given period of time. The employee does not actually buy or receive any stock. Stock appreciation rights, typically, are granted at a set price; they generally have a vesting period; and an expiration date. Once a stock appreciation right vests, an employee can exercise it at any time prior to its expiration. The company will pay the proceeds in cash, shares, or a combination of the two, depending on the rules of an employee's plan. If the employee receives the proceeds in shares, they can be treated as any other shares of stock in a brokerage account. For those who receive shares, if they sell them at a later point, the appreciation in value of the shares from the time of exercise to the time of sale will be treated as a capital gain or loss. Whether it is a long-term or short-term gain or loss will depend on how long the recipient has held the shares.

There are no federal income tax consequences to the employee when the company grants a stock appreciation right. But when the recipient exercises the right, he or she must recognize income on the fair market value of the amount received at vesting. Federal tax withholding applies, which is usually handled by the employer. The remaining net proceeds will be deposited into a brokerage account.

Insider Trading

When dealing with company stock, it is important to be aware of insider trading issues. Insider trading is a term that most people associate with illegal conduct. But the term actually includes both legal and illegal conduct. Legal insider trading occurs when corporate insiders—officers, directors, and employees—buy and sell stock in their own companies and report their trades to the SEC. Illegal insider trading refers generally to buying or selling a security, in breach of a fiduciary duty or other relationship of trust and confidence, while in possession of material, nonpublic information about the security.

Rule 10b5-1 addresses the issue of when insider trading liability arises in connection with a trader's "use" or "knowing possession" of material nonpublic information. This rule provides that a person trades "on the basis of" material nonpublic information when the person purchases or sells securities while aware of the information. However, the rule also sets forth several affirmative defenses to permit persons to trade in certain circumstances where it is clear that the information was not a factor in the decision to trade.

Rule 10b5-2 addresses the issue of when a breach of a family or other nonbusiness relationship may give rise to liability under the misappropriation theory of insider trading. The rule sets forth three nonexclusive bases for determining that a duty of trust or confidence was owed by a person receiving information.

Practice Management

- Become familiar with general retirement income, taxation, and estate planning issues, as well as related IRS reporting forms. It is not necessary to become an expert on the subjects, but it is important to have a general knowledge in order to be able to "quarterback" a client's team of financial professionals.

- Keep in mind that many nonqualified Roth IRA distributions may be taken tax and penalty free.

- Schedule periodic reviews of a client's potential retirement income sources and retirement income goals.

- Review legacy and estate plans regularly.

- Coordinate meetings with clients' CPAs tax attorneys and other financial professionals to ensure income, estate, legacy, and tax plans are consistent.

Feedback for the review questions can be found at the end of the chapter.

1 Which of the following forms is used to report the application of federal gift tax?

    A Form 23-EP
    B Form 709
    C Form 1099-R
    D Form 5498

2 With respect to an annuity contract, which of the following statements is *TRUE*?

    A The insurance company will guarantee a fixed rate of return on a riderless variable annuity contract.
    B The insurance company will guarantee lifetime payments with a fixed annuity contract.
    C A contract holder must surrender and annuitize a contract before receiving payments.
    D An annuity payment is usually fully taxable.

3 How are distributions of qualified retirement plan pre-tax assets treated for tax purposes?

    A They are not taxable.
    B They are taxed at ordinary personal income tax rates.
    C They are considered long-term capital gains.
    D They are taxed at trust tax rates.

4 What is the result of the Roth IRA distribution ordering rules?

    A Contributed amounts taken within five years of contribution are subject to tax and penalty.
    B Roth IRA owners can include converted amounts in taxable income over a two-year period that they select.
    C Distributions of Roth IRA assets are nontaxable, regardless of when they are taken.
    D Earnings on the Roth IRA are distributed last and may be subject to tax and penalty.

5 What does the 20% federal withholding that applies to eligible rollover distributions that are not directly rolled over represent?

    A A pre-payment of the distribution recipient's income tax liability.
    B An IRS penalty for failing to complete a direct rollover.
    C A special tax applicable to qualified plan distributions.
    D All of the above.
    E B and C only.

1 Which of the following forms is used to report the application of federal gift tax?

    A Form 23-EP
    B Form 709
    C Form 1099-R
    D Form 5498

    A *Incorrect, this is the form an Enrolled Retirement Plan Agent would file to practice before the IRS.*

    B *Correct, a taxpayer subject to gift tax or gift splitting must file Form 709 no earlier than January 1 of the year following the year of the gift, but later than the tax return deadline for the year of the gift.* Chapter 11 Page 251

    C *Incorrect, plan administrators file IRS Form 1099-R to report distributions of retirement plan assets.*

    D *Incorrect, IRA administrators file Form 5498 to report contributions to IRAs.*

2 With respect to an annuity contract, which of the following statements is *TRUE*?

    A The insurance company will guarantee a fixed rate of return on a riderless variable annuity contract.
    B The insurance company will guarantee lifetime payments with a fixed annuity contract.
    C A contract holder must surrender and annuitize a contract before receiving payments.
    D An annuity payment is usually fully taxable.

    A *False, the rate of return on a variable annuity contract without an optional rider will vary depending on the underlying investments.*

    B *True, the insurance company guarantees a minimum rate of return in a fixed annuity contract during the accumulation period.* Chapter 11 Page 258

    C *False, a annuity contract owner may opt for periodic payments, which does not require the owner to surrender and annuitize the contract.*

    D *False, because the amounts used to purchase the annuity contract generally have been taxed, payments will be part taxable and part tax free.*

3 How are distributions of qualified retirement plan pre-tax assets treated for tax purposes?

   A They are not taxable.
   B They are taxed at ordinary personal income tax rates.
   C They are considered long-term capital gains.
   D They are taxed at trust tax rates.

   A *Incorrect, distributions of qualified plan pre-tax assets are taxable as ordinary income.*

   B *Correct, recipients of qualified retirement plan pre-tax assets must include distributions of qualified plan pre-tax assets on their tax returns as income in the year distributed.*
      Chapter 11 Page 239

   C *Incorrect, only the net unrealized appreciation on employer stock distributed from a qualified retirement plan would be eligible for long-term capital gains treatment when the stock is sold.*

   D *Incorrect, distributions of qualified plan pre-tax assets are taxable as ordinary income.*

4 What is the result of the Roth IRA distribution ordering rules?

   A Contributed amounts taken within five years of contribution are subject to tax and penalty.
   B Roth IRA owners can include converted amounts in taxable income over a two-year period that they select.
   C Distributions of Roth IRA assets are nontaxable, regardless of when they are taken.
   D Earnings on the Roth IRA are distributed last and may be subject to tax and penalty.

   A *Incorrect, because of the distribution ordering rules, Roth IRA contributory dollars may be withdrawn tax and penalty free at any time.*

   B *Incorrect, only Roth IRA owners who convert amounts in 2010 may include the taxable amount of the conversion in income in 2011 and 2012.*

   C *Incorrect, earnings taken before the Roth IRA has existed for five years and before the Roth IRA owner is age 59½, has died, is disabled or has purchased a first home are taxable and subject to penalty.*

   D *Correct, because of the distribution ordering rules, contributory dollars are deemed distributed first, followed by conversion assets and, finally, earnings.*
      Chapter 11 Page 238

5 What does the 20% federal withholding that applies to eligible rollover distributions that are not directly rolled over represent?

       A A pre-payment of the distribution recipient's income tax liability.
       B An IRS penalty for failing to complete a direct rollover.
       C A special tax applicable to qualified plan distributions.
       D All of the above.
       E B and C only.

A *Correct, the payer remits the withheld amount to the IRS, and it is credited against the distribution recipient's overall tax bill for the year.* Chapter 11 Page 245

B *Incorrect, while the payer remits the withheld amount to the IRS, it is credited against the distribution recipient's overall tax bill for the year.*

C *Incorrect, it is not a tax but relates to federal withholding on income.*

D *Incorrect, only item A is correct.*

E *Incorrect, only item A is correct.*

CHAPTER 12

Special Rules for Company Stock and Net Unrealized Appreciation

Chapter Goal

Qualified retirement plan participants who hold employer stock as a plan investment may take advantage of special tax rules related to the net unrealized appreciation or NUA in the stock when it is distributed from the plan. These special tax considerations make NUA an important tax management tool, which can result in significant tax savings for the stock holders and their beneficiaries.

Upon completion of this chapter the reader will better understand how retirement plan participants may benefit by taking advantage of NUA when taking a lump sum distribution that contains qualifying employer stock from a qualified retirement plan. Readers will also learn how to identify plan participants who are most likely to be eligible to take advantage of the special tax treatment for NUA.

Learning Objectives

✓ Recognize the five key terms that are used when discussing NUA tax treatment.

✓ Distinguish the three key prerequisites for taking advantage of NUA tax treatment with distributions of employer stock from qualified plans.

✓ Identify the three transactions that could disqualify NUA tax treatment.

✓ Calculate NUA given a fact pattern and differentiate its tax implication from the cost basis.

Overview of NUA

When employer stock is held within a qualified retirement plan, its value is made up of a "cost basis," which is equal to the value of the stock when it was purchased or contributed to the plan initially, and NUA, which is the increase in value of the stock while it is held in the plan. NUA is eligible for special tax treatment under Sections 402(e)(4)(A) and (B) of the Internal Revenue Code.

Unlike stock that is held outside of a qualified retirement plan, employer stock that is held in a qualified retirement plan is generally purchased with either pretax employer contributions or pretax employee contributions. Therefore, when a lump sum distribution is taken from a qualified retirement plan that includes employer stock, generally, the portion of the distribution that represents a return of cost basis will be subject to regular income taxes, while the portion representing NUA is often eligible for long-term capital gains treatment.

This chapter will explain how NUA tax treatment works, as well as define important terms that apply when discussing NUA tax treatment with clients.

Terms to Know When Discussing NUA

When discussing NUA tax treatment, it is important to be familiar with the following terms.

Cost Basis

The cost basis of employer stock is the value of the stock when it was purchased or contributed to the plan initially, without regard to any subsequent increases in value. Assuming the employer stock was purchased with pretax contributions, the cost basis in employer stock will be taxed as ordinary income when the stock is distributed. Upon distribution, note that if the plan participant is under age 59½ without a penalty exception, he or she may be subject to a 10 percent early distribution penalty tax on the taxable portion of the distribution.

NUA

NUA is the difference between the stock's fair market value when it is distributed from the plan and the cost basis in the stock. Put another way, NUA is the increase in value in the employer stock while it is held in the qualified retirement plan. Plan participants may delay taxation on the NUA until they sell the employer stock outside of the plan. When the stock is sold, the NUA is taxed at long-term capital gains tax rates rather than ordinary income tax rates. Retirement plan participants automatically qualify for the long-term capital gains tax rate on the NUA accumulated in employer stock while the stock was held in the plan, regardless of the actual amount of time the stock was held in the plan.

Normally, NUA in employer stock received as part of a lump-sum distribution is not taxable until the securities are sold. However, taxpayers can elect to include NUA in taxable income in the year they receive the stock. The total amount to report as NUA should be shown in Form 1099-R, box 6. Part of the amount in box 6 will qualify for capital gains treatment if there is an amount in Form 1099-R, box 3. To figure the total amount subject to capital gains treatment including the NUA, clients may complete the NUA Worksheet that is part of IRS Form 4972, Tax on Lump Sum Distributions.

Appreciation Outside of the Qualified Plan

If a plan participant holds the distributed employer stock outside of the plan before selling it, the stock may experience additional appreciation. The additional appreciation is determined by calculating the difference between the fair market value of the employer stock at the time of distribution from the qualified plan and the fair market value of the employer stock when it is sold. This additional appreciation will also be taxed at capital gains tax rates. Unlike NUA, however, this additional appreciation will be taxed at long- or short-term capital gains rates, depending on how much time has elapsed between the time it was distributed from the plan until the time it is sold.

Any gain in stock that is held for less than a year is treated as short-term capital gain. Short-term gain is taxed as ordinary income. For stock that is held for more than 12 months, any gain is taxed as long-term capital gain.

Long-Term Capital Gains

Plan participants who are contemplating using a NUA tax strategy should be aware of the changes to tax brackets and long-term capital gains tax rates that took effect in 2013 as a result of the American Taxpayer Relief Act of 2012 (ATRA-12). With respect to the effects on the NUA tax strategy, ATRA-12

- Added a 39.6% tax bracket

- Adjusted the dollar figures for the various tax brackets and

- Increased the long-term capital gains tax rate for the highest tax bracket to 20%

2014 Married Filing Jointly	2014 Federal Income Tax Brackets	2014 Federal Long-term Capital Gains Tax Rate
Up to $18,150	10%	0%
$18,151 – $73,800	15%	0%
$73,801 – $148,850	25%	15%
$148,851 – $226,850	28%	15%
$226,851 – $405,100	33%	15%
$405,101 – $457,600	35%	15%
Over $457,600	39.6%	20%

2014 Single	2014 Federal Income Tax Brackets	2014 Federal Long-term Capital Gains Tax Rate
Up to $9,075	10%	0%
$9,076 – $36,900	15%	0%
$36,901 – $89,350	25%	15%
$89,351 – $186,350	28%	15%
$186,351 – $405,100	33%	15%
$405,101 – $406,750	35%	15%
Over $406,750	39.6%	20%

Lump Sum Distribution

A lump sum distribution is a payment from a qualified retirement plan of a participant's vested balance within one taxable year. The lump sum must be paid out because of the employee's death, attainment of age 59½, separation from service or disability (applicable only to self-employed participants). If the employer stock is part of a non-lump sum payment, then only NUA that is attributable to the participant's nondeductible employee contributions is excludible from gross income.

All of the participant's accounts under like plans of the employer must be distributed in order to be a lump-sum distribution. For example, if an employer maintains a 401(k) and profit sharing plan, they would be considered like plans for lump sum distribution purposes. In contrast, if an employer maintains a 401(k) plan and a defined benefit plan, these plans would not be considered like plans.

Tips for Using NUA Tax Treatment

There are three main prerequisites for using NUA tax treatment.

1 A participant must have qualifying employer stock in his or her qualified retirement plan.

2 He or she must take a lump sum distribution.

3 The employer stock must be distributed in-kind.

Certain transactions can irreversibly disqualify plan participants from taking advantage of NUA tax treatment on amounts invested in employer stock in their qualified retirement plans. Therefore, it is important to carefully consider the impact these transactions may have on plan participants' ability to use NUA tax treatment. These transactions include the following.

Selling Employer Stock Within a Qualified Retirement Plan

If a plan participant sells employer stock within a plan, while the transaction does not result in immediate taxation, it does eliminate the possibility of taking advantage of NUA tax treatment in the future. In a case where there has been a substantial increase in value of the employer stock over the years, selling the stock within the plan, and foregoing NUA tax treatment could greatly increase a participant's future tax burden when he or she eventually begins withdrawing from the plan.

Employer Stock as Part of a Nonlump Sum Distribution

Only lump sum distributions are eligible for full NUA tax treatment. If a plan participant takes a nonlump sum distribution that includes employer stock, only NUA attributable to the participant's nondeductible employee contributions is eligible for the special NUA tax treatment.

Rollovers to an IRA

While rolling over employer stock to an IRA preserves the tax-deferred status of the investment for the participant, the rollover does preclude the participant from using NUA tax treatment on the employer stock when it is later distributed from the IRA. Therefore, it is important to evaluate whether a client would be better off using the tax advantages of NUA vs. the tax advantages of a rollover.

How NUA Tax Treatment Works

The following working examples illustrate a participant's tax ramifications when a participant takes a lump sum distribution that includes employer securities. These assumptions are based upon current tax law (as of December 2011). Future legislative changes could significantly alter the results illustrated. Taxes and possible early withdrawal penalties are typically due when an individual takes withdrawals from a tax-deferred investment.

EXAMPLE 1:

Liz participates in a 401(k)/profit sharing plan through her employer, Concord, Inc. A portion of the plan assets are invested in Concord common stock. The Concord stock was worth $15,000 when contributed to her account. Liz's cost basis is $15,000. Today, Liz's Concord stock account balance is worth $350,000. Therefore, Liz has NUA of $335,000 ($350,000 - $15,000 = $335,000).

Upon termination of employment, Liz takes a lump sum distribution that includes the employer stock. In the year of distribution, she will pay ordinary income tax on her cost basis of $15,000. Assuming Liz is in the 33% tax bracket, her tax liability in the year the stock is distributed would be $4,950. She will not be taxed on the NUA portion ($335,000) until she eventually sells the stock.

Three years after receiving the distribution of employer stock, the value of Liz's shares has increased to $400,000. Assuming Liz sells the shares, the NUA would be taxed at the long term capital gains rate of 15%, which means Liz will owe $50,250 in taxes on the NUA ($335,000 x 15% = $50,250).

The additional $50,000 increase in the stock's value also would be taxed at the long-term capital gains rate because of the length of time she held the stock outside of the plan. The $50,000 of additional gain would result in a tax liability of $7,500 ($50,000 x 15%), for a total tax bill of $57,750 ($50,250 + $7,500).

EXAMPLE 2:

Assume the same facts in example 1, except that Liz does not sell the stock, but instead holds it outside of the plan until her death, five years after receiving the $350,000 distribution of employer stock. At the time of her death the securities are worth $500,000. The tax implications to Josh, her beneficiary, are as follows.

Value of employer stock at the time of Liz's death	$500,000
Amount previously taxed (Liz's cost basis)	$15,000
Potential taxable amount ($500,000-$15,000)	$485,000
Original NUA	$335,000
Remaining portion (gain on stock from date of distribution until Liz's death)	$150,000

Liz's beneficiary, Josh, will pay taxes on the original NUA ($335,000) at the long-term capital gains tax rate when he sells the stock. Assuming 15%, the tax bill would be $50,250.

The remaining $150,000 of appreciation is Josh's new stepped-up basis, and is not subject to capital gains or ordinary income tax. Any additional gain on the stock from the point of Liz's death until Josh sells the stock will be taxed at the short- or-long-term capital gains rate, depending on the length of time Josh holds the stock.

Impact of NUA Treatment for Beneficiaries

According to the IRS, NUA represents income in respect of a decedent, which is not eligible for a stepped-up basis at death (Rev. Rul. 75-125). Especially in cases where NUA represents a substantial portion of the employer stock that is inherited, it is important to understand that the beneficiary will not get this portion tax-free upon the death of the original stockholder. The NUA will be taxable to the beneficiary at the long-term capital gains rate when the stock is sold. However, the beneficiary will experience a stepped-up basis on the additional appreciation in the stock that occurs between the time of the original distribution of the stock from the plan and the date of death of the plan participant. The Tax Relief, Unemployment Insurance Reauthorization and Job Creation Act of 2010 reinstated the step-up basis rules for 2011 and later years. If the value of the stock on the date of the decedent's death was less than its adjusted basis, the property takes a stepped-down basis when it passes from a decedent's estate. The heirs recognize any appreciation or depreciation in the stock when they sell the property. For 2010 only, a limited carry-over basis rule applied. Under the carry-over basis rule, a recipient's basis in property acquired from a decedent was the lesser of the adjusted basis of the property at death or the fair market value (FMV) on the date of death. Each estate was permitted to increase the basis of assets owned by the decedent and transferred at death by an additional $1.3 million. Assets left to a spouse could have received an additional $3 million basis increase. The carry-over basis rule expired at the end of 2010. This is why it is important to keep good records to substantiate which portion of inherited employer stock represents cost basis, which part represents NUA, and which part represents additional appreciation.

Does a NUA Tax Strategy Make Sense?

There are several questions clients should answer before they elect to use—or not use—a NUA tax strategy. Some of these questions include the following.

- How important is it to the client to own the stock?

- Does the plan impose any limitations on distributions of employer stock?

- Does the client understand that there is a possibility that the stock will go down in value?

- Is the client subject to the 10 percent early distribution penalty tax?

- Does the client have funds to pay the taxes that will be due on the cost basis at the time of the distribution?

- Are the initial costs of embarking on an NUA strategy outweighed by the value of deferring taxes through a rollover strategy?

- What will the expected tax impact be on the client's beneficiaries?

In some circumstances, a NUA tax strategy does not make sense. For example, if the client's NUA is relatively insignificant compared to the cost basis, it may not make sense to pay a large amount of taxes upfront for a relatively small tax savings on the NUA.

Option	Pros	Cons
NUA strategy	NUA is tax-deferred until stock is sold outside of plan	Must have lump sum distribution
	Lower capital gains tax rate applies to NUA	Taxes due on cost basis when stock is distributed
	Beneficiaries benefit from partial step up in basis	
Sell stock within plan	Immediate liquidity	NUA lost
	Diversification of portfolio	Capital gains tax rate not available
	Lump sum not required	Distributions taxed at current income tax rate
Rollover to IRA	Employer stock remains tax deferred	NUA lost
	Tax-deferred growth	Capital gains tax rate not available
	Diversified portfolio	Distributions taxed at current income tax rate
	Greater beneficiary options	No step up in basis for beneficiaries

When dealing with employer stock held in a qualified plan, the most prudent approach is to weigh the pros and cons of each of the plan participant's options. The following table may be helpful in that process.

Finding Clients Who May Be Eligible for NUA Tax Treatment

Thirty-eight percent of 401(k) participants have employer stock as a retirement plan investment option available to them. This represents a dramatic increase over the last several years, when the availability of employer stock went from 30 percent in 2007, 26 percent in 2008 and 24 percent in 2009.[1]

Most plans that currently offer employer stock as an investment option will continue to do so in the coming years because it remains an appealing investment option for both participants and employers sponsoring plans. That said, more plan sponsors are intending to educate participants about the potential pitfalls of under diversified invest-

[1] Employee Benefits Research Institute, Issue Brief, December 2012

ments, and some intend to impose a plan limit on the percentage of assets that may be invested in employer stock.

It is far more common to find employer stock in plans that are sponsored by large employers. One way to find employers that offer employer stock is to use a database that stores IRS Form 5500 information (such as www.efast.dol.gov), and to search for employers that offer employer stock as an investment.

Expanded Company Stock Diversification Rules

Although the law generally does not limit the amount of company stock that any one participant can hold in a defined contribution plan, the plan sponsor still has a fiduciary duty to manage the plan in the best interest of the participants. This includes, among other responsibilities, the obligation to select investment options that are appropriate for a retirement plan, and to monitor those investment options on an ongoing basis to assure that they remain suitable investments for plan participants. If a plan offers company stock as an investment option or makes matching contributions with company stock, the employer must make a disinterested, prudent assessment as to whether the stock is an appropriate investment for the plan's participants. A portfolio concentrated in a single security is subject to sudden and dramatic losses. The impact on participants and their retirement security could be devastating should they over invest in stock of the sponsoring employer.

The Pension Protection Act of 2006 allows employees more opportunity to diversify their retirement plan holdings away from company stock. As a result, effective beginning with the 2007 plan year, all participants with employee salary deferrals and after-tax contributions invested in employer securities must be permitted to direct that such amounts be invested in alternative investments. With respect to employer-provided contributions (e.g., nonelective and matching contributions), participants with three years of service (and certain beneficiaries) must be permitted to direct that such amounts be invested in alternative investments. In both cases, the alternative investments must consist of a selection of at least three investment options (other than employer securities), each of which is diversified and has materially different risk and return characteristics. For 2007-2009, transitional rules applied to the diversification of employer-provided contributions. The transition rule did not apply to plan participants who had three years of service and who had attained age 55 by the beginning of the first plan year beginning after December 31, 2005.

Plan Year	Percentage
Year 1	33
Year 2	66
Year 3	100

EXAMPLE 1:

Suppose that the account of a participant with at least three years of service held 120 shares of employer common stock contributed as matching contributions before the diversification requirements became effective. In the first year for which diversification applies, 33 percent (i.e., 40 shares) of that stock is subject to the diversification requirements. In the second year for which diversification applies, a total of 66 percent of 120 shares of stock (i.e., 79 shares, or an additional 39 shares) is subject to the diversification requirements. In the third year for which diversification applies, 100 percent of the stock, or all 120 shares, is subject to the diversification requirements. In addition, in each year, employer stock in the account attributable to elective deferrals and employee after-tax contributions is fully subject to the diversification requirements, as is any new stock contributed to the account.

Practice Management

- Obtain plan statements from clients to determine if their plan balances include employer stock that may be eligible for NUA special tax treatment.

- Discuss NUA issues with clients, and offer to complete for them a "NUA Analysis," which is a detailed review of their employer stock holdings. The NUA Analysis will give them their NUA amount and help them understand their options.

- It is the responsibility of the sponsoring employer to provide documentation to the plan participant that reflects his/her employer stock holdings and NUA (e.g., account statement and Form 1099-R, box 6).

- Postpone any action involving the employer stock until you have discussed a strategy with the client.

- Quarterback the team of professionals involved to determine the best approach.

Chapter Review Questions

Feedback for the review questions can be found at the end of the chapter.

1 When taking a lump sum distribution from a qualified plan and a portion represents net unrealized appreciation (NUA), this portion is often eligible for what type of tax treatment?

    A Tax-free
    B Ordinary income tax
    C Short-term capital gains
    D Long-term capital gains

2 What is the definition of net unrealized appreciation (NUA)?

    A The value of the employer stock at the point it is contributed to the qualified plan.
    B The value of the employer stock at the point it is distributed from the qualified plan.
    C Any gains in the value of the employer stock while it is held in the qualified plan.
    D The value of the employer stock when it is rolled to an IRA.

3 What happens if a plan participant rolls employer stock distributed from a qualified plan to an IRA?

    A The stock remains tax deferred.
    B The special tax treatment for NUA is preserved.
    C The stock is registered listing the IRA as owner.
    D All of the above.
    E A and C

4 Which of the following would constitute a lump sum distribution for the purposes of using the special tax treatment for NUA?

    A The lump sum is payable pursuant to a hardship over a two-year period.
    B The lump sum is payable pursuant to attainment of age 59½ within one year.
    C The lump sum is payable pursuant to death and is rolled to the spouse beneficiary's IRA.
    D The lump sum is payable pursuant to separation from service in three annual installment payments.

5　Which of the following statements with respect to beneficiaries and net unrealized appreciation is *TRUE*?

　　A　Beneficiaries may use the special tax treatment for NUA and they will receive a step up in basis equal to the appreciation on the stock from the original date of distribution from the plan until the date of death of the plan participant.

　　B　Beneficiaries will receive a step up in basis equal to the NUA and any appreciation of the stock from the date of distribution from the plan.

　　C　NUA is taxable to the beneficiaries at the short-term capital gains rates.

　　D　The date of death value of the employer stock is included in the beneficiaries' ordinary income in the year of death.

Chapter Review Questions Feedback

1　When taking a lump sum distribution from a qualified plan and a portion represents net unrealized appreciation (NUA), this portion is often eligible for what type of tax treatment?

　　A　Tax-free
　　B　Ordinary income tax
　　C　Short-term capital gains
　　D　Long-term capital gains

　　A　*Incorrect, NUA is taxable at the long-term capital gains tax rates.*

　　B　*Incorrect, amounts other than NUA are generally taxable as ordinary income.*

　　C　*Incorrect, NUA automatically satisfies the holding period to be eligible for long-term capital gains tax treatment.*

　　D　**Correct, pursuant to IRC Sec. 402(e)(4)(A) and (B), NUA qualifies for taxation as a long-term capital gain.** Chapter 12 Page 284

2　What is the definition of net unrealized appreciation (NUA)?

　　A　The value of the employer stock at the point it is contributed to the qualified plan.

　　B　The value of the employer stock at the point it is distributed from the qualified plan.

　　C　Any gains in the value of the employer stock while it is held in the qualified plan.

　　D　The value of the employer stock when it is rolled to an IRA.

　　A　*Incorrect, the value of the employer stock at the point it is contributed is the cost basis.*

　　B　*Incorrect, this is the cost basis of the employer stock plus any gains while it is held in the plan.*

C *Correct, the NUA is the difference between the value of the employer stock when it was contributed to the qualified plan and the value when it is distributed.* Chapter 12 Page 284

D *Incorrect, this is the fair market value of the stock. NUA is lost when the stock is rolled to an IRA.*

3 What happens if a plan participant rolls employer stock distributed from a qualified plan to an IRA?

    A The stock remains tax deferred.

    B The special tax treatment for NUA is preserved.

    C The stock is registered listing the IRA as owner.

    D All of the above.

    E A and C

A *Incorrect, in addition to retaining the stock's tax-deferred status, the stock is registered listing the IRA as owner and the ability to use the special tax treatment for NUA is lost.*

B *Incorrect, the IRA owner looses the ability to use the special tax treatment for NUA when the employer stock is rolled to an IRA.*

C *Incorrect, in addition to re-registering the stock listing the IRA as the owner, the stock remains tax-deferred and the ability of the IRA owner to use the special tax treatment for NUA is lost.*

D *Incorrect, statements A and C are correct, but statement B is incorrect; the IRA owner looses the ability to use the special tax treatment for NUA following a rollover of the stock to an IRA.*

E *Correct, statement B is incorrect; the IRA owner looses the ability to use the special tax treatment for NUA following a rollover of the stock to an IRA.* Chapter 12 Page 287

4 Which of the following would constitute a lump sum distribution for the purposes of using the special tax treatment for NUA?

    A The lump sum is payable pursuant to a hardship over a two-year period.

    B The lump sum is payable pursuant to attainment of age 59½ within one year.

    C The lump sum is payable pursuant to death and is rolled to the spouse beneficiary's IRA.

    D The lump sum is payable pursuant to separation from service in three annual installment payments.

A *Incorrect, hardship is not a qualifying event for a lump sum distribution and the payment must be made to the recipient within one taxable year.*

B *Correct, attainment of age 59½ is one qualifying triggering event for a lump sum distribution; and the lump sum must be paid to the recipient within one taxable year.* Chapter 12 Page 286

C *Incorrect, while death could be a qualifying triggering event, if the lump sum is rolled over, the ability to use the special tax treatment for NUA is lost.*

5 Which of the following statements with respect to beneficiaries and net unrealized appreciation is *TRUE*?

  A Beneficiaries may use the special tax treatment for NUA and they will receive a step up in basis equal to the appreciation on the stock from the original date of distribution from the plan until the date of death of the plan participant.

  B Beneficiaries will receive a step up in basis equal to the NUA and any appreciation of the stock from the date of distribution from the plan.

  C NUA is taxable to the beneficiaries at the short-term capital gains rates.

  D The date of death value of the employer stock is included in the beneficiaries' ordinary income in the year of death.

A *Correct, NUA represents income in respect of a decedent; therefore, NUA is taxable to the beneficiary at the long-term capital gains tax rate. Any step up in basis is limited to the gains on the stock while it was held by the participant outside the plan.*
Chapter 12 Page 288

B *Incorrect,, NUA represents income in respect of a decedent, therefore, it cannot increase a beneficiary's basis. Moreover, any step up in basis is limited to the gains on the stock while it was held by the participant outside the plan.*

C *Incorrect, NUA is taxable to the beneficiary at the long-term capital gains tax rates.*

D *Incorrect, NUA is taxable to the beneficiary at the long-term capital gains tax rate when the stock is sold; gains on the stock while it was held by the participant outside the plan are tax free to the beneficiary; and gains on the stock from the date of death until the date of sale are taxed as long or short-term capital gains depending on the length of time the beneficiary holds the stock.*

CHAPTER 13

Retirement Income Planning Strategies

Chapter Goal

Retirement is the number two reason workers cite for saving, after emergencies. However, less than half have a plan for reaching their savings goals.[1] At retirement, retirement savers shift from saving for retirement (wealth accumulation) to drawing down assets to pay for retirement (wealth harvesting). This transition involves a significant shift in investment focus, which will seem unfamiliar to many retirees, as well as to many financial professionals who, in the past, have focused more on wealth accumulation than on wealth harvesting issues.

Upon completion of this chapter the reader will understand potential risks to retirement income and strategies that may help to mitigate such risks.

Learning Objectives

✓ Identify the eight key risks associated with wealth harvesting.

✓ Associate management strategies to specific types of risks to wealth harvesting.

✓ Recognize the six steps of the retirement income planning process.

[1] CFP Board, Consumer Federation of America Household Financial Planning Survey, 2012

Retirement Income and Risk Management

"To be alive at all involves some risk." Harold MacMillian

Managing risks throughout our lives is essential to success. It should come as no surprise then that successful retirement income planning begins with a thorough understanding of the types of risks that have the potential to affect a retiree's income. Once retirees identify and understand their retirement income risks, they can consider targeted strategies as part of the income planning process to help mitigate the various risks.

Although there may be others, this text identifies eight basic risks to retirement income, and suggests strategies to consider for managing each risk. The eight risks addressed herein include

- spending risk,
- longevity risk,
- inflation risk,
- market risk,
- health care cost risk,
- public policy risk,
- household shocks risk, and
- legacy risk.

Spending Risk

Simply stated, spending risk is overspending and running out of money. A person's spending risk can be assessed based on three factors: spending rate, asset allocation, and mortality. For example, if a retiree increases spending while maintaining the same investment allocation and return, then the probability of running out of money increases.

Managing Spending Risk

Two methods of managing spending risk are 1) determining a sustainable withdrawal rate for the retiree and, 2) maintaining an appropriate asset allocation.

Sustainable Withdrawal Rate

A sustainable withdrawal rate is one that, based on a given portfolio mix, will allow for payments for a set period of time. The retirement industry has used the "six percent withdrawals for 20 years" as a rule of thumb for retirement income planning purposes. But a person's actual sustainable withdrawal rate is based on several variables, including the portfolio mix (i.e., the percentage of cash to stocks to bonds), and the number of years in retirement.

The following graph attempts to answer the question: How many years (with a 90 percent or greater probability) could a specific withdrawal rate provide income, given a portfolio mix of 30 percent bonds, 60 percent equities and 10 percent cash, inflated annually at three percent.

For example, a six percent withdrawal rate from this hypothetical portfolio has a 90 percent or greater chance of lasting 20 years. This illustration gives some credence to the "six percent withdrawals for 20 years" rule of thumb. However, since today's retirees are living longer, it may be far more realistic and prudent to consider 25-, 30-, and 45-year payout periods when determining a sustainable withdrawal rate. Consequently, rather than using a six percent withdrawal rate, a sustainable withdrawal rate may be closer to four percent for a 35-year payout period in this hypothetical example.

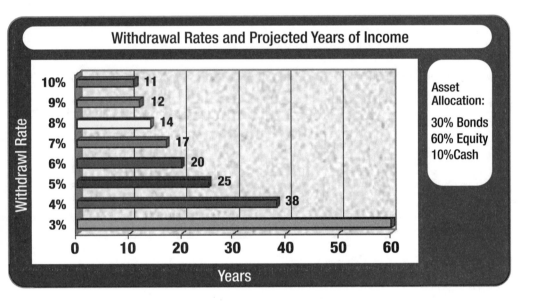

This graph illustrates withdrawal percentages and projected years of income provided based upon a 10,000-iteration Monte Carlo simulation. Assumes portfolio of equity (60%), Bonds (30%), and Cash (10%) as represented by the historical performance of the S&P 500, US Intermediate-Term Government Bonds, and 30-Day T-Bills. Annual withdrawal is inflated at 3% per year. Actual inflation rates may be more or less. This chart is for illustrative purposes only and is not indicative of any investment. Past performance is no guarantee of future results. The S&P 500 is an index consisting of 500 stocks chosen for market size, liquidity and industry grouping, among other factors. The S&P 500 is designed to be a leading indicator of U.S. equities and is meant to reflect the risk/return characteristics of the large-cap universe. Unlike a mutual fund, indices are not investments, do not incur fees or expenses, are not professionally managed, and are used as broad measures of market performance. It is not possible to invest directly in an index.

The Monte Carlo Analysis is a mathematical technique based on the statistics of probability, to estimate the likelihood that an account may realize a target goal within the time frame indicated based on hypothetical risk and return assumptions as well as inflation assumptions. This data is intended as guidelines for reasonable expectations and are not a guarantee or prediction of performance. It is possible for investors to lose more money than is illustrated. Results will vary based on the particular situation.

Asset Allocation

An asset allocation strategy goes hand in hand with a sustainable withdrawal rate in helping to manage spending risk. Asset allocation is generally defined as the apportionment of an investor's portfolio among a number of major asset classes (i.e., stocks, bonds, and cash) based on the investor's risk tolerance (on a scale from conservative to aggressive), time horizon, and overall financial situation. The goal is to achieve portfolio survivability by aligning an optimal asset allocation with a sustainable withdrawal rate for the number of anticipated years in retirement.

Generally, an investor seeking a longer income stream may want to consider delegating a larger portion of his or her portfolio to stocks in order to increase the potential return of the portfolio over time. Keep in mind that asset allocation does not ensure a profit or guarantee against loss.

Investors must exercise caution so that asset allocation does not become another risk in and of itself. Asset allocation as risk is the risk that a retirement savings portfolio is invested so aggressively that it doesn't take into consideration the need to pay for current expenses from the investments, or so conservatively, that the retiree fails to benefit from the potentially better long-term returns generally offered by equity-based investments.

Longevity Risk

Longevity risk is the risk of outliving one's assets, or running out of money. Although it is common practice for financial professionals to base retirement income analyses on average life expectancy, this approach can leave a considerable margin for error.

The average life expectancy at birth today is 78.49 years.[2] However, retirement income planning must be based on the time expected to be spent in retirement. According to life expectancy figures from the National Center for Health Statistics and based on U.S. Life Tables, a 65-year-old has a 50 percent chance of living another 19.2 years to age 84.2.

Because a full 50 percent of individuals who retire healthy at 65 are expected to live longer than the average life expectancy, and medical advances are expected to

[2] Central Intelligence Agency (CIA) Factbook, 2012

extend life expectancies even further in the future, using a longer than average life expectancy may be a more conservative assumption when evaluating wealth harvesting scenarios.

Managing Longevity Risk

There are several strategies that may be used to help effectively manage longevity risk. Two of the strategies—determining a sustainable withdrawal rate and determining appropriate asset allocation—were outlined earlier in the text. Other strategies for fighting longevity risk include considering annuity products with optional riders, and other options that may offer lifetime income streams, implementing a phased approach to retirement, and adjusting retirement spending. Note that any guarantees in variable annuity contracts are subject to the claims-paying ability of the issuing insurance company. A variable annuity has different types of fees and charges that should be considered prior to investment. These may include a sales charge, mortality and expense risk charges, surrender charges, administrative fees, as well as additional charges for optional features that may be elected.

Annuities and Other Lifetime Income Streams

One strategy to help offset longevity risk is to consider the use of annuities with optional riders and other options that may offer lifetime income in a similar manner as Social Security payments and pension plan income.

Social Security benefits, presumably, represent guaranteed income which a person cannot outlive. Pension plan income can represent another type of guaranteed lifetime income, depending upon the payout option selected by the participant.

When an annuity is converted to an income stream, it becomes a guaranteed source of income, and variable annuities often offer optional riders that may have anti-inflation features to help protect the annuitant's buying power. Any guarantees in variable annuity contracts are subject to the claims-paying ability of the issuing insurance company. A variable annuity has different types of fees and charges that should be considered prior to investment. These may include a sales charge, mortality and expense risk charges, surrender charges, administrative fees, as well as additional charges for optional features that may be elected.

With an annuity strategy, a harvester could take a portion of his or her portfolio to purchase an annuity, which would provide a consistent income stream. The harvester may then invest the rest of the portfolio in a more aggressive asset allocation mixture to take advantage of the greater long-term earning potential. Such a strategy could provide the harvester with the ability to pay for his or her essential living expenses from the annuity proceeds, while still providing some flexibility to take additional withdrawals from the assets that are invested in the market when the market is up, or to leave them untouched in years when the market is down. Of course, the harvester should consider potential taxes, fees and penalties that may apply when a withdrawal is taken.

A downside of purchasing an annuity is that an annuitant loses a certain amount of control over his or her assets. Of course, some flexibility may be maintained by only putting a portion of a client's retirement investments in an annuity product and leaving a portion that can be invested at his or her discretion.

A variable annuity should only be considered if the insurance and annuity features meet the client's individual needs. Variable annuities are designed to be long-term investments, to meet retirement and other long-range goals. Variable annuities are not suitable for meeting short-term goals because substantial taxes and insurance company charges may apply if the investor withdraws money early. Variable annuities also involve investment risks, just as mutual funds do. Investors should consult with their financial professionals as to whether a variable annuity product is suitable for them.

Phased Retirement

The concept of retirement is changing. Delaying full retirement may be a viable option to stave off the effects of longevity risk. Today, many people view retirement as an opportunity to have greater control over their lives. When the American Association of Retired Persons (AARP) polled pre-retirees about their anticipated retirement, most said that they planned to stay active and work in retirement, but on their terms. For some, this meant changing occupations, achieving a better balance between work and their personal lives, or learning something new. The good news is that the desire and ability to work in retirement can greatly ease the financial burden for those making the transition.

There are many compelling reasons for individuals to put off retiring until after age 65, and even older, if they are healthy. Some of these reasons include the ability to delay receipt of Social Security benefits, which will ultimately result in them receiving a larger benefit than those who choose to retire before reaching their full Social Security retirement age. Furthermore, if an individual is a participant in a traditional company pension plan, depending on plan design, there is a chance that delaying retirement could not only allow the individual to accrue a larger benefit, but could also cause pension payouts to be significantly larger than if they had retired earlier because payouts would be calculated over a shorter life expectancy.

Even the IRS accommodates employees who want to work into their retirement years. In addition to giving a person a longer opportunity to invest and accrue a benefit in his or her 401(k) plan (if available), if a person continues to work past age 70½, many plans allow participants to delay taking required distributions until they retire, which would further preserve retirement assets.

Furthermore, many employees are shocked to find out how expensive it is to carry their own medical insurance once they retire. Staying employed later into retirement could save some individuals that are covered by employer medical coverage hundreds of dollars every month in out-of-pocket medical expenses.

Reducing Retirement Spending

While perhaps somewhat unpalatable, it may be necessary for a retiree to reduce retirement spending in order to avoid running out of money. Of course adapting this strategy generally will be much easier for a person who, during his or her wealth accumulation years, abstained from excessive discretionary spending, than it will be for someone who is not use to exercising financial discipline.

Inflation Risk

Inflation, over time, decreases the purchasing power of money. For example, a dozen eggs and a pound of bacon in 1950 cost $0.49 and $0.35 respectively. Today, similar measures of eggs and bacon cost $1.54 and $4.48 respectively! By not accounting for inflation, retirees run the risk of running out of money to cover expenses.

Inflation affects retirees by reducing the value of their retirement nest egg, and increasing the cost of future goods purchased. Consequently, it is essential that retirees consider investments that can outpace the rate of inflation. Individuals who invest their retirement assets too conservatively often have ignored the potential damage that inflation risk can inflict on the purchasing power of their portfolio. Although inflation is a concern during wealth accumulation, it can really wreak havoc on the portfolio of an individual who must depend on his or her existing investments to pay for current and future living expenses.

Managing Inflation Risk

Inflation risk may be mitigated by purchasing investments that have higher potential of outperforming inflation over the long-term. Historically, equity-based products have been one alternative for this objective.

Also, variable annuity products may offer optional riders that could provide anti-inflation protection, whereby payouts will increase in conjunction with cost-of-living increases. Any guarantees in variable annuity contracts are subject to the claims-paying ability of the issuing insurance company. A variable annuity has different types of fees and charges that should be considered prior to investment. These may include a sales charge, mortality and expense risk charges, surrender charges, administrative fees, as well as additional charges for optional features that may be elected.

Real estate investments may also provide a hedge against inflation in some cases. Given the sometimes speculative nature of many real estate investments, however, these sorts of options should be carefully considered with a trusted financial professional.

Finally, investors may want to consider purchasing inflation-adjusted government securities, either Treasury Inflation-Protected Securities, also known as TIPS, or Series I Bonds. TIPS are securities whose principal is tied to the Consumer Price Index. With inflation, the principal increases, with deflation, it decreases. When the security matures, the U.S. Treasury Department pays the original or adjusted principal, whichever is greater.

Series I bonds are a new type of bond designed for investors seeking to protect the purchasing power of their investments and earn a guaranteed real rate of return. Series I Bond interest rates have two parts: a fixed rate that lasts for 30 years, and an inflation rate that changes every six months. (For more information on TIPS and I Bonds, see www.publicdebt.treas.gov)

Market Risk

The rise and fall of the stock market can have a profound effect on the value of retirement income assets. Consider that down markets can have a disproportionately negative impact on assets during the early harvesting years vs. the later years. This is significant even when subsequent market upswings occur.

If a harvester takes distributions from assets that are depressed in value, it can be extremely detrimental to the longevity of the overall portfolio. The following graph illustrates the effect that market fluctuations can have on the value of retirement assets.

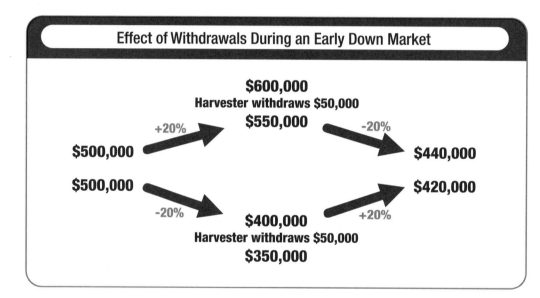

Assume an investor begins with a $500,000 plan balance, and the market goes up 20 percent early on (new balance is $600,000), and he or she takes a $50,000 withdrawal, the remaining balance is $550,000. Assume then that the market drops 20 percent. The investor's ending balance is $440,000.

Now compare that to an early down market scenario. Assume that instead of going up, the market drops 20 percent early on (new balance is $400,000), and the investor takes a $50,000 distribution. His or her remaining balance is $350,000. The market rebounds and goes up 20 percent, but the investor's ending balance is $420,000.

Challenges With Clients At or Near Retirement

Impact of Early Down Markets on Retirees is Huge

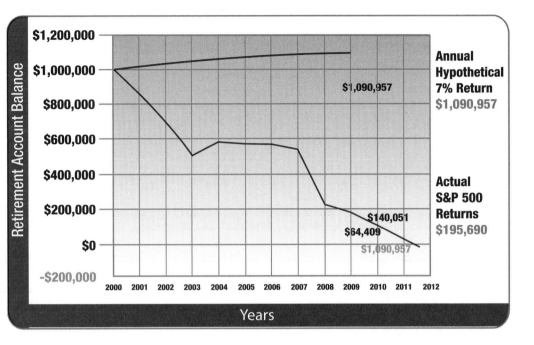

*Actual S&P 500: Actual rates of return for the S&P 500 for years 2000—2012; assumes an annual $50,000 withdrawl; inflated annually at 4%; Annual Hypothetical 7%: Assumes an annual $50,000 withdrawl, inflated annually at 4%; hypothetical 7% return for all years. **Performance is historical and does not guarantee future results.** It is not possible to invest directly in an index.

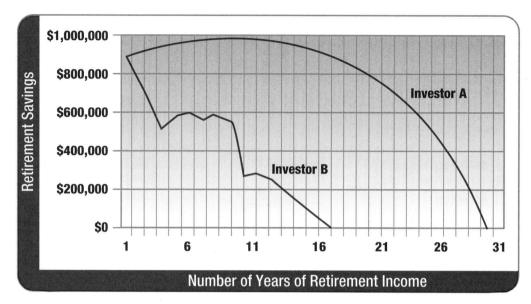

Investor A: Assumes an annual $50,000 withdrawal, inflated annually at 4%; hypothetical 7% return for all years. Investor B: Actual rates of return for the S&P 500 for years 1–13 (years 2000–2012); assumes an annual $50,000 withdrawal; inflated annually at 4%; hypothetical 7% rate of return for years 14–33 (years 2013–2032). **Performance is historical and does not guarantee future results.** It is not possible to invest directly in an index. This chart is not intended to project the present or future value of any particular mutual fund investment.

Managing Market Risks

In order to help manage market risks, investors may want to consider limiting withdrawals during down markets, adjusting asset allocation, incorporating less volatile investment vehicles (e.g., low BETA investments), and/or purchasing annuity products with optional riders that may provide principal, withdrawal, and/or income guarantees. Any guarantees in variable annuity contracts are subject to the claims-paying ability of the issuing insurance company. A variable annuity has different types of fees and charges that should be considered prior to investment. These may include a sales charge, mortality and expense risk charges, surrender charges, administrative fees, as well as additional charges for optional features that may be elected.

In today's redefined retirement, the individual retiree bears the risk in volatile markets. Today, retirees must learn to both manage their down-side risk and exercise spending discipline.

This means that capturing up-market returns over the long-term is essential for participants and retirees alike to accumulate sufficient assets to reach retirement income goals and to keep pace with inflation Today's market volatility creates the need for all participants to develop better risk management strategies. There is no guarantee that traditional stocks and bonds will perform as well as they have in the past.

In fact if a down-market occurs in the late stage of retirement accumulation and the early stage of retirement income, it can have a disastrous effect on an individual's retirement income plans.

- Participants may not be able to afford to retire and
- Retirees may have to radically down-shift their lifestyle or return to the workforce.

For all of these reasons, financial professionals play a crucial role in helping participants and retirees clients find solutions that capture up-market returns and minimize down market exposure.

Investing in the financial markets involves risk. To mitigate the risk of having retirement income run out, diversification alone may not be enough. It may be necessary to use a variety of investment products and strategies—even some that are relatively new to the market.

There is a dramatic paradigm shift taking place in the investment needs of today's participants as they prepare to move from the accumulation phase to the distribution and retirement phase. Portfolios today can be more complex than they were in the past and need to last longer. As participants look for ways to achieve more predictable investment returns, it is clear that traditional portfolio management theory and asset allocation models may not be sufficient for today's retirees' needs.

Relying solely on these traditional strategies may leave a retiree's portfolio overly exposed to the risks of market volatility. Participants transitioning into their retirement years are looking for investment solutions that help manage market risk.

Why should pre-retirees and retirees consider new investment approaches? Traditional investment strategies are geared toward the accumulation stage of an investor's lifecycle. These strategies leave a pre-retirees and retiree's savings exposed to risks and market volatility that we have just talked about.

Other long-term institutional investors including corporate and public pension funds, foundations and endowments have been capturing return and managing market volatility for several years now by adding alternative asset classes to enhance diversification and protect their portfolios.

Pre-retirees and retirees should consider adding alternative asset classes to their own portfolios for the same reasons.

Alternative asset classes are defined as low correlated asset classes that do not move in the same direction at the same time as traditional asset classes. An alternative asset class can benefit investors during various market cycles by providing a higher level of diversification and potentially reducing risk. As many investors have seen with traditional asset classes, the performance of individual asset classes can fluctuate from one year to the next. The same holds true for alternative asset classes. So, having exposure to a diversified mix of alternative assets is important in the battle to control market risks.

Health Care Cost Risk

The risk that the rise in health care expenses will outpace gains in retirement assets is health care cost risk. Increasing costs, eroding retiree health benefits, and limited benefits from Medicare and Medigap programs means that retirees should expect to use a sizable portion of their retirement savings for their health care costs. For example, without employment-based health insurance, a retired couple could need about $387,000 to cover medical expenses in retirement.[3]

Overall spending on health care services will increase at an annual average rate of 4.2 and 3.8 percent for 2012 and 2013. In 2014, it is projected to rise to 7.4 percent.[4] Just as health care costs are rising at unprecedented rates, fewer and fewer companies are offering retiree health care benefits.[5] This trend is only expected to worsen as Baby Boomers place greater and greater strains on the health care delivery system.

The failure to account for expenses that are not covered by Medicare or Medicaid, not to mention possible long-term care expenses, could quickly devour a retiree's entire retirement savings.

Managing Health Care Cost Risk

There are a couple of strategies a retiree can consider to help minimize the health care expense risk, including securing cost effective health insurance to bridge any gap in Medicare or Medicaid coverage, and purchasing long-term care insurance.

Health Insurance

Medicare is a federal health insurance program primarily for people age 65 and older. Qualifying patients must pay part of their medical expenses through deductibles, and Medicare pays the remaining amount. Medicare has two parts, Part A (Hospital Insurance) and Part B (Medicare Insurance). Most people receive Part A coverage for free, but those who want Part B coverage must pay for it. The monthly Part B premium for 2013 for most retirees is $104.90. If your income is above $85,000 (single) or $170,000 (married couple), then your Medicare Part B premium may be higher.[6]

Medicare pays for many health care service and supplies, but it doesn't pay all health care costs. To help cover extra health care costs, an individual typically has two options: purchase a Medigap policy, or purchase employment-based health insurance (if available from a former employer).

A Medigap policy is a health insurance policy sold by private insurance companies. The Medigap policy must follow federal and state laws, and must be clearly identified as "Medicare Supplement Insurance." If an individual buys a Medigap policy, he or she will pay a monthly premium to the private insurance company offering the policy. In all states except Massachusetts, Minnesota, and Wisconsin, a Medigap policy must be

[3] Employee Benefits Research Institute, Notes, October 2012   [4] National Health Expenditure Projections 2011-2021, cms.gov   [5] Employee Benefits Research Institute, Issue Brief No. 377, October, 2012   [6] www.medicare.gov

one of 12 standardized policies (Plans A–L) so the purchaser can easily compare them. Each plan has a different set of benefits.

A few lucky retirees will have the option to purchase health insurance coverage through their former employers, but the number of employers offering coverage is dwindling. Only 25 percent of private employers offer health insurance to early retirees, and 16 percent offer it to Medicare-eligible retirees.[7]

Long-Term Care Insurance

Another option to help offset health care cost risk, and one that is usually best exercised prior to, or early in retirement, is to purchase long-term care coverage. One out of every two people will need long-term care at some point in their life time; and over 70 percent of those over 65 will require long-term care.[8] In general, the insurance industry has recommended getting a policy no later than age 65, and getting a policy earlier than age 65 only if there is a chronic disease, or a history of serious illness in the family. The reasoning behind this general rule relates to premiums. The annual premium for a low-option policy for a person at age 50 is about $850; at 65 that same policy costs about $1,800; and at 79, about $5,500.[9] If a policy is purchased after age 65, the premiums are higher, and the individual may not be able to pass the necessary medical tests.

Public Policy Risk

The risk that legislative activity will change the rules for retirement income and income planning is, arguably, one of the most unknowable risks that retirees face. The last major overhaul of retirement policy took place in 2006 when the president enacted the Pension Protection Act. Congress continues to consider new pension reform bills, as well as bills that would shore up Social Security.

Managing Public Policy Risk

One strategy for managing public policy risk is to be aware of pending legislation that may affect retirement income planning. This can be accomplished by reading related news reports and monitoring government web sites that deal with the subject matter (for example, http://thomas.loc.gov/).

A second, more aggressive strategy would be to become a political activist for retirement-related legislation. There are several organizations that are advocates for retirees, the most well known being AARP (http://www.aarp.org).

Household Shocks Risk

Life is unpredictable, and even the best laid plans of mice and men—and retirees—may go awry. Household shocks risk is the risk that unforeseen occurrences, for example, the early death of a spouse or divorce, may lead to earlier-than-expected portfolio depletion. Unfortunately, individual's have little to no ability to predict household shocks that may affect their retirement income.

[7] Employee Benefits Research Institute, Issue Brief No. 377, October 2012
[8] www.helpguide.org/elder   [9] Health Insurance Association of America

Strategies for managing household shocks risk may include the following:

- setting aside a reserve fund to be used only in the event of unforeseen emergencies;
- updating beneficiary information regularly;
- purchasing life insurance policies;
- seeking competent advice when dealing with qualified domestic relations orders and/or divorce decrees in the event of divorce;
- ensuring wills and estate plans are up to date; and
- reviewing the retirement income plan regularly for needed adjustments.

Legacy Risk

Legacy risk is the danger that a person's goal to provide for a beneficiary after death will not be fulfilled. The unfulfilled goal may come as a result of poor or no legacy planning, or changes in circumstances which require the benefactor to use more income than anticipated to cover his or her own living expenses.

Managing Legacy Risk

Strategies for managing legacy risk could include conducting periodic beneficiary audits, the use of trusts, and purchasing life insurance.

Beneficiary Audits

Financial professionals can provide a value-added service to their clients by conducting beneficiary audits to help ensure that desired legacy planning and continuity objectives will be carried out based on their beneficiary designations.

Prime candidates for beneficiary audits include individuals who

- are over the age of 50,
- have recently married,
- have recently lost their partners due to death or divorce, or
- have recently added a child or grandchild through birth or adoption.

Trusts

Trusts can be very effective legacy planning tools. Generally, a trust is a legal agreement between three parties:

- the grantor (also known as the settlor or trustor);
- the trustee; and
- the beneficiary.

A grantor transfers legal title to some of his or her property to a trust, then a trustee manages the property for a beneficiary. There are many types of trusts that serve many different purposes, so it is essential for individuals who want to use trusts to manage legacy risk to speak with a competent expert.

Life Insurance

Life insurance can provide an income tax-free death benefit for a beneficiary that far exceeds the premiums paid. Proceeds from a life insurance policy paid because of the death of the insured are generally excludable from the beneficiary's gross income for federal income tax purposes.[10]

Conclusion

Understanding retirement income risks is a key element in effective retirement income planning. Retirees can manage retirement income risks more effectively if they set realistic expectations and execute strategies appropriate for their individual situations. Above all, retirement income planning must be viewed as an ongoing process. Regular reviews of the retirement income plan are necessary to address changes in circumstances and potential risks.

The Retirement Income Planning Process

"Good plans shape good decisions. That's why good planning helps to make elusive dreams come true." Lester R. Bittel, *The Nine Master Keys of Management*

Creating a retirement income/risk management plan is really a process that can make the transition from wealth accumulation to wealth harvesting as smooth and rewarding as possible. Developing the retirement income/risk management plan involves six basic steps.

Step 1: Identify client needs and potential risks
Step 2: Identify and sort client resources
Step 3: Consolidate assets
Step 4: Convert resources into income
Step 5: Manage retirement income risks
Step 6: Monitor the process and adjust, if necessary

The first step in developing a retirement income/risk management plan is to identify the client's income needs in retirement and potential risks to retirement income. During this step, effective financial professionals really get to know their clients. They explore the client's financial history, determine the client's retirement goals, identify obstacles to attaining those goals, determine which retirement income risks are most likely to affect the client, and include spouses and other family members in any planning discussions as appropriate.

[10] Section 101(a)(1) of the Internal Revenue Code

As a result of Step 1, the client and financial professional will create a breakdown between the client's anticipated fixed retirement expenses, and his or her anticipated discretionary retirement expenses. Additionally, the team will determine which risks to retirement income are most likely to affect the particular client.

Step 2: Identify and Sort Client Resources

The second step in the retirement income/risk management planning process is identifying the income sources the retiree will have at his or her disposal. They may include some or all of the following:

- Social Security benefits,
- employer-sponsored plans (e.g., 401(k) and/or pension plans),
- annuity payments,
- personal savings,
- real estate income,
- investment income,
- cash value of life insurance,
- business income,
- work income, and
- inheritance.

According to the Employee Benefits Research Institute, "on average," a person will receive 40 percent of his/her retirement income from Social Security. But remember averages can be misleading. If one were to look at sources of retirement income based on household income, one would find that those in the lowest income bracket rely more heavily on Social Security income in retirement than those individuals in the highest of income brackets.

Once the sources are identified, they must be sorted as to whether they are fixed sources (e.g., Social Security and pension income), or fluctuating sources (e.g., 401(k) and real estate).

Step 3: Consolidate Assets

Asset consolidation is important. It is in the client's best interest not to have islands of assets. When clients consolidate their assets, they potentially reduce the need to track multiple accounts. Other benefits of asset consolidation they may realize include:

- more effective retirement income planning,
- maximum investment buying power,
- reduced fees,

- enhanced beneficiary management and options,
- consistent service, and
- streamlined paperwork.

With respect to asset consolidation, financial professionals may get the most return on investment of their time by focusing on retirement plan rollovers. The rollover opportunity is huge. The Economic Growth and Tax Relief Reconciliation Act of 2002 greatly increased the portability of retirement plan assets between various plan types.

The Rollover Market Opportunity

The annual rollover market is estimated to exceed $450 billion by 2017.[11] Rollovers are projected to increase at an annual rate of 8 percent, annually.[12]

Assets that are eligible for rollover do not appear to be "sticky." 70-80 percent of rollovers move to new providers,[13] and the younger the lump sum recipient, the less likely he or she is to roll it over. Rollover rates range from 64 percent for near retirees to 15 percent for the youngest workers.[14]

Consequently, if a financial professional does nothing else but focuses on retirement plan rollovers, he or she stands to gain considerable assets under management. Who are rollover targets? In a nutshell, they are job changers, retirees, and workers who have "in-service" distribution options.

Job changers

On average, a worker will hold 11 jobs from ages 18 to 42.[15] A job change can be a rollover opportunity that could trigger the need for advice—and an opportunity for a financial professional to establish a long-term investing relationship. The average job-changer rollover is estimated to be $33,000.[16]

Retirees

Retirement asset distributions annually reach over $1 trillion dollars in traditional retirement products alone, as a result of the rapid growth in the retired population.[17] The average plan balance of a participant in his or her 60s with 20 years of service is $160,000.[18]

Workers with "In-Service" Distribution Options

Many 401(k)/profit sharing plans allow participants to take eligible rollover distributions while they are still working. Effective in 2007, pursuant to PPA-06, employers may offer in-service distributions from their defined benefit plans to participants who have at least attained age 62. To determine whether a plan participant may take in-service distributions, a review of the governing plan document is necessary. The terms of the plan document will determine whether in-service distributions are available, and the conditions, if any, under which they may be taken.

[11] Cerulli Report, 2012 [12] Ibid [13] McKinsey, The Asset Management Industry: Outcomes are the New Alpha, 2012

[14] EBRI, Fast Fact #115, 2009 [15] Bureau of Labor Statistics, 2012 [16] Employee Benefits Research Institute, Issue Brief, #380, December 2012 [17] Cerulli Report, 2012 [18] Employee Benefits Research Institute, Issue Brief No. 380, December 2012

Step 4: Convert Client Resources into Retirement Income

The fourth step in the retirement income/risk management planning process is to convert the identified retirement income sources into retirement income. This is done by first matching fixed expenses with fixed income streams. If an income gap results, clients must then use a systematic withdrawal plan to secure payments from fluctuating income sources to cover the gap. Finally, any remaining amounts based on the systematic withdrawal plan can be used to pay for discretionary expenses such as travel and entertainment costs.

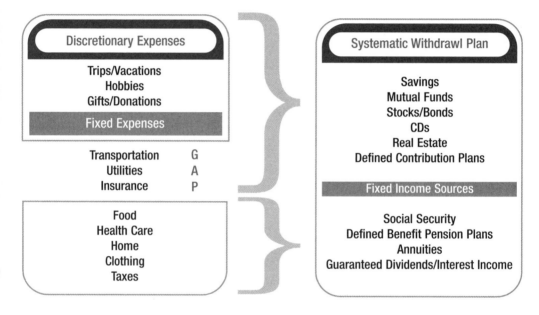

Step 5: Manage Retirement Income Risks

Refer to the first section of this chapter for information on the risks to retirement income, and potential strategies for reducing the risks' effects.

Step 6: Monitor and Adjust

The retirement income/risk management planning process is not a one-time, "set-it-and-forget-it" approach to retirement income security. As alluded to earlier, it is an ongoing process. Financial professionals and their clients should review retirement income/risk management plans at least annually, and adjust them to meet changing circumstances.

The Retirement Income/Risk Management Process

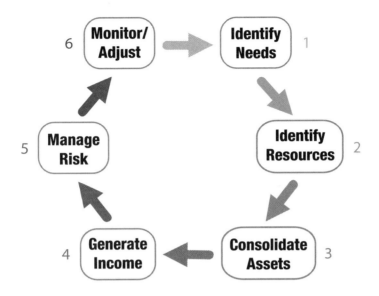

Practice Management Application

- Financial professionals can play the role of "quarterback" for clients' professional advisors (e.g., CPAs, tax attorneys, financial planners, etc.). Proactive interaction with professional advisors increases credibility, and ensures synchronized efforts are made towards clients' retirement goals.

- Demonstrate an understanding of technical concepts related to retirement income planning; this also builds credibility.

- Manage clients' fears related to retirement income risks through proper planning and risk management.

- Emphasize the need for discipline.

- Reinforce and manage expectations on an ongoing basis.

- Remember that retirement income planning is an ongoing process.

Chapter Review Questions

Feedback for the review questions can be found at the end of the chapter.

1 Of the following, which best represents the order of steps in the retirement income planning process?

    A Convert resources into income; manage risks, monitor the process; identify needs and risks; identify resources; and consolidate assets.

    B Identify needs and risks; monitor the process; identify resources; manage risks; consolidate assets; convert resources to income.

    C Monitor the process; manage risks; convert resources to income; consolidate assets; identify resources; and identify needs and risks..

    D Identify needs and risks; identify resources; consolidate assets; convert resources to income; manage risks; monitor the process.

2 What would be a strategy that an investor might employ to meet his/her fixed expenses in retirement?

    A Align the fixed expenses with stocks and real estate.

    B Align the fixed expenses with Social Security benefits and annuities.

    C Align the fixed expense with mutual funds..

    D Align the fixed expenses with defined contribution plans.

3 Which of the following, generally, is NOT a risk to retirement income?

    A Market volatility

    B Longevity

    C Spending

    D Deflation

4 What role can a fixed annuity play as part of the retirement income planning process?

    A Annuitized payments represent a source of guaranteed income.

    B Fixed annuities can be a good investment vehicle to maximize growth.

    C Annuities provide the broadest selection of beneficiary options.

    D All of the above.

5 To secure adequate assets; achieve a desired lifestyle; and meet legacy objectives are goals of what?

    A Asset diversification

    B Annuitization

    C Retirement income planning

    D A sustainable withdrawal rate

1 Of the following, which best represents the order of steps in the retirement income planning process?

    A Convert resources into income; manage risks, monitor the process; identify needs and risks; identify resources; and consolidate assets.

    B Identify needs and risks; monitor the process; identify resources; manage risks; consolidate assets; convert resources to income.

    C Monitor the process; manage risks; convert resources to income; consolidate assets; identify resources; and identify needs and risks.

    D Identify needs and risks; identify resources; consolidate assets; convert resources to income; manage risks; monitor the process.

    A *Incorrect, the correct order is Identify needs and risks; identify resources; consolidate assets; convert resources to income; manage risks; monitor the process.*

    B *Incorrect, the correct order is Identify needs and risks; identify resources; consolidate assets; convert resources to income; manage risks; monitor the process.*

    C *Incorrect, the correct order is Identify needs and risks; identify resources; consolidate assets; convert resources to income; manage risks; monitor the process.*

    D *Correct, since each step is dependent on the step that precedes it, this order represents the logical flow of planning steps.* Chapter 13 Page 311

2 What would be a strategy that an investor might employ to meet his/her fixed expenses in retirement?

    A Align the fixed expenses with stocks and real estate.

    B Align the fixed expenses with Social Security benefits and annuities.

    C Align the fixed expense with mutual funds.

    D Align the fixed expenses with defined contribution plans.

    A *Incorrect, stocks and real estate can be volatile assets and would not be among the best options to meet the need for fixed income.*

    B *Correct, Social Security benefits and annuities represent fixed income sources, which would be among the best options for meeting fixed expenses.* Chapter 13 Page 314

    C *Incorrect, mutual funds can be volatile assets and would not be among the best option to meet the need for fixed income.*

    D *Incorrect, since defined contribution assets are not guaranteed; they would not be among the best option to meet the need for fixed income.*

3 Which of the following, generally, is NOT a risk to retirement income?

    A Market volatility

    B Longevity

C Spending

D Deflation

A *Incorrect, stock market volatility can have a great effect on the value of retirement income assets.*

B *Incorrect, people are living longer which increases the risk they will out live their retirement assets.*

C *Incorrect, spending too much can deplete retirement income sources too rapidly.*

D **Correct, inflation-not deflation-reduces the purchasing power of retirement income.**
Chapter 13 Page 303

4 What role can a fixed annuity play as part of the retirement income planning process?

    A Annuitized payments represent a source of guaranteed income.
    B Fixed annuities can be a good investment vehicle to maximize growth.
    C Annuities provide the broadest selection of beneficiary options.
    D All of the above.

A **Correct, when an annuity is converted to a stream of payments, it can provide income for the lifetime of the annuitant.** Chapter 13 Page 301

B *Incorrect, fixed annuities generally offer a low, fixed rate of interest and, therefore, are not used as an investment vehicle to maximize growth.*

C *Incorrect, beneficiary options are annuity products are more restrictive than for other types of investment vehicles.*

D *Incorrect, B and C are incorrect.*

5 To secure adequate assets; achieve a desired lifestyle; and meet legacy objectives are goals of what?

    A Asset diversification
    B Annuitization
    C Retirement income planning
    D A sustainable withdrawal rate

A *Incorrect, asset diversification is a tactic that an investor can use to secure adequate assets, achieve a desired lifestyle and meet legacy objectives as part of a retirement income planning process.*

B *Incorrect, annuitization is a tactic that an investor can use to secure adequate assets, achieve a desired lifestyle and meet legacy objectives as part of a retirement income planning process.*

C **Correct, ensuring an investor does not outlive his/her assets, is able to achieve the desired lifestyle he/she wants in retirement and to satisfy objectives for transferring wealth after retirement are key goals of the retirement income planning process.** Chapter 13 Page 298

D *Incorrect, maintaining a sustainable withdrawal rate is a strategy that an investor can use to secure adequate assets, achieve a desired lifestyle and meet legacy objectives as part of a retirement income planning process.*

GLOSSARY

401(k) plan A funding arrangement, also known as a cash or deferred arrangement, attached to a profit sharing or stock bonus plan that allows participants to set aside a portion of their compensation as pre-tax salary deferrals or after-tax qualified Roth contributions.

403(b) plan A defined contribution plan similar to a 401(k) plan available exclusively to public schools, colleges, universities, churches, public hospitals and IRC Sec. 501(c)(3) tax-exempt entities.

412(e) plan A type of defined benefit pension plan funded exclusively with life insurance or fixed annuity contracts.

457(b) plan A type of nonqualified deferred compensation plan exclusively for state and local governmental units, certain educational organizations and certain tax-exempt entities.

457(f) plan A type of nonqualified deferred compensation plan exclusively for state and local governmental units and tax-exempt entities that fails to meet one or more of the requirements under IRC Sec. 457(b).

Administrative roadblocks to rollovers Logistical problems with the plan provider, product or employer sponsoring the plan that prevent a rollover.

Annuity A contract that pays a fixed amount of money for a specified period of time.

Asset allocation The process of dividing assets among various investment options.

Automatic enrollment A 401(k) arrangement where the employer withholds a predetermined percentage of pay to contribute to the plan if an eligible participant fails to opt out or to elect a different level of deferral.

Baby boomer A member of the generation born between 1946 and 1964.

Beneficiary determination date September 30 of the year following the year of the IRA owner or plan participant's death.

Capital gains A special 20% capital gains tax election that may apply to the portion of a lump sum distribution of assets that accrued before 1974, which is available to retirement plan participants who were born before January 2, 1936.

Cash balance plan A type of defined benefit pension plan where the retirement benefit is based on a hypothetical account balance derived from a pay credit and interest credit.

320

Cash out A distribution of plan assets without the consent of the plan participant.

Class exclusion A group of employees as defined by the plan sponsor that may be excluded from participation.

Conversion A taxable rollover of non-Roth assets from an eligible plan to a Roth IRA or qualified Roth account.

Cost basis The value of the employer stock when it is purchased or contributed to the retirement plan.

DB(k) A hybrid plan that combines elements of defined benefit and 401(k) plans.

Defined benefit pension plan A type of tax-qualified, employer-sponsored retirement that specifies the retirement benefit participants will receive.

Defined contribution plan A type of tax-qualified, employer-sponsored retirement plan that typically offers a discretionary annual employer contribution.

Designated beneficiary The beneficiary of an IRA or retirement plan whose life expectancy may be considered for distribution calculation purposes.

Direct rollover A tax-free, custodian-to-custodian movement of cash or other assets from one retirement savings plan to another.

Distribution triggering event An occurrence as defined by the retirement plan document that allows a participant to receive all or a portion of his or her plan benefit.

Early distribution penalty tax An IRS penalty that generally applies to payments of plan benefits prior to age 59 1/2 where no exception applies.

Employee plans compliance resolution system A series of IRS correction programs to address plan qualification issues.

Employee stock ownership plan A type of stock bonus plan that is designed to invest primarily in the stock of the sponsoring employer.

Estate tax A federal and sometimes state tax that may apply to the taxable estate of a decedent.

Fiduciary adviser Financial advisers that deliver investment advice to plan participants under an arrangement the meets certain Department of Labor requirements.

Five-year clock A five-year period that applies for qualified Roth IRA and conversion distribution purposes.

Five-year rule A beneficiary distribution option that requires the IRA or retirement plan assets be paid out by the end of the fifth year following the year of the IRA owner or plan participant's death.

Gift tax A federal and sometimes state tax that may apply to the value of gifts of money or/and property.

Hardship distribution A payment of plan benefits to a participant for purposes of covering an immediate and heavy financial need that does not exceed the amount necessary to satisfy the need.

Health care cost risk   The risk that the rise in health care expenses will outpace gains in retirement savings.

Household shocks risk   The risk that unforeseen occurrences may lead to earlier-than-expected retirement savings depletion.

Income averaging   A special tax option for plan participants born before January 2, 1936 who receive lump sum distributions.

Income in respect of a decedent   Generally, the taxable amount remaining in a decedent's IRAs and retirement plans on the date of death that will pass to beneficiaries.

Indirect rollover   An eligible rollover distribution that is paid to the account owner and redeposited to another eligible retirement savings plan within 60 days.

Inflation risk   The risk that increases in prices for product and services will decrease the purchasing power of a retiree's retirement savings.

In-service distribution   A payment of plan benefits while the participant is working for the employer maintaining the plan.

IRA   Individual retirement annuity or individual retirement account.

IRS Form 706   The IRS form that must be filed when federal estate taxes apply to a decedent's estate.

IRS Form 709   The IRS form that must be filed when a taxpayer is subject to gift tax or split gifting.

Joint and last survivor table   An IRA life expectancy table for use by IRA owners and plan participants whose spouses are more than 10 years younger, and are the sole beneficiaries of their retirement plans.

Legacy risk   The risk that a person's beneficiary goals will not be fulfilled.

Life expectancy payments   A beneficiary distribution option that bases annual payments on a single life expectancy.

Longevity risk   The risk that a retiree will outlive his or her retirement savings.

Long-term capital gain   The increase in value of a qualifying investment, which is subject to lower tax rates than the general income tax rates.

Lump sum distributions   For purposes of special tax options, a payment in one taxable year of a plan participant's entire balance from all of his or her employer's qualified plans of one kind because of 1) death, 2) attainment of age 59 1/2, a participant's separation from service (n/a for selfemployed), or a participant's disability (self-employed only).

Market risk The risk that the stock market's volatility could cause a retiree to prematurely deplete his or her retirement income savings.

Modified adjusted gross income   Adjusted gross income from IRS Form 1040 without taking into consideration certain deductions.

Money purchase pension plan A type of defined contribution plan that guarantees an annual employer contribution.

Net unrealized appreciation The increase in value of stock of the sponsoring employer while the stock is held in the retirement plan.

Nonperiodic payments Retirement plan distributions that are other than annuity-type payments or corrective distributions.

Nonqualified Roth IRA distribution A Roth IRA distribution that is not a qualified Roth IRA distribution.

Nonrecalculation For distribution calculation purposes, life expectancy is set in a particular year by referring to the appropriate life expectancy table, and reducing the life expectancy figure by one for all subsequent years.

Nonrollable assets Cash or other assets from a retirement savings plan that are not eligible for rollover.

Nonrollable plans Retirement savings plans the assets of which are not eligible for rollover.

Ordering rules The order in which the IRS deems Roth IRA assets to be distributed.

Periodic payments Retirement plan distributions that are paid at regular intervals for a period greater than one year.

Plan document roadblocks Plan document language that prevents a rollover.

Profit sharing A type of defined contribution plan that provides for discretionary employer contributions.

Psychological roadblocks Bad past experiences of a plan participant related to rollovers that prevent a rollover.

Public policy risk The risk that legislative changes will affect the rules for retirement income planning.

Qualified charitable distribution A distribution by an IRA owner or IRA beneficiary age 70 1/2 or older that is paid directly to a qualified charitable organization, $100,000 of which is excludable from taxable income.

Qualified default investment alternatives A life-cycle or target-date fund; balanced fund; or managed account that meet certain Department of Labor requirements.

Qualified disclaimer The means by which a beneficiary refuses to accept a whole or partial interest in inherited property.

Qualified domestic relations order A court and plan sponsor approved document that addresses the disposition of plan assets to an alternate payee.

Qualified Roth IRA distribution A withdrawal from a Roth IRA that occurs 1) at least five years after the Roth IRA owner contributes to a Roth IRA; and 2) after the Roth IRA owner attains age 59 1/2, becomes disabled, qualifies for a first-home purchase, or dies.

Qualified trust For beneficiary purposes, a trust that meets certain requirements which then allows the beneficiaries of the trust to be treated as if they were named as beneficiaries directly on the IRA or retirement plan, with some exceptions.

Recalculation For distribution calculation purposes, life expectancy is re-determined each year by referring to the appropriate life expectancy table.

Regulatory roadblocks Rules in law or regulation that prevent a rollover.

Required beginning date The date by which an IRA owner or plan participant must begin taking required minimum distributions from their retirement plans.

Required minimum distribution (RMD) A mandatory minimum annual payment from a retirement savings plan.

Retirement income planning process A six-step planning process that helps prepare an individual for retirement from a financial planning standpoint.

RMD aggregation The rules that allow an IRA owner with multiple IRAs to total the individual RMDs required from each IRA and remove the sum amount from one IRA.

Rollable assets Cash or other assets from a retirement savings plan that are eligible for rollover.

Rollable plans Retirement savings plans the assets of which are generally eligible for rollover.

Rollover A tax-free, movement of cash or other assets from one retirement savings plan to another.

Rollover notice A participant disclosure, also know as a 402(f) notice, that is required when the individual will be receiving an eligible rollover distribution.

Rollover target An individual who is eligible to receive a distribution for rollover purposes; generally someone changing jobs, retiring or with in-service distribution options.

Roth IRA A personal retirement savings plan that is either an individual retirement account or annuity that allows for nondeductible contributions and potentially taxfree earnings.

Safe harbor 401(k) A special 401(k) plan design that allows sponsoring employers to automatically satisfy certain nondiscrimination testing provided they make mandatory contributions, among other requirements.

Salary reduction simplified employee pension (SARSEP) plan A SEP plan that permits employee salary deferrals.

Savings incentive match plan for employees (SIMPLE) IRA A type of IRA with a funding arrangement that allows employers with 100 or fewer employees to make contributions and that also permits employee salary deferrals.

Severance from employment When a common law employment relationship with an employer maintaining a retirement plan has ended.

Simplified employee pension (SEP) plan
A funding arrangement that allows employers to make contributions to traditional IRAs for their employees.

Spending risk   The risk that a retiree will over spend causing him or her to run out of money in retirement.

Split gifting   A married couple can give up to the twice the maximum gift tax excludable amount provided they file a gift tax return to show the gift splitting.

Statutory exclusion   Groups of employees as defined by law that a plan sponsor may exclude from plan participation.

Stock bonus plan   A type of defined contribution plan, similar to a profit sharing plan, except that benefits must be payable in the form of stock of the sponsoring employer.

Stretch IRA   A type of distribution strategy that allows beneficiaries to base IRA payouts on the longest life expectancy permitted under the circumstances.

Substantially equal periodic payments   Regular annual payments that are made for the life (or life expectancy) of the employee or the joint lives of an individual and a beneficiary.

Systematic withdrawal plan   A payment schedule that allows an investor to receive to receive specific payment amounts at regular intervals.

Taft-Hartley plan   A plan for union employees established under the Taft-Hartley Act.

Target benefit plan   A type of money purchase pension plan where employer contributions fund a stated "target" benefit.

Thrift savings plan   A retirement savings and investment plan available to certain government employees.

Traditional IRA   A personal retirement savings plan that is either an individual retirement account or annuity that allows for deductible or nondeductible contributions and taxdeferred earnings.

Unified credit   A amount that an individual can use to offset both estate and gift tax liabilities.

Uniform lifetime table   An IRS life expectancy table for use by unmarried IRA owners and plan participants, married IRA owners and plan participants whose spouses are not more than 10 years younger, and married IRA owners and plan participants whose spouses are not the sole beneficiaries of their retirement plans.

Wealth accumulator   Individuals who are saving money to acquire assets to be used for retirement income.

Wealth harvester   Individuals who are spending their retirement savings.

INDEX